Rebirth

as Doctrine and Experience

ABOUT THE AUTHOR

Francis Story (Anagārika Sugatānanda) was born in England in 1910 and became acquainted with Buddhist teachings early in life. For 25 years he lived in Asian countries—India, Burma, and Sri Lanka—where he deeply studied the Buddhist philosophy of life. With that background and endowed with a keen analytical mind, he produced a considerable body of writings, collected and published in three volumes by the Buddhist Publication Society. At the age of 61 he passed away at a London hospital after a severe case of bone cancer.

From the time of his early contacts with Buddhism, Francis Story had a special interest in the subject of rebirth, which grew keener during his years in Burma when he encountered cases of individuals who could actually recall their previous lives. He wrote prolifically on the doctrinal side of the Buddhist rebirth teaching and on its correlate, the doctrine of karma. His interest in cases of rebirth memories finally led him to assist Dr. Ian Stevenson in tracing, investigating, and studying such cases in Sri Lanka, Thailand, and India. How fruitful this cooperation proved to be is vividly told in Professor Stevenson's Introduction and documented by the case studies included in this book.

Dr. Ian Stevenson was born in Montreal, Canada, in 1918 and received his medical training in various institutions in Canada and the United States. He was Professor and Chairman of the Department of Psychiatry at the University of Virginia School of Medicine, and Carlson Professor of Psychiatry and Director of the Division of Parapsychology at the University of Virginia School of Medicine. Professor Stevenson has had an almost life-long interest in parapsychology and has been actively engaged in research in this field since 1957, specializing in cases of the rebirth type. He has made numerous field trips to investigate such cases in Asia and other parts of the world. He was frequently accompanied on such trips by Francis Story until the latter's death in 1971. His publications include: *Twenty Cases Suggestive of Reincarnation, Xenoglossy,* and three volumes of *Cases of the Reincarnation Type: Vol. 1. Ten Cases in India; Vol. 2. Ten Cases in Sri Lanka;* and *Vol. 3. Fifteen Cases in Thailand, Lebanon and Turkey.* These are all published by the University Press of Virginia, Charlottesville, Virginia 22901, U.S.A.

Rebirth
as Doctrine and Experience

Essays and Case Studies

Collected Writings
Volume II

Francis Story
(Anagārika Sugatānanda)

Introduction by
Ian Stevenson, M.D.

Buddhist Publication Society
Kandy • Sri Lanka

Buddhist Publication Society
P.O. Box 61
54, Sangharaja Mawatha
Kandy, Sri Lanka

First edition 1975; reprinted 1988
Second edition   2000
Retypeset edition: 2010

Story Francis

Rebirth as Doctrine and Experience: Essays and Case
Studies / Francis Story – Kandy: Buddhist Publication Society, 2000 – p.vii, 223 ; 22 cm
272p.; 22cm

ISBN 955–24–0176–3

i. 294.34237   DDC 21   ii. Title
1. Reincarnation (Buddhism)
2. Buddhism – Doctrines

ISBN 978-955-24-0176-3

Typeset at BPS

Printed in Sri Lanka by
    Ruchira Offset Printers
    Kandy—Sri Lanka

Contents

Editor's Preface   vii
INTRODUCTION by Ian Stevenson, M.D.   ix

Part One: Essays on Rebirth   1

I. The Belief in Survival   3
II. Rebirth and its Investigation   6
III. The Buddhist Concept of Rebirth   14
IV. What is Reborn?   19
V. Rebirth and the Western Thinker   24
VI. Rebirth, Karma, and Modern Science   42
VII. Karma as a Factor in Disease   51
VIII. The Karmic Force in the Rebirth Process   55
IX. The Buddhist Doctrine of Rebirth in Subhuman Realms   58
X. Did the Buddha Teach Rebirth?   91
XI. A Change of Heart   96
XII. A Question of Terminology   102
XIII. From Life to Life   105

PART TWO: CASES OF REBIRTH MEMORIES   111

XIV. Types of Rebirth Cases   113
XV. A Case of the Reincarnation Type in Ceylon   116
XVI. Another Case of the Reincarnation Type in Ceylon   132
XVII. The Siamese Sergeant   148
XVIII. The Metamorphosis of a Mother   153
XIX. Rebirth or Possession   162
XX. What Happens Between Incarnations   169
XXI. Miscellaneous Cases of Rebirth Memories   177

PART THREE: THE CASE FOR REBIRTH   197

XXII. The Case for Rebirth   199

NOTES   245

Editor's Preface

While the first volume of the late Francis Story's Collected Writings, *The Buddhist Outlook*, covers a wide range of subjects relating to Buddhist teachings, this second volume deals with one single topic, that of rebirth. This seems justified for several reasons. Firstly, one connected with the author himself (and this reason need only be mentioned in this brief Preface). The subject of rebirth had occupied his thoughts and his activities in an increasing degree. During his years in Burma, cases of rebirth memories occurring in that country had roused his keen interest, and this finally led him to assist Dr. Ian Stevenson in the tracing, investigation, and study of such cases in Sri Lanka (Ceylon), Thailand, and India. How fruitful this cooperation was is vividly told in Professor Stevenson's Introduction, which he so kindly contributed to this volume; and it is documented by the Case Studies forming the Second Part of this book.

It had been the intention of Francis Story to write a larger book on the subject of rebirth, and a tentative Table of Contents found among his papers shows that this work was planned to be wide-ranging and deeply reaching. That this book remained unwritten is a great loss to those interested in the subject. The present volume can be regarded only as a meagre substitute for it. The essays collected in the First Part were written at different periods of the author's life. They are mostly short and do not deal with the subject in a systematic way. It was, therefore, thought advisable to supplement them by the author's largest connected piece of writing on the topic, *The Case for Rebirth*, which first appeared in the series "The Wheel." It is here reproduced in Part Three, with a few amendations and some additions to the Appendix.

A valuable addition to this volume are the case studies of rebirth memories. The Editor is grateful to Professor Stevenson for his kind permission to reprint here those case studies which he had co-authored (Chapters XV and XVI), as well as for helping to edit the notes on Miscellaneous Cases (Chapter XXI) and for contributing material to them which was not among the late Francis Story's papers preserved in Ceylon. Besides, Professor Stevenson has given much valuable advice and suggestions to the Editor, personally and in letters.

It is hoped that this volume will contribute to stimulate further thought and research on the problem of rebirth, which is of deep human, philosophical, and psychological concern.

Nyanaponika Thera

Forest Hermitage, Kandy, Sri Lanka
September 1974

Introduction

Before his untimely death in April, 1971, Francis Story had projected a book on rebirth. He never completed it—indeed he never really began it—and thus gave his friends and readers one more reason to regret his passing. For he could have written an excellent work on the subject, one that would have combined his deep knowledge of Buddhist texts and literature with his extensive acquaintance with cases of the rebirth type in South Asia and of the peoples among whom these cases occur. And he would have illuminated the whole with his rigorous logic and lucid style of writing. I am sure the book he wanted to write would have greatly surpassed the one the reader now has before him. It is even possible that Francis Story will look down disapprovingly from the *deva* realms on the collection of his papers on rebirth which the Ven. Nyanaponika has so skillfully edited. For a number of the chapters included in this volume derive from mere drafts or field notes, which the author would certainly have developed further and revised if he had lived and had wished to publish them. I make this comment in an explanatory rather than an apologetic spirit. The friends of Francis Story have agreed that the importance of his contributions to the study of rebirth cases justify making them available to a wider circle of readers despite imperfections which he would have removed if he had lived longer. The reader should attribute any defects to those of us who wanted to see this work published rather than to the author, who had no chance to correct them himself.

Francis Story began to investigate cases of the rebirth type when he was living in Burma in the 1950s. At that period he started, at first almost casually, to jot down notes of cases he encountered. Gradually he became more systematic in his recording of the data he collected. In 1961 he accompanied me during my first trip of investigations in Sri Lanka, to which he had moved in 1957. Thereafter he joined me during every field trip I made in Sri Lanka until 1970. In addition, he helped me during two field trips in India and Thailand and he made trips of investigation by himself in India, Burma, and Thailand in the 1960s. At the time of his death he had some personal experience with most of the cases in Sri Lanka, Thailand, and Burma of which we then had any information. Many of them he had investigated entirely by himself.

His strong conviction about the truth of Buddhism gave him a certain advantage in the study of the cases in which respect I have felt myself at times deficient. He had become convinced of the essential truth of the Buddha's teaching when only sixteen years old. His acceptance of Buddhism then and later had nothing to do with evidence from case studies. This happened because first, there was little of such evidence available until we began our investigations, and secondly, because Buddhism's appeal to him in no way depended on evidence. He accepted Buddhism on rational rather than on empirical grounds. For me, on the other hand, the truth of Buddhism, and hence my acceptance of it, depended at least to some extent on whatever evidence of rebirth the investigation of the cases could generate. This attitude led me to treat the cases sometimes as if they were fragile and as if the loss of a case would lessen, if only by a little, my own wavering convictions about Buddhism. Not so Francis Story. For him all the evidence from the cases could have collapsed into nothing and he would have remained unshaken in his belief in the truth of the Buddha's teachings. With this background he approached the cases as a neutral and sometimes stern critic of informants. Discrepancies about details such as occur commonly enough in human testimony of the kind obtained in these cases vexed and occasionally angered him. He sometimes cross-examined witnesses in a manner that made the targets of his penetrating questions uncomfortable and observers wonder why he had not taken up the law as a profession. He had an unusual gift for pursuing small details, although he rarely allowed the lesser aspects of a case to decide his assessment of it as a whole.

Some persons may nevertheless think that his bias toward Buddhism could have influenced his interviews and his analysis of the data that emerged from them. From the observations that I could make of him during the many months we spent together I do not think this occurred. And this was so not only because, as I have said above, he was rather indifferent to the outcome of the investigation of any single case—although not to the research as a whole—but also because he had the detachment of the true scientist. (This is a virtue in Buddhism also and his Buddhism made him a better scientist.) He always gave facts primacy over theory and when some element of a case conflicted with what Buddhist teachings had led him to expect he unhesitatingly questioned the teaching rather than the data, provided that he had satisfied himself of their authenticity. I need hardly add to the probable readers of this book that the Buddha himself taught us to learn by our own experiences rather than accept on faith anyone else's statements—including his own. And Francis Story found nothing incompatible between Buddhism and true science, although he could be scathing about scientism—the tendency to think that current beliefs held by scientists have value for all time.

He sometimes expressed a keen disappointment that the cases had not brought out more evidence of retributive karma. He had hoped that they would yield some evidence not only for rebirth—which they do—but also for the operation of processes such as karma. He admitted that his convictions about Buddhism had led him to expect more support for the teaching of karma than the cases provided, which was in fact very little. (This is not to say that karma does not occur, only that if it does, its workings must be vastly more complicated and more subtle than most students have suspected.) And yet he never attempted to twist the interrogations of the informants or the interpretation of their testimony in a way that would have made the evidence for karma—or anything else—appear stronger than it was.

Despite the fact that he did not think the evidence from cases would alter his own beliefs one way or the other, he was widely read in the general literature of modern science and he knew that carefully studied cases might eventually have some influence in changing opinions about the nature of human personality and of man's destiny. And therefore he entered tirelessly into the work of investigating them.

Although he never had an opportunity to investigate cases in cultures outside those of South Asia, one could never satisfy his curiosity about them. As I remember our conversations, it seems to me that when we were not talking about the immediate case under study then, almost all the time Francis was either expounding Buddhism to me or pumping me about the details of cases I had studied elsewhere.

I hope the readers of this book enjoy physical comforts far superior to those usually encountered in the field investigations of cases of the reincarnation type in Asia. The average Western reader holding a finished case report and seated in his own deep armchair cannot easily conceive the practical difficulties and sometimes physical hardships which the investigator has had to endure in order to provide him with this material. Francis Story took all these travails in good spirit. Once he went to study a case in India after we had separated there in 1964. He later wrote me about how he had to wade through a river to reach the village of the case, but had managed to keep his notes dry by holding them over his head. He added characteristically that he found these incidental hazards of the work added to its overall interest for him. On another occasion, when we were together in Thailand, a jeep became flooded crossing a river in a particularly remote rural area. We had to wait many hours for some new vehicle, but such a mishap and detention merely gave Francis Story another opportunity to discuss Buddhism. Even his rare complaints about the conditions of our work always had humour in them. Once when we were rushing hectically to catch a train at a crowded railway station in a South Asian country he remarked: "This is an impossible country. You cannot even count on the trains departing late!" On another trip, when we had almost exhausted our informants and ourselves and had partaken of nothing since breakfast but chopped open coconuts, he allowed himself to say, toward 5:00 PM, "I have quite stopped thinking about lunch. My only concern now as regards food is whether I shall have any supper!"

In view of his willingness to undergo deprivations of this kind, it is not surprising that the first symptoms of his fatal illness came on when he had to stand for hours during a long train journey taken to investigate a case in eastern Sri Lanka. He spent much of this time with his chest against a rather sharp ledge. Afterwards he had persistent pain in the area of his chest where the ledge had pressed him. Examination showed that he had developed at that place a pathological fracture of a rib. That was early in 1970. By the autumn he was severely weakened, in much pain, and using a cane. But he accompanied me just as usual throughout most of my investigations in Sri Lanka during November of that year.

His cheerful tolerance of the austerities of field investigations represented the least important contribution he made to the study of the cases. He and I both regarded these as merely incidental features in the gathering of the data. Far more important was his participation as an analyst of the evidence and an assessor of its value. Almost always on our field trips we worked until late at night in going over the notes of the day's interviews. Francis Story's agile mind constantly thought of new questions for the next day's work or new ways of understanding the testimony we had already obtained.

The discussion of cases with him gave me not only pleasure, but an assistance whose true worth I did not appreciate until much later. As I think now about my ignorance of South Asian peoples in the early 1960s I realize that if I had allowed myself to become aware of it then I would never have made my first journey for investigations. I should have lost my nerve before departure. I only realized much later the good fortune I had in that, from the very beginning of my field work, Francis Story made his rich experience of South Asian peoples available to me. Many times his extraordinarily wide knowledge of the cultures of the area clarified some discrepancy or obscure item in the informants' statements or the behaviour of the subject. One of his other friends told me quite credibly that in at least some

Introduction

matters Francis Story knew much more about the peoples of South Asia than they knew themselves. This was not said as a shallow repetition of the cliché according to which we never see ourselves as others see us. Francis Story had a lively interest in all sorts of subtle differences of custom which made him an unrivalled expert on the peoples among whom he lived. I sometimes wondered why, during all the years he lived in Asia, he had never learned a modern Asian language; but perhaps if he had done so the time and effort would have left him with less to devote to the study of other aspects of the cultures of the region.

He was not, however, satisfied with the mere collection of data. He wanted to learn—and even to anticipate—the patterns which began to emerge from the cases. He constantly thought and talked about their similarities and differences and their relationship to the Dhamma. It is altogether appropriate therefore that about half of the present volume consists of writings on what we might call the theoretical aspects of rebirth. But the essays of Francis Story on the theory of rebirth, in my opinion, stand far above those of most theorists of the subject. For although most of them have never been near a case, Francis Story from personal experience could see the relevance of Buddhist texts to cases and of cases to texts. His report and subsequent comments about the case of the Karen houseboy with appalling deformities (reprinted in Chapter XXII of this volume) provide only one example of his unusual powers of integration.

He was particularly interested in "international cases," those in which a subject claims to have lived a previous life in another country. The case of Ranjith Makalanda (reported in Chapter XXI of this volume) provides an excellent example of the type. The subject, a Sinhalese boy of Sri Lanka, claimed that he had been an Englishman in his previous life and he had certain English habits that harmonized with his (unfortunately unverified) statements about the previous life he claimed to remember. Francis Story liked to muse over how such an event as a Christian Englishman being reborn a Sinhalese Buddhist could happen. Occasionally he talked about his own particular fondness for Chinese and Indo-Chinese peoples and a few odd likings and other traits he had which made him speculate that he himself might have had a previous life as a Chinese.

The reasons why a person might be reborn in one particular family (of the same culture) rather than in another also fascinated him. The fact that the subject's birth often occurred near the place of death—verified or conjectured—of the previous personality drew his attention. Some of us finally developed "Story's Law" which says: "Other things being equal, a person will be reborn where (or near where) he dies." Francis Story needed no reminding that other things are rarely equal. Nevertheless he sensed that regular processes govern rebirth and that further investigations might allow us to develop at least provisional concepts of their "laws."

If a reader of the present volume should happen to come to it with no knowledge of what Francis Story called "the case for rebirth" he will not put it down without being cured of that ignorance. And although the essays and case reports of this book may not convince anyone of the truth of rebirth—their author never intended that they should—they will at least leave no doubt in his mind that the cases provide some evidence—however future generations may weigh it—which justifies a belief in rebirth. Belief can precede proof and often does.

During the past three or more centuries, since the beginning of European colonialism in South Asia, hundreds of thousands of Europeans have lived in the area as administrators, diplomats, soldiers, traders, or missionaries, and in other capacities. These persons were surrounded by abundant cases of the rebirth type. And yet of all these thousands of Europeans only a handful paid any attention to the cases. One thinks of Fielding Hall and W.F. Yeats-Brown (both of whom gave short summaries of some cases in their books) and—who else? The list is pitifully short. But Francis Story is on it and in my opinion is its most outstanding member to date. The modern anthropologists have been no more attentive to the cases since nearly all have gone to Asia as captives of Western ideas on human personality. On furlough from their doctrinal prisons in Europe or America they could not see in Asia what they knew to be impossible. Francis Story was a different type. Here was a man who did his own thinking and who lived among South Asians not with the idea of teaching them something—although he could—but with that of learning from them. He penetrated farther than any of his predecessors into what I call the empirical basis of South Asian religions. I predict that his contributions to the scientific investigations of rebirth will make his name better known and remembered with gratitude by future generations.

IAN STEVENSON, M.D.

Division of Parapsychology
Department of Psychiatry
School of Medicine
University of Virginia
Charlottesville, Virginia 22901

I

Essays on Rebirth

I

The Belief in Survival

Man has always found it difficult to believe that his life comes to an end with the dissolution of the physical body. The question, "Do we live on after death?", has always been prominent in human speculation, for it links up with every fundamental problem of man's being and purpose on this earth.

All religions, from the earliest times, have been unanimous in affirming that life continues beyond the grave, but doctrines differ widely on the question of what form the survival takes. Every theory presents its own special difficulties, the chief of them being that of deciding what constitutes individual personality. Theological distinctions between "spirit" and "soul" have never been able to free themselves from animistic associations; but the idea of a developing personality that is subject to the conditions of temporal existence is hard to reconcile with the notion of a spiritual entity that does not alter in the transition from time to eternity.

Primitive man found it easy to believe that his personality had a solid, unchanging core of selfhood that could persist in some way apart from the body, and this idea lay at the root of most religious thinking. Philosophers, on the other hand, have seldom attained the same degree of certainty. In ancient times the cleavage between religion and philosophy was not so sharp as it has become in our own day, but there has always been a marked difference between the charismatic utterances of the priest and the speculations of independent thinkers. When science took its own course, and insisted on the rejection of every belief that could not be subjected to the kind of tests that had been found valid for physical phenomena, science and religion came into direct conflict, with the ordinary man, who is neither scientist nor mystic, poised uneasily between them.

Nevertheless, the mass of humanity continues to believe in some form of survival, as it has done throughout the ages. In view of the virtual impossibility of establishing the truth of survival by empirical methods, this persistent belief is remarkable enough in itself to carry considerable force. It strongly suggests an area of experience that is accessible to the insights of

---

The title has been supplied by the Editor.

religion but is not open to the methods of investigation accepted by science. Philosophy itself is circumscribed by facts of the known world; it proceeds on assumptions drawn from observable phenomena; but religion draws its inspiration from personal intuitions in which these facts take on a different aspect, and in some circumstances cease to have the same relevance. The intuitive religious mind may thus become capable of reaching certain general conclusions that are true, by way of ideas that are not themselves true, or are at best only relative truths. This would account for the variety of different forms in which survival after death has appeared to people of different religious backgrounds.

One of the most serious objections to the belief in survival, that those who hold it cannot agree on the form the survival takes, or the conditions surrounding it, is removed if we consider that human thought can express itself only in terms of what is generally understood and believed. So the Christian, the Hindu, and the Muslim interpret what they feel to be true in terms relative to their own religious experience. The validity of what they have grasped does not in any way depend upon the truth or falsity of any conventional ideas from which it springs, but only on the authority of the universal truth that speaks through them.

In the West, spiritualism claims to have proved survival, and its adherents now include many people who have investigated it scientifically and have been convinced of its reality. There has been a revolutionary change in the attitude towards psychic phenomena in recent years. Many things which were once dismissed as fantasies of the imagination have become the subject of serious study. Intensive work carried out by the Society for Psychical Research in England, the Parapsychology Foundation of America, and similar organizations in several European countries has produced a great mass of evidence to show that there are forces at work in the cosmos which lie beyond the range of our present knowledge. The result of all this has been that such phenomena as telepathy, clairvoyance, and psychometry have come to be acknowledged as facts; the only point still open to conjecture is what it is that causes them. Even xenoglossy, the ability of certain people while in trance to speak languages unknown to them in their waking state, is now admitted to the list of supernormal faculties that have been demonstrated.

Nor is physical and objective evidence lacking for telekinesis, the moving of solid objects by intangible forces, which has been observed under test conditions. It is found in cases of "poltergeist" hauntings, the physical levitation of mediums, and the appearance of "apports," the last being objects which are transported from a distance independently of any physical agency, and sometimes projected into a closed chamber from outside.

It is now conceded that these phenomena actually take place; but they are not necessarily supernatural. They belong to an order of reality that lies beyond the space-time conditioned universe of physics, but which is governed by its own natural laws. To what extent and in what circumstances these laws are able to mingle with and modify the operations of the familiar world has yet to be established; but that they can, and occasionally do, cause interference with the ordinary processes of nature is a fact which cannot be dismissed.

Apart from the question of survival, the implications of the range of psychic phenomena are far-reaching both as regards the nature of the mind and its powers, and the character of the universe we live in. They suggest, in the words of Sir Oliver Lodge, "that an enlarged psychology, and possibly an enlarged physiology—possibly even an enlarged physics—will have to take into account and rationalize a number of phenomena which so far have been mainly disbelieved or ignored."

It is against this background that we must approach our inquiry: If we continue to exist after death, is it not reasonable to suppose that we have also lived before?

II

Rebirth and its Investigation

Once when Napoleon was having a dispute with his generals over strategy he suddenly stormed at them: "Don't you know who I am? I am Charlemagne! Don't you understand? *Charlemagne!*"

Whether the Man of Destiny really was Charlemagne reborn we shall never know. Self-identification with great historical characters is not unknown, but it is somewhat rare outside of mental homes. Napoleon was taking a risk with his reputation.

This idea suggests that there may be more sane people with a conviction that they have lived before than we should be inclined to suppose, and that for reasons of prudence they keep the knowledge to themselves. This may, indeed, be one explanation of the fact, often pointed out by critics, that memories of previous lives are more often found among children born in a Buddhist or Hindu environment than in the West. Many children are subject to elaborate fantasies, the creation of so-called dream worlds, in which they sometimes show surprising knowledge of things entirely outside their normal experience. One example of this, which happens to be known because of its connection with English literature, is that of the Brontë children, who wrote romances around their imaginary kingdoms, Gondal and Angria. Years later, on meeting Hartley Coleridge, Branwell Brontë was interested to learn that the son of the poet had also created a fictitious country, peopled by personalities that were very real to him, in early childhood.

Most children in the West are discouraged from leading such imaginary internal lives. If these are in fact based upon residual memories of former existences, they are very quickly suppressed by unsympathetic treatment, and the immediate impressions of the new life take their place. It may be that the comparatively new trend in education towards encouraging self-expression may release more information about the mental lives of children which will enable psychologists to trace the sources of these fantasies.

Some further help may come from the relaxing of religious attitudes,

Title supplied by the Editor. This section and the following one ("The Buddhist Concept of Rebirth") were intended as Chapters I and II of a larger book which remained unwritten. A few references to later chapters of that planned work have been deleted.

which in the West have acted as inhibiting factors preventing children from expressing what they are taught to look upon as false or unorthodox ideas. It is rather significant that when, some few years ago, a number of children attending English state schools were asked to fill up a questionnaire on religion, one question of which was: "What do you think happens to us after death?", an unexpected percentage of them answered something like "I think we sort of come back again, to learn more and become better." Most of the children who were questioned were from very ordinary homes where it was unlikely that they would have heard anything about rebirth. Despite unfavourable environments, cases are reported from time to time of children claiming to remember previous lives even among Roman Catholic and Muslim communities. For each one of these that has received publicity, adequate documentation, and investigation, it is fairly safe to assume that there are any number of others which are never revealed. It is only when something sensational is connected with them that they break into the news.

Parapsychology is a term which denotes the study of all kinds of extrasensory perception (ESP) and in general whatever functions of the mind may, on the evidence, be considered paranormal. It is beginning to give scientific respectability to the investigation of claimed memories of previous lives, as it has already done to that of other *psi* phenomena such as clairvoyance, precognition, telepathy, and a whole constellation of allied phenomena. Today there are research workers all over the world devoting themselves to the study of unexplained psychic faculties. But whereas it is possible to investigate, let us say, the ability of certain people to guess the order of cards turned up at random without seeing them, as Dr. J.B. Rhine of Duke University and others are doing, under very rigid test conditions, and so arrive at a statistical estimate of the subject's paranormal perceptive faculties based upon the law of averages, the case is very different with the investigation of claimed memories of previous lives. There, the possibilities of a controlled experiment are at the best limited; in some cases they are totally absent. Thus it is far more difficult to eliminate the possibility that the factual evidence so laboriously gathered by the investigator may be information that has reached the subject (usually a child) through normal channels, by subconscious observation, or even through the possession of some other paranormal faculty such as clairvoyance or psychometry. The extreme care which has to be taken in eliminating as far as is humanly possible all alternative explanations of the phenomena will be shown later on when we discuss the methods of investigating rebirth cases. At times the difficulties of placing the evidence on a firm scientific basis seem to be almost insurmountable. But by trial and error and the repetition of certain investigational methods over a large number of cases a technique is being formulated which has already yielded highly significant results.

Among other things, a general pattern of experience connected with rebirth is beginning to emerge from the mass of evidence that has accumulated. This pattern shows features that are quite independent of the religious, cultural, and social background of the subjects. The parapsychologist draws his net wide: one outstanding pioneer worker in this field has carried out on-the-spot investigations of cases suggestive of rebirth in parts of the world that have scarcely any feature in common, religious, cultural, or ethnic, with one another.[1] Places as far apart as India, Alaska, North Africa, America, and the European countries have all yielded their quota of what I shall call, for the sake of brevity, rebirth cases. And when it is discovered that through all the most seemingly authentic of these there runs a thread—or several threads—of common experience, the fact is surely something that must be taken into account. I shall mention here just two of these features which are encountered again and again with but slight variations: the similarity of descriptions of after-death or "between-lives" experiences given by those who claim to remember them, and the important role that birthmarks play in the continuity of identity between one life and another. The second feature is especially prominent in cases from Alaska and Burma, where it is actually used as a means of identifying a reborn personality, but it also occurs elsewhere.

My own investigations of rebirth cases began on a very minor scale in Burma in 1952. As a Buddhist, I had been for some time past interested in the stories that were current in Burma regarding rebirth. Several of them were narrated to me by persons who claimed that they had occurred to people personally known to them, or to relatives. As my informants were in the main people of some social standing and included judges, doctors, and government officials, I considered their testimony at least worth putting on record, and started making notes. At that time I had not read Fielding Hall's *The Soul of a People*, which gives some rather typical Burmese rebirth stories, so I approached the matter without any preconceived ideas.

Many of the people named in the cases were still living, but unfortunately I was not at that time able to carry our full-scale investigations. I was kept fully occupied with my work as Director-in-Chief of the Burma Buddhist World-Mission, which I had founded in 1949, and with my position on the

8

English Editorial Board of the Union of Burma Buddha Sāsana Council, which produced the Buddhist magazine *The Light of the Dhamma*. In addition to this, most of the rebirth cases reported to me were in parts of Burma which were occupied by insurgents, and it was impossible—for a foreigner, particularly—to visit them without incurring the suspicion of the Burmese authorities. For the time being, at least, Burma is off the map as regards rebirth investigation by parapsychologists from the West.

Nevertheless, one highly interesting example of rebirth with physical malformations happened to come under my own observation in Rangoon. That was the case of the Karen houseboy which I have described in my book *The Case for Rebirth*.[2] For the reasons I have mentioned above I was not able to follow up with interviews with the boy's parents or childhood associates, but I questioned him closely, obtained a medical opinion on his congenital malformations, and satisfied myself by psychological tests that he was speaking the truth. I had two reasons for believing him: first, the Karens are noted for their general truthfulness and integrity, and this particular houseboy had never given me any reason to doubt his word in other connections; and secondly, no matter how closely I cross-examined him with trick questions he never contradicted any detail of his account, but remained entirely consistent from first to last. Furthermore, the marks on his body were of a highly unusual kind, and corresponded perfectly with the account he gave of the circumstances of his death.

Critics of this particular case have told me that they would have believed the boy's evidence if I had used a lie-detector. A comment of this kind shows only a complete ignorance of psychology and of the way lie-detectors function. The lie-detector works by registering the physiological changes in a guilty person who knows that he is speaking falsehood and cannot control his nervous reactions. If a person under test is suffering from a genuine delusion and fully believes that he is speaking the truth when he is not, the lie-detector will report him as speaking the truth. A lie-detector is therefore worse than useless in such a case, since it will serve only to confirm as truth what is nothing but a fantasy.

This is not to say that the use of such instruments as the lie-detector and the encephalograph is completely worthless in all cases. There may be circumstances in which conscious lying by the subject or by witnesses can be exposed by such means, and investigations in future may be carried out with their assistance. All I wish to make clear is that in the case of the Karen houseboy, and in all cases where the subject fully believes that he is speaking the truth, whether he is or not, such devices as the lie-detector cannot be expected to give worthwhile results.

Since my first rather crude attempts at investigating rebirth cases in Burma I have been able, through the encouragement and support of an American university, to extend my field work on the subject in India, Thailand, and Ceylon. Before undertaking this research I had already developed my own techniques of investigation. My methods were later supplemented from the experience of other researchers whose study had covered more diverse cultures and a far wider geographical area than my own, and I have been greatly helped by the pooling of information that resulted from these contacts. I have been given reason to believe, also, that my own contribution to the pool has not been without value. It must be remembered that this particular branch of parapsychology is still in its infancy. Not only is it of far more recent origin than the research into other types of ESP, but it is encountering even more opposition from orthodox scientific circles than did Dr. Rhine's experiments in extra-sensory communication. It is a sad reflection on the essentially unscientific nature of human thinking that this opposition comes almost as strongly from psychical investigators who, although for many years they have been engaged in trying to prove survival after death, show an unreasonable objection to the idea that survival should take the form of rebirth. On the other hand, there is an increasing number of Western spiritualists who have come to accept what they call "reincarnation" as a fact—simply because it is the only theory that can account for some of the gaps and inconsistencies in spiritualist belief.[3]

Sometimes I am asked whether there is decisive "scientific" proof of rebirth. The question is a rather naive one. I can only reply that at the present stage of investigations there is no conclusive proof, and that it is rather too much to expect. Actual conviction lies only with those who have the subjective experience of remembering a previous life, and a purely subjective experience can never carry absolute authority with those who have not shared it. We may have the testimony of many outstanding men and women who for various reasons, philosophical or intuitive, have believed in an unending series of lives, although it is not part of their traditional religious faith,[4] but all that goes for nothing with the average man who bases his attitudes upon just the information which his own senses provide him as to the nature of the world he lives in. Similarly, any number of people may testify that they can remember having lived on earth before, and neither lie-detectors nor any other device will help them to convince anyone but those who have the same kind of memories. We therefore have to rely upon the careful sifting and weighing of evidence from many different sources, an operation which has to be carried out not only with a sound knowledge of psychology, both normal and abnormal, but also with a grounding in the techniques used in other branches of psychical investigation. The investigator must also have a thorough knowledge of all that is at present known about telepathy, psychometry, clairvoyance, and every other branch of ESP, for each of them impinges at some point or other upon his analysis and assessment of a rebirth case.

The ideal rebirth investigator would in fact be a combination of private detective, examining magistrate, psychologist, philosopher, and newspaper reporter—the last to enable him to avoid publicity rather than to exploit it. Above all, it need hardly be said, his attitude must be strictly objective and he must have a veneration for truth which no temptation can shake. If this branch of parapsychology is ever to take its place as a form of research commanding scientific respect it must have no connection with propagandists or with those who are satisfied with slack and unmethodical work, or who are lacking in the training and experience which would enable them to distinguish between facts which could have become known to a subject under examination by normal means, or through one of the extra-sensory faculties, and information in his possession which he could not have gained through any of these channels, and which only paranormal memory of a former existence could account for.

The Buddhist principle of avoiding the two extremes is as sound in rebirth investigation as it is in all other human activities. The investigator must not be anxious at all costs to make out a case for his own theory or religious belief in rebirth; on the other hand, he must not be prejudiced against it. The one is as bad as the other.

Apropos of this, I feel it due to the reader to give a brief description of my own position. I have been a Buddhist since the age of sixteen, having accepted the Dhamma first on purely intellectual grounds. Over the years, and with gathering experience, my faith has become confirmed. This being so, rebirth—as it is understood in Buddhism—stands as a fact which needs no external evidence to support it. It is sufficient for me that there is nothing in scientific knowledge which is inconsistent with it. I therefore feel no desire or need to convince either myself or others through the evidence afforded by the claimed memories of previous lives. So far as I am personally concerned, they could all be proved explicable on quite other grounds,

11

whether it be fraud, delusion, dual or multiple personality, or even spirit-possession. I should be quite ready to throw them all out of the window if necessary. If I have come to the conclusion that a large percentage of them cannot be explained away by any of these hypotheses it is not because I am a Buddhist, but because the nature and weight of the evidence would have brought me to that view in any case. In all the rebirth investigations I have conducted personally I have recorded the testimony of subjects and witnesses with impartiality, noting where there are discrepancies and making no attempt to conceal or gloss them over. The evidence in a great many of the cases fills bulky files. Many of the cases I have had to reject as being insufficiently supported by the evidence. Such cases nevertheless serve as useful guides in the study and evaluation of others; they provide instructive psychological information as well as indicating various ways of guarding against self-delusion and downright fraud on the part of subjects or witnesses.

Other cases have been so rich in evidential detail that they could be dealt with adequately only by making them the subject of a separate book, which ideally should include a full discussion of the case on its individual merits. This is particularly so where interesting psychological features are prominent, as for example in cases involving change of sex in rebirth. This in itself represents a rather startling challenge to Western psychological concepts, and promises to give a new orientation to all accepted ideas. When more is known about it, the fresh knowledge may result in a totally different attitude towards sexual maladjustments, and, it may be hoped, a more reasonable and humane one.

One feature of the investigations has been found in conflict with my own earlier view: namely, the fact that certain persons claim to have been "reincarnated" in the bodies of babies conceived, and sometimes even born, before the death of their previous personality. Whatever opinion we may hold of them, such cases are on record and they come from various parts of the world, including Buddhist countries. They have to be taken into consideration and fitted into the general pattern. Long before this branch of parapsychology reaches maturity we may be obliged to revise many of our ideas on the subject of rebirth, and indeed of what it is that really constitutes human personality. If that is so, we must be prepared to do it. But once the central fact is established we shall have advanced a long way towards being able to examine the apparently disharmonious details with a better understanding of just what the rebirth process entails.

At present the work of the investigator is to gather as many well-attested facts as possible, subject them to exacting scrutiny and critical analysis, and by comparison of a great number of cases try to discover their points of agreement and disagreement; to trace cultural and religious influences where they exist, and to present as unbiased a picture of the progressive results as he can from time to time, without necessarily committing himself to any final interpretation of the phenomena.

III

The Buddhist Concept of Rebirth

Every scientific discovery has begun with a hypothesis of some kind, and the need to remain uncommitted as to details does not prohibit the parapsychologist from holding certain beliefs concerning rebirth, nor does the possession of such ideas disqualify him as an investigator of the phenomena. That is, so long as he possesses the ideas, and the ideas do not possess him. He must be prepared to follow the example of a certain famous astro-physicist who, after firmly holding to the steady-state theory of the universe for over twenty years, finally rejected it when he found that it no longer fitted the latest facts. This is the kind of sacrifice that science demands, and which the scientist must be at all times prepared to make in the interest of truth and progress.

On that understanding I propose, before going any further, to define what is meant by rebirth in Buddhism.

Regarding the question of survival after death, human thinking has in general followed one of two philosophical currents: annihilationism and eternalism.[5] The first holds that after the dissolution of the physical body the personality ceases to exist; it is equivalent to materialism. The second maintains that the individual personality persists after death in a recognizable form, as an entity variously named the "soul," "spirit," or "self." This belief, in some form or another, is the basis of all theistic religion. There are many theories as to what happens to this soul-entity after death, from the ancient Egyptian belief that it continued to inhabit the mummified body—or alternatively, went on a hazardous journey through the underworld until it became united with the Osiris—to the Christian belief in a resurrection of the body—or alternatively, the spiritualistic idea that it continued its conscious existence on a spiritual plane. In all of them the common factor is the belief in the immortality of the individual, his preservation of the same identity throughout all eternity. Vedantic Hinduism offers a modification of this theory in the doctrine of a final absorption of the individual Ātman in the Brahman.

Buddhism rejects both of these opposing views. The first was stigmatized by the Buddha as being erroneous and harmful. If there were no continuity of life in any shape after death there would be no moral law of *kamma* and *vipāka* (actions and results) operating in the universe. All life would be meaningless and there would certainly be no object in practising self-restraint or endeavouring to free oneself of the craving which brings suffering in its train. The Buddha's entire doctrine of Nibbāna, the path to it and the reasons for following that path, would be redundant if death were followed by complete extinction. There are certain persons today who try to maintain that the Buddha did not teach rebirth. Whether they propagate this view in the mistaken belief that by so doing they make Buddhism more acceptable to the modern mind, which they imagine is completely wedded to materialism, or because they wish to convert Buddhism and Buddhists to the materialist-annihilationist view which the Buddha expressly repudiated, their ideas need not detain us here. They are sufficiently refuted in every expression of the Buddha's teaching, from his first sermon at Isipatana to his last exhortation before his Parinibbāna.

As to the second view, that of eternalism, the Buddha's teaching was equally emphatic. He perceived, and showed conclusively, that there is no stable, enduring entity in human personality—that it was not possible for what we understand as the *total personality* of a being to survive death. It is this teaching, the *anattā* doctrine, which is at once the distinguishing feature of Buddhism, the one that marks it out from all other religious concepts of life after death, and at the same time the most difficult doctrine to grasp. Its full realization is in fact so difficult to attain that the Buddha himself, when he first penetrated it, doubted whether he would ever be able to make it intelligible to others. With a little superficial thinking it is easy to accept annihilationism or eternalism, and to believe that there is no alternative to them; but to understand the Buddhist teaching of rebirth and *anattā* is a tougher proposition altogether. Many people imagine that they understand it when they do not. Yet it is in a sense the most important issue of Buddhism, the doctrine around which all the others revolve and the one thing needful above all others for the right understanding which leads to the destruction of craving and the painful round of rebirths. Suffering arises from craving, and craving is grounded on the illusory concept of a "self"; therefore the first of the ten fetters to be broken for release from the round of existence (*saṃsāra*) is called "illusion of selfhood" (*sakkāya-diṭṭhi*).

It is not my purpose here to go into the ethical implications of *anattā*, or its bearing upon the doctrine of Nibbāna. I shall confine myself to such description of it as is necessary for an understanding of the Buddhist position regarding rebirth.

15

As long ago as the beginning of this century William James wrote something to the effect that in studying the mind we come across mental operations and processes, a continual flux of events, but nowhere any stable, enduring entity. It is precisely this truth that the Buddha discovered and taught as an essential part of his Dhamma.

In Buddhism the sentient being is a psycho-physical complex made up of five aggregates: material form, sensation, perception, mental formations, and consciousness. These constitute the total personality, or *nāma-rūpa* (literally, name-and-form). The division of material and psychical corresponds in a sense to the Western concept of the flesh and the spirit, but in Buddhism it does not imply a dichotomy: the four immaterial aggregates depend upon and are conditioned by the existence of a body, and the nature of their functioning is determined by the sensory apparatus of that body. Likewise, in the process of its arising and formation the body is conditioned by the mind. The two aspects of personality are therefore interrelated and interdependent. How this comes about can be understood by viewing their relationship in terms of a cyclic process: it cannot be said that mind precedes body, or that body precedes mind.[6] The Buddhist doctrine of dependent origination,[7] or arising by way of condition, completely excludes the need for a first cause, since it makes the temporal sequence of causality a purely arbitrary notion. Without going into the philosophical complexities of dependent origination, some idea of the relationship subsisting between the aggregates of personality may be gained from the following description of their nature and functioning.

Material form (rūpa): This is simply the physical body, equipped with the sensory organs appropriate to it. It comes into being through the genetic processes, its nature and the quality of its sensory apparatus being determined by the kamma of a being who has lived previously.

Sensation (vedanā): This is the feeling that arises through contact between the organs of sense and objects which produce sensory stimulation. The "fields of sense perception" are six: visual, auditory, olfactory, gustatory, tactile, and mental. The mind is included as one of the senses for two reasons: it depends upon a physical organ (the base of consciousness) and it correlates and organizes all the information received through the other senses, while at the same time having a sensory activity of its own, the capacity for ideation.

Perception (saññā): The conscious awareness of sensation. This is made a distinct aggregate because the quality of perception varies with different

16

organisms and even between individuals of the same organic composition: i.e., what is perceived as pleasant by one may be unpleasant to another. These distinctions depend upon the predilections or aversions produced by past kamma.

Mental formations (saṅkhāra): This is the most difficult of the terms to define in brief. It includes memory, habit formations set up in the past, and, most important of all, the capacity for volition. In a sense it is equivalent to character. Although the mental formations, as the term implies, are largely conditioned by the nature of past activities, they are yet capable of producing willed action within a more or less limited field of choice. Considered from the ethical point of view, therefore, it is correct to include kamma, the power to act according to decision, among the mental formations. This production of kamma, with its good or bad results (*vipāka*), is the most decisive feature of personality.

Consciousness (viññāṇa): The stream of conscious existence fed and supported by the other aggregates. Consciousness is not an entity; it consists of an endless series of point-moments of awareness which arise and pass away with inconceivable rapidity. As each point-moment passes away it is followed immediately by its successor. It is in this way that the "world-line" of identity is maintained. There is also a submerged stream of identity, which consists of the causal continuity of the process (*santati*) on the organic and mentally subconscious levels.

In Buddhism, then, personality is seen as a series of events; it is a process in time, wherein the subjective notion of self-identity depends upon the ability to recall past states, and objective identity between one state and another state that succeeds it lies in the temporal relationship of causality subsisting between them. To put it more simply, a man of sixty may remember his boyhood and enough of what has happened to him in the time between to be able to say that he is the same person as the boy he remembers having been. But he is the "same" person only in a conventional sense. Actually, there is no single item of his psycho-physical complex that is the same as it was when he was a boy. In terms of what actually exists it can only be said that the man of sixty belongs to the same line of causal continuity as did the boy that he remembers having been: he is the end-product of an infinite series of connecting states of being—or rather, of coming-to-be—which make up his individual world-line. If he were to suffer damage to the brain resulting in total amnesia, his sense of personal identity would be lost; there would then be nothing but the unconscious

17

stream of causality left to identify him with the personalities of his infancy, youth, and maturity. His friends would "recognize" him whereas he himself could not.

We are now in a better position to answer the vexing question: If there is no soul, what is it that is reborn? The first thing that becomes apparent is that the word "rebirth" is not a very satisfactory one. It is better, certainly, than "reincarnation," yet still it implies that there is a something that after death takes on flesh again. The Pāli word used in Buddhism to denote the process simply means "arising";[8] there is nothing but a continuous "arising by way of cause."[9] And this "arising by way of cause" denotes not only the arising of a new mind-body complex at birth, as the result of the kamma of one that has existed before; it also stands for the arising of the point-moments of consciousness as they succeed one another in the causal continuum of one lifetime. Each point-moment of consciousness is a little birth and a little death; and this alternation of birth and death is going on all the time. It is for this reason that Buddhism defines all existence as *anicca, dukkha, anattā*—impermanent, subject to suffering, and void of self.

The life-stream may be likened to a current of electricity, for its flow is the result of the generation of units of energy from moment to moment. The sustaining factor in this continual generation of psychic energy is desire or craving (*taṇhā*). This craving manifests itself as a clinging to the elements of existence, the will to live, and it expresses itself in action. All intentional action can therefore be traced back to desire of some kind, the only exception to this rule being that of the arahat, the fully purified human being who has extinguished every form of craving.

(*Here the manuscript ends.*)

IV
What Is Reborn?

Extracts from a letter to a friend

In your letter you asked about rebirth, and I'd better admit straight away that I can't "explain" it in so many words. Words, which are just symbols, can only deal precisely with matters of common experience, for which we have a common stock of corresponding ideas; and even then they sometimes go astray badly, because we each draw our own interpretation of their meaning from our own individual sum of knowledge and our own personal way of interpreting the facts of experience. For the rest, they're just approximations to the reality they express, and that "reality" in itself is subject to various modes of cognition; it is only relative and can therefore only be "known" in the context of other assumed realities. Each of us is apt to see, or understand, things, events, and situations in an entirely different way both from other people and even from ourselves at different stages of our ever-changing mental and psychic progression. For this, it's only necessary to cite the difference between the child's world and that of the adult; between that of the sane "normal" person and the psychopath, without taking extreme cases. There is a world that is normal for the child and one that is normal for the adult, yet at the same time this normalcy is purely theoretical; it can only be known by deviations—some degree of the infinite range of which is to be found in everybody.

"*Cogito, ergo sum*" sounds very convincing, but we must define just what we mean by "I am." Right at the start, it's not a static entity. The child who says "I exist" becomes a man and continues to say "I exist" with the same confidence, but he is not talking about the same thing when he says "I." Everything that constitutes it has changed, no doubt imperceptibly and in some cases to a much lesser extent, psychically, than in others (here I make no quarrel with your observation of yourself, because in some people the character of the mind does change comparatively little—"nevertheless, it changes") and the "I" of the man of forty is by no means the "I" of the

From *The Light of the Dhamma* (Rangoon), Vol. III, No. 2 (1956).

child of, say, twelve. Or of any of the innumerable stages in between. Yet it is the *result* of that former "I," without the pre-existence of which it could not have come into being; there is a causal continuum that links them, just as there is a continuum of the bodily process that, through all the cellular changes and physical developments or deteriorations, makes the body of the grown man the *result* of the body of the infant. Here, the only "reality" we can trace is the reality of a causal process, and it cannot well be anything but that process that we mean when we say "I am." Now, we may call this a "life process," and for certain purposes that is a satisfactory definition. But not for all, because the process applies equally to inanimate things, and to give it its true significance we must raise it to a cosmic level, where the words "alive" and "lifeless" cease to mean what they meant on the plane of relative reality, or on the subjective level of the individual's own self-awareness. A process of de-personalization—something more than mere objectivity—must come into play to enable us to realize the nature of the "self" as merely a part, or a succession of momentary manifestations, of a universal principle.

The impression we receive of a persisting identity throughout the unbroken succession of experiences, together with the conviction of selfhood, comes about through the individuality of the current of awareness and its insulation from all other currents, whether they be parallel or transverse, not through the actual persistence of any unit of personal identity such as we commonly mean when we use the word "myself." When we say, "Yesterday I did so-and-so," we are speaking in conventional terms; to be more nearly precise we should say, "Yesterday the aggregate of physical and mental elements that constituted what was then called 'I,' and which was the causal forerunner of what is called 'I' today, did so-and-so." And this introduces another important factor in the persistence of the identity-concept—that of memory. To a certain extent, varying greatly in different people, we do have the ability to retrace our steps, as it were, through the line of the causal continuum, marking various points at which the time-flow cuts across it; but this is also characterized by gaps, periods of which we can recall nothing because the points of intersection did not mark any significant interruption of the real current, which is subconscious (in Pāli it is called *bhavaṅga)*. When conscious attention is turned towards any external object or event there is an interruption of this unconscious causal current, and it is these points which, to a greater or lesser extent, according to their strength and the consequent impression they make, we remember.

Now, if we accept this view of the "personality" as we study it in ourselves or any other living being, it becomes much less important to know *what* it is that is reborn. The whole question takes on a different aspect, and we even begin to suspect that it is wrongly put—there ceases, in fact, to be any justification for such a question. "Not he, yet not another," the Buddha tersely said, and the reply fits equally the case of the adult man and his causal predecessor the child, and the being that comes into existence (or rather, the re-emergence of the same causal current) after what we call "death." All we are justified in assuming is a causal cosmic principle which connects the child with the adult, and the "self" of this existence with the "self" of the next and all subsequent ones. The actual determinant of the nature of this current is the willed activity we generate—if you like, the life-urge (which is *taṇhā*—craving) and the actions to which it gives rise, which form the kamma. At any given point we are subject to the results of past kamma, but our present kamma with its future results is subject to us; we cannot unmake the past, but we are continually creating the future.

Here, two further difficulties present themselves, of which I'll deal with the simplest first. Since memory does not usually bridge the gulf between two existences (although it in fact does so much more often than is commonly supposed, and can certainly be cultivated to do so), how can it be said that there is any kind of identity between the past, present, and future personalities, and even if an identity of a sort be admitted, can it be truly said that the new being is suffering or enjoying the results of his own actions? Is he not justified in saying, "Since the person who suffers the results of my bad actions will not be myself, in the sense in which I understand it, why should I trouble about possible consequences?"

For the answer to this we have to return to the concept of personal identity that we constructed from our comparison of the child and the (consequent) adult; and where concrete examples can be used it is always best to use them. Supposing, then, the child loses an arm or leg through an accident. The man that he becomes, despite all physical and mental changes and what may be quite justly called a completely reconstructed personality, will still continue to be a person minus an arm or leg, as a direct result of what happened to the child that he once was. He will be suffering, in fact, for something that happened to *a being that was, yet at the same time and in another sense was not,* himself—and that despite the fact that he may not be able to recollect any of the circumstances of the accident. Yet would one say that a child need not take any special care in crossing the road because if he loses a limb it will not be he who will suffer in the future but another person whose existence he cannot even foresee? To carry the analogy forward in another direction and incidentally bring in the moral considerations that are inseparable from any view of kamma, it is possible for an elderly man to be suffering the physical and mental consequences of follies committed in his youth; yet would one say to any youth about to commit such follies that he should go right ahead, since their results would be endured not by him but by another person who would be merely the result of his present existence? Obviously one wouldn't; yet the relationship between the youth and the old man is precisely the same as that existing between the "personality" of the present life and that of the future—simply that the one is the result, in a causally connected sequence, of the other.[10]

There is yet another aspect to this question, with its ethical implications. With the gradual liberation from the concept of personal identity and all it implies of selfhood, and consequently of exclusive self-interest, the ego inevitably becomes merged in the wider cosmic operation, and it becomes of the first importance to avoid the propagation of suffering in any form, whether it is oneself that suffers or any other sentient being. Long before self-identification—the real objective and purpose of compassion—is achieved, the question of whether it is oneself or another that suffers in the future recedes into insignificance, until it is finally found to have no meaning whatever. The "self" as we understand it may not be real, but suffering is real. In the widest philosophical interpretation all *vedanā* (sensation) is *dukkha* (suffering), whether it appears in the form of pain or pleasure. This is so because it is a stimulation, an agitation, a disturbance of the mind's tranquillity; and also because it is transitory and yields only temporary satisfaction. Pleasure, particularly physical pleasure, is only the release of a tension, the momentary gratification of a craving that is incessantly renewing itself, and which grows in intensity with what it feeds upon. What we call pleasure and pain are so intimately associated that in certain experiences it is impossible to say at what point the one becomes the other or to what extent the two are commingled and identified.

What it all comes down to is that we have to discard the old terms of reference and adopt new ones, substituting the idea of a dynamic process of causality for the conventional and grammatically necessary "I," which means that the problem of rebirth is largely one of semantics. In any case, we have to begin like Confucius, by examining and "rectifying" terms, finding out just how closely they can be made to correspond to the ideas they represent, before we can establish whether the ideas themselves are true.

The chief thing in the quest for understanding is to allow the ideas to sink in—neither striving to accept nor to oppose—until by a gradual readjustment the mind comes to a decision. There are some things one can understand, yet cannot express in words. It's just this point I've tried to make in my articles in the *Light of the Dhamma* and elsewhere. Naturally people want to know about rebirth, and how the Buddhist idea differs from "reincarnation," "transmigration," and so on. One can only say that these ideas are simplifications of it—reductions of the highly abstract truth to popular and animistic terms.

V

Rebirth and the Western Thinker

EDITORIAL NOTE IN "THE LIGHT OF THE DHAMMA":

We have received the following letter from a reader in Australia who is a sincere student of Buddhism. The points it raises are of such general interest and so typical of the queries that must arise in the minds of Western students of Buddhism that we are publishing the letter in full, together with a reply by Mr. Francis Story, who has made Buddhist philosophy vis-a-vis Western thought his special subject.

We wish to take this opportunity of reminding our readers all over the world that we welcome such queries as this, since they afford us an opportunity of showing how Buddhism meets the challenge of present-day knowledge.

Kedron, Brisbane, Australia
Dated the 28th December 1957

Dear Sir,

What puzzles me most concerning kamma and rebirth is how one can correlate it with new developments and findings in modern psychology and genetics. I received from Professor F.A.E. Crew, M.D. (Edinburgh), who is a lecturer in genetics, the following reply some time ago:

As to whether or not the doctrine of reincarnation is inconsistent with the findings of the geneticist, I really cannot give you a satisfactory answer. I take it that reincarnation or rebirth means the reappearance of the same individual with the same inborn potentialities and therefore, presumably, with the same genetic constitution. This would mean that the individual in each of his several reappearances would perforce have to belong to the same species and that many of his attributes would be the same in every succeeding generation—e.g., his blood group, the colour of his eyes and skin, his fingerprints, and the like. On the other hand, since so much of the characterization of the individual is due to the interaction of genetic constitution and the circumstances and conditions of the external world, differences in experience in successive appearances would tend to yield different personalities.

From *The Light of the Dhamma* (Rangoon), Vol. V, No. 2 (1958).

A Rationalist writer, J. Bowden, on rebirth writes as follows:

It seems to me that the science of genetics has definitively disposed of the rebirth theory. It has been established beyond a shadow of doubt that every person manifests not only the physical but the mental characteristics of both its parents—not in equal proportions, of course; the traits of one parent may predominate. The parents will carry the characteristics of their parents, and so on.

Ancestral traits comprise the hereditary equipment of every child at birth. Environmental influences then come into play, the personality which results being the product of hereditary and environmental factors.

On the rebirth theory the child cannot be the offspring of its parents other than in a physical sense, although he or she may be an incarnation of some remote ancestor, i.e., it may be its own great-great-grandparent.

But it has been demonstrated that the psychic life of each of us commences from the moment of conception and that this "soul" develops with the growth of the embryo. What of this "soul"?

True, the mind of the child at birth is a *tabula rasa* (except in so far as it may—and this is doubtful—carry impressions of its intra-uterine existence); but of ideas it has none. All that it has is a brain and nervous system (built up of elements derived from both parents) which enable the child to acquire ideas. But what ideas shall be acquired depends upon the nature of its environment. A child born in China of Chinese parents will develop a peculiarly Chinese "psyche," one which no European can properly understand.

All these facts are commonplaces of social psychology. The rebirth theory makes nonsense of it all. On that theory the "soul" is an intruder; it does not develop from within, it enters from without; it had been waiting for a greater or lesser period in the ethereal region for a suitable body to inhabit.

Several questions present themselves. Is the "soul" during its sojourn in the ethereal region conscious or unconscious? If the former, why is it that we do not recall our experiences in that region? If the latter, then how does it find its way into the embryo or foetus? (If not unconscious before, it certainly becomes unconscious when it enters the embryo: consciousness does not dawn until some time after birth. The first discovery of the child is of itself, through the sense of touch. Then it begins to "take notice" of its mother, and gradually takes in other factors of its environment.)

25

The dictum of the physiological psychologist that there can be no mind without a brain completely negates the belief that a "soul" can exist in the interval that believers in rebirth necessarily assume between the departure from one body and the entry into another. To the physiological psychologist, mind is the activity of the brain and the nervous system (or, to put it the other way, the activity of the brain and nervous system is "mind").

It has been demonstrated that injury to a particular brain area, say the centre for sight, will render one blind; injury to or disease of the auditory centre will result in deafness, and so on. What happens when the entire brain is destroyed? Where is the "mind"—"the soul"?

The brain is an extremely delicate organ. Its functioning can be deranged by alcohol or other drugs. A blow on the head may bring unconsciousness. And yet we are expected to believe that if the brain is completely crushed a functioning mind still persists. One may as well (it is just as logical) contend that a particular current of electricity generated by a primary cell will continue to flow when the cell is destroyed.

There is no individual, no "person," until the fusion of male and female germ cells takes place. There can be no psychic life until there is a psyche and I (Bowden) am not able to believe in a psyche existing before there is a completed brain. Those who argue that "mind" is possible without a brain are invited to explain why a brain is developed at all.

Ideas are complex mental formulations, and it seems to me to be self-evident that before ideas can exist there must be material for thought. Impressions have to be registered on the brain, and these impressions are derived from the external world via the sensory nervous system. How can impressions be registered before there is a nervous system capable of picking up impressions? The argument that a personality already equipped with a stock of ideas enters into the developing embryo only puts the problem further back. How did the first "personality" acquire its ideas?

The eyes of the new-born child are expressionless. By watching the child as it grows one can also see the dawn of intelligence. Its eyes roam; it begins to "take notice" and gradually builds up a world of mental experiences, a storehouse of ideas. But the nature of the ideas thus acquired depends upon the nature of the environment. Of course the quality of the brain has to be taken into account. We can be certain that had Edison been born in Paleolithic times he would, by virtue of his superior brain power, have discovered a new and better way of making fire; but he could not have invented the incandescent lamp.

It seems to me (Bowden) that the theorists of mind have overlooked that the word "mind" is merely an abstraction, a convenient term for mental experiences. We speak of mind and brain, but that is for convenience of expression. It is lost sight of that what is separable in thought is not necessarily separable in fact. We should say that brain and mind are two aspects of the same thing. Those who refuse to consider mind in terms of brain function should tell us what is the brain's function if it is not mental. We know that the brain is a living functioning organ. What is its function if it is not mind? It would perhaps be best to regard "mind" as the brain at work.

How does one account for "identical twins" on the rebirth theory? When such twins are brought up together they not only show many characteristics in common; they often react in a similar manner to environmental influences; their ideas follow a similar pattern. On the rebirth theory we have to suppose that every time identical twins are on their way, two virtually "identical" souls enter into the developing embryos.

Identical twins result when an ovum that has been fertilized splits into two separate parts which then develop independently, unlike twins who are the outcome of the fertilization of two different ova. On the rebirth theory, there is no reason why if identical souls can enter the embryos in the first case they should not do so in the second, and the physically unlike twins possess the same mentality. But it is notorious that unlike twins may differ so widely in their outlook as scarcely to have an idea in common. In such cases one twin has a predominance of maternal characteristics and the other of paternal characteristics. Only in the case of identical twins are the characteristics evenly distributed.

On the rebirth theory we have to suppose an extraordinary series of coincidences. We have to believe that identical "souls" are forever hovering around awaiting their opportunity to enter the bodies of identical twins, and those only; they "pass up" the chance of entering the bodies resulting from two independently fertilized ova. The problem is complicated further when we consider triplets, quadruplets, etc. And what happens when one of the set dies at birth? What happens to this twin "soul"? Does it return to the empyrean, there to await another chance for rebirth? But then it will have to enter into an entirely different body—one which may be malformed or have a defective brain."

I do not think J. Bowden is correct in his statements on identical twins. Even though they result as he says I do not think they are as completely identical as he says. Minor differences are present. However, I will try to get Professor Crew's opinion on the matter as he specializes in genetics.

I would be much interested as to the views of Buddhists on the above matters. The subject of kamma and rebirth is indeed a vast one and I do not expect any details as I know you have much work to do. Kamma and rebirth is for me, and I think most Westerners, a very difficult subject to understand. Incidentally, does rebirth mean plurality *of lives on earth*?

May the Buddha-Dhamma form a bridge of understanding between East and West!

With best wishes and greetings from Australia,

Sincerely,

Sd./A.G.

P.S. I suppose my quotations from Mr. J. Bowden all sound academic (for Buddhism is a practical way of life) but it is on such questions that I'm ignorant of Buddhist concepts.

A.G.

THE REPLY

Much misunderstanding of the Buddhist doctrine of rebirth has been caused in the West by the use of the words "reincarnation," "transmigration," and "soul."

The last concept in particular presents a stumbling block to the true understanding of what may be thought to happen when rebirth takes place. "Soul" is an ambiguous term that has never been clearly defined in Western religious or philosophical thought; but it is generally taken to mean the sum total of an individual personality, an enduring ego-entity that exists more or less independently of the physical body and survives it after death. The "soul" is considered to be the personality factor which distinguishes one individual from another, and is supposed to consist of the elements of

28

consciousness, mind, character, and all that goes to make up the psychic, immaterial side of a human being. A very good non-religious definition is given by Max Loewenthal who says: "The entity which is known by the names of mind, soul, spirit, consciousness, or psyche, may be defined *as the organic whole of an inner world consisting of associated conscious impressions and activities all of which are felt as belonging to a conscious unit or ego."* (*Life and Soul: Outlines of a Future Theoretical Physiology and of a Critical Philosophy,* 1935).

The idea of such a "soul" transmigrating after death into another body, in the Pythagorean sense, is inherently improbable. Theories of a "reincarnating soul" ask us to believe that this complex psychic entity can be transferred from one physical habitation to another of an entirely different psychophysical order, as when the "soul" of a fully matured man, replete with knowledge and experience, is said to "reincarnate" in the body of a newborn infant. Obviously there can be no identity between the mind of the man who died and the undeveloped psychic faculties of the infant who is said to be his "reincarnation." When the theory is extended to "transmigration" into animal forms of life it becomes totally unacceptable.

In any case, all the evidence is against the existence of such a "soul" even during the course of one lifetime. The "entity," the "conscious unit or ego" of Max Loewenthal, is merely a subjective impression derived from the continuity of successive moments of conscious experience. William James, one of the pioneer psychologists, declared that no such entity could be found, but in its place only an ever-changing process. This process is not only the ordinary process of change of which we can be sensible in everything around us, but is actually, as Buddhism teaches, an "existence" made up solely of the arising and passing away of momentary units of consciousness. Those who have difficulty in conceiving a flux of change without a "thing" that changes will find the idea presented very convincingly in Henri Bergson's *Creative Evolution.*

In the journey from cradle to grave the personality alters with the accumulation of experience, the growth of understanding, and the changes wrought in it by external circumstances. It is also subject to alterations due to physical degenerations and accidents. Nothing can be found in the psychic side of man's nature that is permanent; very little that is even consistent. All we can distinguish are certain tendencies to think and react in recognizable patterns of behaviour which can remain fairly constant throughout life if they are not affected by any irresistible influences. It is the sum of these tendencies which we call character; but even they are not predictable in all circumstances. To the scientist they appear as partly the results of heredity and partly of environmental influences, and there can be no doubt whatever that these factors in their interaction account for a great deal of human personality. Whether they account for *all* of it we shall be in a better position to decide at a later stage of this discussion.

The Buddha categorically denied the existence of a "soul" in the sense defined above. Buddhism recognizes the fact that all conditioned and compounded phenomena are impermanent, and this alone makes the existence of such a "soul" impossible. A being is a compound of five *khandhas*—physical body, sensation, perception, tendencies, and consciousness—all of which are in a continual state of flux.

What then is the "identity" between a person in one life and the "same" person in another which justifies the use of the word "rebirth?" The answer is that it is purely a serial relationship—an "identity" of a certain kind which can only be described in terms of a causal continuum. Actually, this is the only kind of identity that can be found between the various different stages of life of a being throughout a single life span. The "identity" between the newborn infant and the old man it becomes, say eighty years later, is *only* an identity of causal succession. Everything that makes up the individual, both mental and physical, at any particular moment, is the product of a series of antecedent and causally related personalities, and when we say it is the same person we use the expression merely in a conventional sense; what we really mean is that the infant is the causal antecedent of the old man, and the old man is the effect-product of the infant. Instead of an enduring "soul" we find a dynamic process of cause and effect to be the only link between the various stages of an individual life.

The relationship between the human being who dies and the human or other being that is born as the result of his kamma in the process called "rebirth" is of precisely the same order as the relationship between the newborn child and the old man it is destined to become. It is the same as the relationship between the infant, the child, the adolescent, the youth, the adult, and the elderly person. It is purely and simply a causal relationship; the one is the result of the other—"not the same, yet not another." The "dying and being reborn" process is actually continuous throughout life, for consciousness consists of a succession of thought-moments, or *cittaviṭhi* (courses of cognition), which are like beads strung on the connecting thread of *bhavaṅga, or the unconscious life-continuum.* Each conscious moment in its arising and passing away is a little birth and a little death. To go into this in detail would involve a discussion of Abhidhamma, which is not the purpose of this article. It is sufficient to state that what we know as sentient life is the various forms of momentary consciousness that arise from contact between the organs of sense and the objects of sense.

But in addition to the five seats of sense perception recognized by Western thought, Buddhism adds a sixth, the *manāyatana* or mind-base, which is the centre of the thought processes. It is proper that this should be included with the external sense organs because it also produces sensations and awareness, and can do so independently of them, even though these impressions may exist only in imagination or as functions of memory.

Manāyatana corresponds to "mind" in the Western sense, but it is quite different from the idea of "soul." It now becomes necessary to ask ourselves what we mean by "mind." All we can say from observation is that mind is a function, as the quotation given above states. But a function of what? Is it a function of a physical organ, the brain, or of something immaterial and transcendental? Until recently, science rejected the latter theory as belonging to the realm of the mystical and fanciful. But before we go into the Buddhist explanation let us take a look at some of the latest hypotheses. The following quotation is from *Psychical Research* by R.V. Johnson, M.A. (Oxon), PhD., D.Sc. (London), English Universities Press, 1955. It summarizes the conclusions to be drawn from experiments made by Dr. J.B. Rhine of Duke University (United States of America), Professor Gilbert Murray, G.N.M. Tyrrell, and other investigators in the sphere of general extrasensory perception (G.E.S.P.):

> The mind of a person is certainly linked with his brain, and permits both of action of the person and the receipt of impressions at the point of space where his body is. The mind of the person must not, however, be assumed as "in" space at all. A part of its activity, and in particular its relation with other minds, is apparently on a level to which our familiar spatial considerations do not apply.

Another quotation from the same work:

> That the only modes of communication between minds should be such indirect methods as speech, writing, and signalling would, I think, have always been regarded as an unreasonable supposition *had it not been for the (now obsolete) theories of the causal dependence of mind on brain.*

31

Here we have a very significant statement indeed, and one that gives a somewhat different picture of the mind and its nature from that offered by J. Bowden on the basis of orthodox physiology. The brain is still seen to be an instrument of the mind, but the mind itself, as a force, seems to be able to perform certain of its functions independently of a physical medium and without an express location in space. It operates, perhaps, in spatial dimensions other than those familiar to us. The incalculable rapidity of the "courses of consciousness" described in Buddhist psychology (Abhidhamma) seems to indicate that this is in fact the case. It is a matter of common knowledge that time as we know it is annihilated in the dreaming state, and that the mind is capable of creating a time-dimension of its own when released from the ratios of the external world.

> The belief that all mental activities are confined to gray matter, more particularly that of the cerebral cortex, is another of those prejudices, jealously adhered to and never given up without a struggle, which act like grit in the machine of human progress. Its inception probably dates back to the time when ganglion cells were first seen in the microscope, and were forthwith, and are still hailed, as the units of consciousness. Berry asks: "If the ideas are not in the brain cells, where are they?" and Dubois-Raymond uttered the blasphemy: "Show me ganglion cells in the universe, and I will believe in a God." But these cells are only found in gray matter. What was more natural than that the largest and phylogenetically latest expanse of gray matter, the cerebral cortex, should be looked upon as the sole abode of the mind? A number of physiological experiments and pathological observations seemed to lend support to this view. Other accumulations of gray matter in the brain-stem, the cerebellum, the spinal cord, and the peripheral nervous system are separated from the cerebral cortex by white matter supposed to be insensible, and a consciousness dwelling only in cells and groups of cells cannot therefore be shared by isolated accumulations of gray matter. But the observations and experiments admit of different interpretations, and the arguments already advanced, and others presently to be submitted, will show that this view which looks upon the cellular constituents of gray matter as the sole carriers of consciousness is quite untenable.
>
> (Max Loewenthal, *Life and Soul*)

The same author later sums up his findings as follows:

Since the mind must derive its information regarding the spatial properties of outer objects from somewhere, it follows that portions of the mesotype other than the cerebral portion supply this information. In fine, the brain, including the gray cortex, is

(a) neither an organ of sensory perception,

(b) nor the exclusive seat of consciousness.

Life and Soul, Ch. 2, 52, pp. 217, 218, and 225

This agrees with the Buddhist concept of mental activity. The *manāyatana* of Buddhism has a physical base (it was identified by the classic Buddhist commentators with the *hadaya-vatthu* or "heart-base," but this was merely in conformity with the almost universally accepted ideas of the period); yet Buddhism maintains also the possibility of mental activity taking place without a physical organ, or at least by means of an organ of such fine substance as to be, from our point of view, immaterial. This state obtains in the *arūpa-loka* or realm of formless beings, which is a "Brahma-world" of pure thought. Leaving this aspect of the matter aside, however, there is sufficient evidence available to point to the fact that some form of mental energy, wheresoever it may be generated, has apparently the power of annihilating space, and that it can operate without a material medium over great distances and can to a certain extent overcome temporal barriers. The simplest explanation may be that it does not exist in space as we know it at all. Our own space-time continuum is not necessarily the only one in the cosmos; it is merely the only one that our ordinary senses are able to cognize.

At this stage of our enquiry it may be useful to resort to an analogy from physical science. Not a perfect analogy, because no analogy can be exact; but one that at least provides a parallel to the case under consideration. Electricity is a form of energy that is generated either artificially or by a combination of natural circumstances in the atmosphere or in material substances. This energy, the precise nature of which is still unknown, is itself invisible and unsubstantial; what we perceive is not the electric current, but its manifestations as heat, light, sound, or power. Undoubtedly it consists of particles which can be measured, but these particles are not detectable until they are transformed into one or other of the visible and tangible manifestations. The same current of electricity can be used to produce any or all of these several effects, according to the nature of the substance on which it is made to operate. If we visualize mental energy as something similar to electricity we get perhaps as close an approximation to it as is possible. For the electric generator we may substitute the brain, remembering

33

always that under certain conditions electricity can be produced without the artificial apparatus we use for the purpose. If mental energy can be generated or stored in the cells of the brain as electricity is stored in the cells of a battery, there is no reason why it should not share some of the other characteristics of an electrical charge. This much at least we can say: as in the case of electricity, we know of the existence of mental energy only when it manifests in some sensible operation. It is now being ascertained that the range of such operations is far greater than has been commonly attributed to it. It is these hitherto uninvestigated aspects of its nature and power that are the subject of the present experiments in extrasensory perception, telepathy, telekinesis, and allied subjects.

We shall return to the analogy of the electric current again later.

Buddhism teaches that one of the most important, if not the most important, functions of the mind is that of *willing*. Under this aspect the mind is called *cetanā*, which denotes its capacity for willed intention. And *cetanā*, the Buddha declared, is *kamma* (volitional action). The will to act is followed by the action; action in its turn is followed by result (*vipāka*). Thought is therefore a creative act. It was from this that Schopenhauer derived the central theme of his *The World as Will and Idea*, which makes will the dominating factor in the universe. The creative act of thought may be good or bad, but whichever it may be, it can only produce results of a like nature to the causes it originates. The moral principle of the universe is a scientific law.

But what of the varying degrees of power exhibited by the mind? The experiments in extrasensory perception have indicated that the largely unpredictable nature of the results obtained is caused by the uncertainty as to how such conscious or unconscious willing can be generated. Common observation of psychic phenomena (of telepathy, visions of the dying, and so on) shows that the communication of telepathic impressions depends most of all on the amount of emotional stimulus behind them. This means, in effect, that thought is able to operate over great distances without physical means of communication only when its generation is accompanied by a very strong desire, an emotional reaching-out as it were, towards its object. Only in such circumstances can minds communicate with one another on some extraspatial level. It is this which makes the scientific investigation and measuring of the mind's nature and powers so extremely difficult and inconclusive, for emotion cannot be generated under laboratory conditions. But to know that it is so is highly important when we come to consider the vital part that desire, or craving (*taṇhā*), plays in the mind's activities.

Craving and ignorance (*avijjā*) conjointly are the bases of the rebirth process; "craving" because it is the "will-to-live," the desire for continued conscious experience; and "ignorance" because without ignorance life would be seen as it is—intrinsically painful and therefore undesirable. The mind, therefore, is the generator of a force of craving. Schopenhauer's *World as Will and Idea* is a world of desire and thought-projections of desire. The "will-to-power" and the "will-to-enjoy" are only facets of the fundamental "will-to-be" which is common to all forms of life but is most consciously self-aware and complex in man.

We have now reached the stage at which we are able to see the mind as an energy flowing out from the centre of cognition, where it is generated by the impact of sensory apperceptions from the external world. In this form it is able to operate upon matter in direct and indirect ways: indirectly when it is limited by temporal and spatial relationships imposed by the physical body, and directly when it is realized as a force outside of space-time conditions. If, as the E.S.P. experiments seem to prove, it is capable in special circumstances of operating independently of physical media while the conditions of its normal functioning still obtain (i.e., during life), there is no difficulty in conceiving it as a continuing projection of energy after the cessation of the physical functions in death.

This is in fact what happens. The thought-energy, an impersonal force carrying with it only its craving-impulse and the potentialities it has generated (its *kamma*), is released at death, the last thought-moment it generates conditioning the rebirth-consciousness. Like any other form of energy, it is attracted to a suitable medium for its new physical manifestation, and the nature of that medium is determined by the quality of the dominant mental impulse, or in other words, its kamma-formation (*saṅkhāra*).[11] Just as the electric current can manifest under suitable conditions as heat, light, sound, or power, so the thought-energy being drawn to a suitable combination of genetic conditions, works upon them to produce a new manifestation according to its peculiar nature. If its past characteristics, revivified in the last thought-moment, are of a low order, it finds its new sphere of manifestation in a low order of being; that is to say, in the realms of suffering or the animal world. If of a high order, it produces its effect (the new life) in one of the heavenly or spiritual realms. If it is neither more nor less than human it produces a human rebirth. By a law of attraction it gravitates towards the conditions to which it has been attuned by past

35

volitional activity. Unlike the current of electricity which, as Bowden mentions, cannot continue after the destruction of the primary cell, the thought-energy does not merely expend itself in producing a final effect, but flows out to animate a new cell, which thereafter proceeds to generate new impulses.

I have mentioned higher and lower forms of rebirth, but it is with human rebirth that we are mainly concerned in this discussion. Precisely how is human rebirth accomplished? The answer is that the thought-force is attracted to the physical conditions of human procreation which will enable it to re-manifest and thus give expression to its craving-potential. The released energy in some way operates on and through the combination of male and female generative cells on much the same principle as that of the electric current working on the filaments in the lamp to produce light. The blind creative power of the craving-potential then adapts and develops them, moulding the structure of their growth in such a way as to make it serve its purpose within the limitations it carries with it in its *kamma*. In this it is also restricted, of course, by the general characteristics of the racial group and other distinctive categories to which the parents belong, but even within this limiting framework there are still infinite variations of physical and mental characteristics to be developed by the influence of the past *kamma*. To infer that all Chinamen are alike, only because what is most noticeable to us is the manner in which they differ from ourselves, is as absurd as to say that all Englishmen or all Russians are alike.

To illustrate the process, let us take an extreme case, that of the genius. Let us say that a man dies who has devoted his life to music. It so happens that music is one of the arts which can so dominate the mind as to become almost an obsession, and it thereby creates a very powerful craving-force— a constantly recurring craving-impulse associated with the pleasure derived from sound patterns. This mental energy, on its release at death, will be attracted to the conditions that offer it the fullest opportunity of following its bent. It may be drawn to parents who are themselves musical and whose hereditary endowment will thus favour it to the greatest extent. But this does not always happen; sometimes the craving-force is sufficiently developed to be able to dispense with all help from the parents. Mozart was born of parents who were only moderately musical, yet so highly concentrated was the musical tendency in the infant that he was an accomplished musician almost before he could read. It could only be a tendency created by past kamma. Cases of children of genius being born of mediocre parents are less common than those of subnormal children born to average parents, but both illustrate the same principle, that while heredity is often an important factor in character and ability, it is not invariably so.

In its power to modify the development of growing tissue, the thought-force from the past life is actually capable of setting the pattern of the brain cells. A craving for a physical instrument of a certain kind has been developed in the past life and so, according to degree of intensity of the craving, a suitable brain-formation is obtained in the new birth. Is it not possible, even in a single lifetime, to develop certain faculties in oneself if one has sufficient willpower to do so? To deny this is to make nonsense of all methods of mind development and character moulding. But whereas a man may make himself a passably competent musician, scientist, or architect by hard work, it takes something extra to make him a genius; something that cannot always be found in his heredity or opportunities. Buddhism teaches that this something extra is the *kamma* from the past life, transmitted by natural processes through a series of causal relationships.

In the theory of biological evolution it is assumed that from simple beginnings more and more complex organisms come into being over innumerable generations, and science is content to explain the process by the allied theory of natural selection. But to give a thing a name is not to explain it. Nobody has yet revealed exactly what is the driving force behind natural selection. It cannot be by mere chance that single-cell protoplasm becomes more highly organized, more sensitive, and more completely master of its environment until it becomes the higher animal and eventually the human being. On the other hand, the evolutionary urge produces too many errors and failures in its progress to be the result of a consciously directed plan from the mind of a higher intelligence. It exhibits the features of a blind, groping desire towards some incompletely defined goal. And these are precisely the features we would expect it to show if it were motivated by this craving-force which Buddhism teaches is the generating energy of life. It is illuminating to interpret the selective processes of biological evolution in this light. Dispensing with the obsolete theological trappings of God and soul, Buddhism shows that the whole pattern of evolution is based upon the blind craving-impulse which works through the natural biological processes towards a progressively realized result. The force that causes rebirth and the force that propels the evolutionary urge are one and the same: it is thought-force acting upon matter.

Here it should be noted that just as the process of rebirth is beginningless in time, so also is the arising and passing away of universes. The *kamma* which begins to operate at the commencement of every universe is *kamma* from the beings of the previous world-cycle. The *kamma*-force of Buddhism provides the "X-quality" which science requires to fill the gap between non-living matter and living, sentient organisms. Since it is the scientist's self-defined task to show how things happen, not why they happen, he should not object if someone else, working on the material he provides, supplies a *raison d'etre* for the natural processes, so long as it does not conflict with the known facts.

From the foregoing it should be clear that what is reborn is not a "soul" but a cause-effect continuum, carrying with it tendencies and potentialities created in the past; it is not a complete set of ego-characteristics. The reader is asked to think back to the cause-effect relationship between the infant and the old man referred to above, and to apply the same principle to the relationship between the person who is "reborn" as the result of the dead personality's *kamma*. They are "not the same (personality), yet not another." In the conventional sense, as when we say the child has "become" the old man, they are the "same"; but in the real sense (*paramattha*) they are only a relationship of cause and effect. The well-known analogy of the leaf which in the course of its decay changes in every perceptible feature—colour, shape, and texture—yet is said to be the "same" leaf throughout, provides a good illustration of the Buddhist principle of *anicca* (impermanence), and therefore also of *anattā* (non-existence of any enduring self-principle). Just as we use the word "leaf" for what is not a self-existing "thing" but only a succession of changing conditions, so we use the word "man" or any other word that denotes an object of composite and impermanent nature. These words are the instruments of communication only; they stand for ideas, not for the reality of the process which we mistake for a "thing." The thing-in-itself, the object of the philosopher's quest, can never be found; but much of our habitual confusion of thought about the phenomenal and the noumenal is due to an inability to distinguish between what is actual and what exists only as an idea. The "thing" is only an idea; the reality is the process of flux and continual arising and passing away of momentary existences.

The arguments against "reincarnation" and "transmigration" therefore do not apply to the Buddhist doctrine of rebirth. By discarding the notion of a travelling entity, Buddhism places the entire concept on a rational level.

Since there is no "soul" there is no need to assume any intermediate existence between births in an "ethereal region." Rebirth is instantaneous, rebirth arising immediately upon death. But here it is necessary to bear in mind that there are many kinds of rebirth besides that in the human realm. Buddhism does not deny the existence of other dimensions, both above and below the human plane. Many beings are reborn after death in the *peta-loka,* in the form of spirits, and have a life span of varying duration according to their *kamma.* Buddhism rounds off its picture of the visible and invisible universe by taking into account those planes of existence which the psychic investigator calls spirit realms. The "spirits" which the medium contacts in the seance room are beings who after death have been reborn on planes of existence not too far removed from our own. The higher planes are inaccessible to him, as are also, of course, the beings who have been reborn in animal forms. This accounts for a fact which has always puzzled spiritualists; namely, that certain departed personalities can be contacted while others cannot. It also explains why it is that departed "spirits" on the whole show no greater knowledge or wisdom than they possessed in their earth life, but frequently much less. Rebirth in one of these states does not necessarily mean spiritual advancement. In the *peta* realms it is accompanied by degeneration of the faculties.

We are now ready to take up the other points raised in the quotations given by our correspondent. It will be seen that many of Professor F.A.E. Crew's objections based on the assumed necessity for the individual in each of his several reappearances to "belong to the same species and to exhibit the same attributes in respect of blood-group, colour of eyes and skin, fingerprints and so on" are irrelevant. These attributes may be considered part of a "soul" personality, but they have no place in the *kamma*-tendency which is what is actually reborn. Genetic constitution and the circumstances and conditions of the external world, together with differences in experience in successive appearances certainly do, as Professor Crew states, tend to yield different personalities; but it has been shown that personality is a flux, and therefore necessarily subject to modification by such influences. They in their turn are largely conditioned by the past *kamma* of the individual concerned which, as I have already said, tends to gravitate towards conditions suitable to its state, and itself creates the situations in which the new personality begins to function. Here the principle of attraction comes into play; the thought-force gravitates naturally towards what is most in affinity with it, and so to some extent creates, and certainly modifies, its circumstances.

These also act upon the awakening consciousness, so that heredity and environment both have a share in moulding the new personality. If the past *kamma* was bad, these external conditions will reflect that "badness," so that it is only by a new effort of will that the mind can rise above their influence and fashion for itself a better destiny. Thus Buddhism takes into account all the factors which the geneticist, the sociologist, and the psychologist insist upon as being ingredients of the fully developed personality, while adding the extra element, that of *kamma*, which is necessary to weld them into a logical pattern.

The quotation from the rationalist writer, J. Bowden, where it deals with the genetic principles, is also covered by this explanation. What he does not mention, however, is that very often children of the same parents, subjected to the same environmental influences, show individual characteristics that cannot be traced to either source, and that such children differ also from one another. It is observable that from earliest infancy characteristic traits show themselves which distinguish one child from others of the same family. Science does not attempt to explain this except by referring the cause back to some remote ancestor. If this is in fact the cause of such differences, is it not be conceivable that the child which bears the characteristics of some great-great-grandparent may be the reappearance of that current of causality in a new birth, after an intermediate rebirth of some other kind? This hypothesis involves no greater mystery than does the transmission of hereditary traits through the generative cells of the parents. It is continually necessary to remind scientific thinkers that in being able to describe the method by which a particular effect is brought about they are not always telling us the reason why it is brought about. The genetic processes require some life principle in addition to the purely material chemical combinations in order to make them work, as surely as does the doctrine of rebirth. As Voltaire put it, there is no greater mystery about being born twice than there is about being born once. The only difference is that we accept the second mystery because we have to do so, while the first we can ignore.

The question relating to the "soul" and its development with the growth of the embryo presents no difficulties when the myth of the "soul" has been discarded once for all. The rebirth theory does not, as Bowden claims, make nonsense of all the commonplaces of scientific knowledge except when rebirth is tied up with belief in a complete psychic entity.

The problem of the existence of mind without a brain has already been dealt with. Regarding injuries to the brain, toxic effects, and the results of disease, these only pose a problem when we try to reconcile them with the idea of "soul." In periods of unconsciousness the thinking and cognizing faculties are suspended but the *bhavaṅga*, or life-continuum, carries on uninterrupted. However, as the quotations I have given from R.C. Johnson show, science has not yet proved that mental activity needs to be located in any specific place, and the identification of the mind with the brain, or to consider the mind as "the brain at work," is no longer thought to be a necessary assumption. The reference to Edison and the inherent qualities of his brain has been covered by the description of the rebirth process and the manner in which it works upon the living cell tissues.

There remains the point concerning the two types of twins. In the first place it should be noted that when J. Bowden says (quite rightly) that "it is notorious that unlike twins may differ so widely in their mental outlook as scarcely to have an idea in common," he is weakening the force of his earlier argument concerning the importance of heredity and environment in shaping personality. The unlike twins share the same heredity and the same environmental conditions, yet still their minds are totally different. This is evidence for, rather than against, rebirth. It can only be explained by their individual kammas.

In this discussion I have intentionally omitted all reference to ethical values. It must be apparent, however, that ethical values are intrinsically a part of the law of cause and effect. They are not artificial standards invented by man for his own utilitarian purposes; neither are they arbitrary laws imposed from without. They are part of the cosmos. The science that can find no place for them is an imperfect science; the rationalism that ignores them is a defective rationalism. By trying to grasp in its entirety the process of rebirth we come closer to the focal point of our being, the source from which we draw the knowledge that enables us to rise in the hierarchy of those who control their own destiny. A single life, meaningless in isolation, becomes charged with meaning when seen against the continuing pattern of rebirth. By it we come to know why we are what we are, and how we may become what we wish to be. The mind that has freed itself of prejudice has taken the first step towards Nibbāna.

VI

Rebirth, Karma, and Modern Science

Thirty-three years ago Dr. Evans-Wentz, lecturing here in Colombo, made a remarkable prediction. He said: "It is highly probable that within another fifty years the belief in rebirth will have been accepted by science as true. In my own opinion it will be so accepted."

Events in our modern world move very rapidly, and since that statement was made at a public meeting in 1925 there have been many advances in science. For the most part they have been on a materialistic level, and they have changed the face of the world and our mode of living very considerably. But while science has been primarily concerned with technical results it has also brought about some radical changes in man's view of life and the laws that govern the universe. The philosophical implications of the new knowledge must be taken into account as well as its practical achievements. While still chiefly interested in the mastery of the physical world, the scientist is constantly presenting us with fresh data that have to be assimilated into our ideas concerning the nature of man and his purpose as a part of the cosmic whole. Every fresh discovery is a challenge that religion has to meet.

The exploration of outer space, for instance, will very soon be a practical possibility. It promises to extend man's knowledge beyond this planet into realms which up to now have been only subjects of speculation. What we shall eventually find there can only be guessed, but we must be prepared to encounter forms of life unknown to us before. We already know that in the vastness of the unexplored universe with its countless planetary systems it is highly improbable that ours is the only world that has produced living organisms. What this means in terms of traditional Western religious beliefs is a matter that is already engaging the attention of theologians. It is a far more revolutionary idea than was Galileo's discovery that the earth is not the centre of the solar system, although that in its time was regarded as so dangerous to religious orthodoxy that its discoverer was tried as a heretic and only escaped the flames by a false recantation. Now we are confronted by evidence that this world and mankind are not special creations with a unique plan of salvation. It is quite inconceivable that the same tragedy

Broadcast talk, Colombo, 3rd July 1958

could not have been enacted wherever there are inhabited planets throughout the universe, and that it will be re-enacted in time to come when others have reached the stage of producing human-type beings in the course of their evolution. In Buddhism this problem does not arise, for Buddhism has always taught that there are countless world-systems in different stages of development, and that the same moral law of cause and effect operates in all of them exactly as it does here. The significance of man's life does not depend upon a single incident which took place in a certain locality at a certain point in history. Buddhism shows that the laws by which we live, and through which we can achieve our liberation, are universal cosmic laws: they prevail everywhere.

One of these cosmic laws is that which operates through *kamma* and *vipāka* to produce rebirth. What, if anything, has science got to say on this subject? As yet it has no definite conclusion to report; but certain lines of investigation are being followed which point unmistakably to the truth of rebirth. There are signs that we are on the threshold of a scientific revelation that will confirm the ancient teachings and cause a revolution in man's thinking. The methods of investigation now being used are techniques for recalling the memory of past existences.

In the Aṅguttara Nikāya the Buddha speaks on the yogic method of remembering past lives as follows:

> "If the bhikkhu desires to be able to call to mind his various temporary states in days gone by, such as one birth, two births, three, four, five, ten, twenty, thirty, forty, fifty, a hundred, a thousand or a hundred thousand births, his births in many an aeon of destruction, in many an aeon of renovation (so as to be able to say): 'In that place such was my name, such my family, such my caste, such my subsistence, such my experience of happiness or of pain, and such the limit of my life; and when I passed from thence I took form again in that other place, where my name was so-and-so, and such my family, such my caste, such my subsistence, such my experience of happiness or of pain, and such my term of life; and from thence I was born here: thus am I able to call to mind my various temporary states of existence in days gone by'—in that state of self-concentration if the mind be fixed on the acquirement of any object, that object will be attained."

Recollection of past lives is one of the *iddhi-bala*, or psychic powers, acquired during the cultivation of the jhānic states. But in making his prophecy concerning the scientific acceptance of rebirth Dr. Evans-Wentz mentioned hypnotism as a means of uncovering the latent memory of previous lives which can be used in the case of ordinary people. Already at that time some highly important research work was being carried out on these lines. It had already been found that the process known as recession could produce some surprising results. Recession is a treatment sometimes given by psychologists to bring back to conscious memory forgotten incidents of childhood. The subject is put into a deep hypnotic sleep and it is then suggested to him or her that he should go back in time to some particular point in childhood, say to the age of six. If the hypnotic trance is complete, this is what happens. The subject's mind reverts to what it was at the time indicated, and all the impressions that were then foremost in the consciousness are recovered. The subject thinks and responds to questions just as he would have done at that particular age. It was found that recession could be carried back to earliest infancy; and from that the next stage was to revive pre-natal memories. At that point the surprising thing happened: it was found that people were remembering a life previous to the present one. When asked their names they would give names other than those they bore in the present life, and would follow up with details which in some cases could be verified from old records.

Such verification, of course, was not always possible. Sometimes the lives they described were too remote in time, or had been lived in other parts of the globe. The subjects sometimes spoke in languages they did not know in their present life. But some striking facts emerged which could be checked against historical records. Altogether a vast body of information on the subject has been gathered during the past twenty years, and it is still being investigated. Attempts were made, and still are being made, to account for the phenomenon by telepathy; but to cover all the evidence it has been necessary to bring in theories that are more far-fetched than the simple fact of rebirth.

Recently there have been several widely publicized cases, among which that of Bridey Murphy in America has provided the most sensational reading. A girl remembered, under deep hypnosis, a previous life in Ireland, when her name had been Bridey Murphy. She gave dates, names of places and people, and descriptions of the life of the period. That period was near enough to our own time to allow of verification from parish registers, old maps, and local history. The case, and the book written about it, aroused a storm of controversy in America. One leading newspaper sent a representative to Ireland to check up on the facts, which in many particulars he was able to confirm. As is always the case, however, there were people who from various motives tried to confuse the issue and suppress the evidence. It is noticeable that whenever there is any reference to rebirth or "reincarnation" in any of the psychic magazines or the popular press there is immediately a deluge of letters attacking the doctrine. The chief source of this hostility is easily recognizable. It is not only anti-religious materialists who are anxious to suppress the truth about rebirth. It is due to the influence of certain powerful religious groups that much of the evidence for it is never made public.

In England there have been similar cases to that of Bridey Murphy. One of them is worth describing in detail. A young married woman in Exeter was asked to submit herself to hypnotism for experimental purposes. She was not told the object of the experiment, but when she was carried back in time she remembered and gave details of two previous lives. In one of them she was Clarice Hellier, a nurse at the beginning of this century. She gave a vivid account of her life and the people she knew, ending with a description of her last illness and death. She then, most astonishingly, gave a description of her own funeral and told the number of the grave in which she had been buried, all of which she apparently saw while in a disembodied state. While relating these memories under hypnosis she showed all the emotions natural to one who was passing through the experiences at the present time. When she emerged from the trance she had no memory of what she had been saying, but was under the impression that she had been in a deep and refreshing sleep.

In subsequent sessions she recalled another former life, in which she had been living in Ireland. Replying to the hypnotist's questions she said: "I am Mary Cohan. I am seventeen. I live in Cork. It is 1697." It was pointed out that Cohan is more like a Jewish than an Irish name, but she insisted that she was Irish and spelt the name in the way she said her mother had taught her. She then proceeded to give a circumstantial account of her life in 17th and 18th century Ireland: how she was married against her will because her mother could no longer support her; how she had two sons, Pat and Will, and how her husband ill-treated her. The name of the village near where she was born she gave as Grener. Later, when enquiries were made, no such place could be identified until in some old papers dating back 250 years mention was found of a hamlet named G–R–E–E–N–H–A–L–G–H and pronounced Grener. Mary Cohan had said that she was married at

45

Rebirth as Doctrine and Experience

St. John's Church, and records in the possession of a parish priest showed that there was at that time a church of that name in Greenhalgh. Several other facts were verified in due course.

One of the most interesting features of the case was the emotional reaction shown by the subject when asked about her married life. In great distress she described her husband's cruelty to her; how he had beaten her and broken her leg. It was exactly as though she were living through the experience, and she became so disturbed that to calm her the hypnotist took her back to her earlier life, when she was thirteen. Then she spoke affectionately of her brother Sean and how they used to play together as children. The name is spelt S–E–A–N, but she gave it its correct Irish pronunciation. Altogether, five of these sessions were held, with the hypnotist taking her from one life to another, and she invariably related the same incidents and repeated the same details. I have in my possession a recording of one of these sessions.

But the case that has gone furthest towards the realization of Dr. Evans-Wentz's prediction is that of an American, Edgar Cayce. Edgar Cayce was born in Kentucky in 1877. As a young man he suffered from a nervous complaint which deprived him of his voice. His condition would not respond to medical treatment, but it was found that he was able to speak normally while under hypnosis. In this state Cayce was able to look at his own body, describe its condition, and prescribe treatment which was afterwards found effective. He actually diagnosed his own complaint while in the hypnotic trance, using medical technical terms that were quite unknown to him in his waking state. He had had only a very moderate education, and when the notes that had been taken of his diagnosis were shown to him he could not at first believe that it was he who had used those unheard-of technical terms. When his self-treatment was found successful he was persuaded to try his power of treating sickness while under hypnosis on other people. The same procedure was followed: Cayce would put himself into a hypnotic sleep and then answer questions relating to the patient, in the same expert manner he had shown when dealing with himself. In every case where the treatment he recommended was followed the patient recovered; if recovery was not possible he said so, and his diagnoses were invariably correct. In the hypnotic state he spoke with complete assurance and authority, but in his ordinary waking state he had agonizing doubt about the rightness of what he was doing and for a long time was in dread of doing harm to someone unintentionally. It was only through the persuasion of his wife

46

and friends that he carried on, but in the end the consistent success of his treatments, particularly in cases where doctors had failed, finally removed all doubts from his mind.

Soon he was treating patients at a distance, whom he had never seen. Then one day a friend who was interested in religion and philosophy asked him while he was under hypnosis whether rebirth was true. Cayce replied at once that it was, and described his own previous life. In this connection he used the word "karma." In reply to another question he said that if asked he could also see the previous lives of other people and would be able to trace the karmic causes of their diseases.

When the notes of what he had said were shown to Cayce on waking he was at first puzzled and then horrified. He had never heard the word "karma" and had no idea what it meant. All he knew of "reincarnation" was that it was a belief held by some Oriental peoples—some kind of "heathen" doctrine, he imagined. It must be understood that Cayce was a very simple man born in America's "Bible belt"; a devout Bible reader with a very limited outlook in religion. All the books written about him stress this point. At first he flatly refused to believe in his own revelations, considering that they were contrary to his Christian faith. But another friend, a Bible scholar who was also a student of Oriental philosophy, told him that there was no passage in the Bible that expressly denied rebirth. On the contrary, there were several cryptic statements that could only be interpreted in the light of rebirth. He quoted the well-known passage: "He that liveth by the sword shall die by the sword." Many people who had lived by the sword, he pointed out, died peacefully of old age, so that if the saying had any truth it could only mean that they must die by the sword in some subsequent life. Cayce read through his Bible again, but could not find any passage that conclusively ruled out the belief in rebirth. Meanwhile, further experiments were being carried out, and under hypnosis he started investigating the previous lives of other people, with the most startling results. From then on he would always include in his diagnosis a tracing of the karma of previous lives which had brought on the ailment from which the patient was suffering. This increased the value of his "psychic diagnoses" very considerably. It enabled him to give valuable advice on questions relating to character and moral conduct and he was able to point out where people were making mistakes in their present life owing to influences from the past.

Ultimately Edgar Cayce's work assumed world-wide proportions. An organization was set up which enabled him to devote all his time to treating the sick and he dealt with cases all over the world. These were people he had never seen, and whose only contact with him was by letter. Several books have been written about his amazing work and it has become widely known. Cayce died in 1945, but the institute he founded in Virginia, now known as the Association for Research and Enlightenment, still carries on, working on the great mass of case histories he left behind.

It would be strange and unaccountable if among all the accurate information Cayce was able to give under hypnosis only the part relating to rebirth were untrue. If the overwhelming number of successful cures are accepted—as they must be since the evidence, fully documented, is available to everyone—the teaching regarding rebirth must be accepted as true also. It is being so accepted by great numbers of people who find in it a rational explanation of the ills and seemingly unmerited sufferings that life brings in its train.

With Dr. J.B. Rhine at Duke University experimenting in para-psychology and extrasensory perception, and other specialists all over the free world conducting investigations of a similar nature and pooling their results, our generation, despite its preoccupation with the materialistic aspects of science, is opening up new visas of knowledge on levels that are not materialistic. Most leading thinkers are now of the opinion that the old materialism is dead; it died with the discovery that matter is a form of energy, not solid and immutable substance. Behind it all they see the operation of a something that resembles mind, but not of the kind that used to be associated with a divine power. It is a groping, fumbling sort of mind which works through trial and error towards an unperceived goal. We find this groping force behind the processes of biological evolution, where science has not been able to account for the cause underlying the development of living organisms. Science so far has only been able to describe the means by which it works, the transmission of hereditary characteristics from one generation to another, and the appearance from time to time of mutations. What it was that caused the various species to differentiate, and to develop extremely complicated sense organs together with the neural apparatus for receiving and recording impressions through them, has not yet been satisfactorily explained. To describe how a thing happens is not the same as explaining why it happens. The science of genetics tells us how, but not *why*, the process takes place. It cannot say why matter became sentient in the first place. One chance event of such a nature might be accepted, even though science does not as a rule approve of chance as an element in any physical processes; but a long series of such chances, culminating in the appearance of a highly complex organism like man, is altogether too unlikely. There must be an activating and guiding principle somewhere behind the complicated evolution of inert matter into organic substance equipped with senses, perceptions, and the faculty of thinking and acting. The more advanced scientists, therefore, have abandoned the old materialistic explanation, or rather have gone beyond it; but they cannot accept the alternative theory of a purposive creator working through nature. If there were such a creator the plan would have been less wasteful and would have been carried out more efficiently.

Buddhism solves the problem with the doctrine of rebirth and karma. The blind, groping force that animates matter to produce living beings is indeed a mind-force. It is the force of craving, mentally generated in the past to make the present, and generated from moment to moment now to create the future—an interminable process of *creativity by craving*.

The first of the Four Noble Truths teaches that all existence is suffering; the second that the cause of this birth and suffering is craving, a craving that can never be satisfied because it is nourished by the food of the senses. It is that craving which is the life-force and it originates in the mind. Now at last science is beginning to recognize that to find out man's true nature it is his mind, not his physical body, that must be studied. In all the investigations into the psychic faculties which I have mentioned, such as the experiments in clairvoyance, clairaudience, and the ability to move objects by mental radiations without physical contact, the subject of rebirth comes up again and again. It is the key which unlocks all the doors; at the same time it is the link that unites the physical with the super-physical. But it is only the Buddhist concept of rebirth without a soul-entity that fits all the facts. In all the phenomena that are being studied at present there is no place for an unchanging ego-principle.

What we find in analysing mental processes is only a succession of states, linked together by a cause-and-effect continuum. This operates simultaneously on the psychic and physical levels. Just as, according to physics, an atom cannot be said to be identically the same atom from one moment to another, so the momentary units of consciousness that arise and pass away in rapid succession are not the same from one thought-moment to another. They are connected only by a causal relationship, the *bhavaṅga,* or life-continuum. One complete unit of consciousness represents a psychic life span; a series

49

of these associated with the same current of physical existence is the life span of a being. When the psychic current and the physical current become dissociated at death—that is, the *jīvitindriya-upaccheda*—the karma of the past carries the psychic current on in a new physical manifestation, the nature of which is determined by the past mental activity predominating in the last moment of consciousness.

When the truth of karma and rebirth is scientifically established man's attitude to life is bound to undergo a radical alteration. Moral values will no longer be in doubt and the ultimate goal for which man should strive, Nibbāna, will be a clearly-perceived necessity. There are many signs that this change is being brought about. Evidence from many different sources is piling up to show that, while man is not a special creation uniquely endowed with an immortal principle, the soul, neither is he a mere accident thrown up by the cosmos from a fortuitous combination of chemicals. Between these opposing and equally untenable theories there lies the Buddhist truth that every living being is the result of karma working through the physical processes.

All forms are but temporary manifestations of the invisible yet all-potent karmic energy. They arise and pass away and there is no goodness or permanence in them.

> *Aciraṃ vata'yaṃ kāyo*
> *Paṭhaviṃ adhisessati*
> *Chuddho apetaviññāṇo*
> *Niratthaṃ'va kaliṅgaraṃ.*

"Soon the body must lie upon the earth, despised, without consciousness, like a decayed log." Knowing this, it behoves the man of wisdom to desire nothing but the final liberation, the ultimate peace of Nibbāna

VII
Karma as a Factor in Disease

I recently met a doctor from Europe who is a specialist in pulmonary diseases, and also a Buddhist. With some surprise I noticed that he was a fairly heavy cigarette smoker. In view of the prevalent fear of cancer through smoking I asked him his views on the subject. He smiled and shrugged his shoulders. The gist of his reply was that he would not recommend smoking, but that there are so many apparent causes of lung cancer, including diesel fumes and a chemically contaminated atmosphere, that it is difficult to see how anyone could avoid developing it, if physical causes alone are accountable. His own opinion, as a Buddhist, was that the essential factor is the karma of the individual. All the physical causes of cancer, such as continual irritation of the tissues, might be present, but unless the karma of the individual was also a predisposing factor, cancer would not develop. On the other hand, if the physical factors and the karmic disposition came into action together, some type of cancer would result.

Taking any other view it is difficult to explain why some people develop cancer while others, in the same circumstances, do not; and also why some cancer cases, even of malignant types involving vital organs, respond to treatment while others take their destructive course to the end. It is a medical fact that in some cases cancers have been known to disappear entirely after the patient had been given up as doomed. Such instances are rare, but they occur. There has been much controversy over the cancer cures claimed by certain specialists, notably those of Dr. Max Gerson in America. The only fact that emerges clearly from them is that treatments which are successful with some patients do not produce results with others. If the unknown factor which decides the issue is the sufferer's karma, the situation can be readily understood. The same may be said of many other diseases besides cancer.

This is not to be taken as an orthodox medical opinion, by any means, and doubtless the doctor in question would hesitate to express it in a scientific convention. But at the same time it does represent a growing tendency among doctors and psychiatrists, especially the latter, to seek further back

First published, under the pen-name Vim Surangkhanong, in *The Buddhist* (Colombo), July 1967.

in the patient's history for causes of a disease which are not apparent in the present life. Why do some people become sick while others, exposed to identical conditions, do not? What is it that decides, in an epidemic, who shall succumb and who shall survive? And how does the mental attitude of the patient affect the course of his disease? The lung specialist whose view I have just quoted was formerly a psychiatrist, and is therefore fully alive to the psychosomatic character of many illnesses. This may still be a long way from admitting the part that karma plays in disease, but for many independent thinkers the step has been made easier by the work of the late Edgar Cayce, whose sensational cures were based upon psychic insight into the patients' past karma.

The extent to which karma and rebirth are being given serious study today is shown by two papers issued by a research institute in the U.S.A. The first is a resumé of a treatise by Prof. Herbert Fingarette, Professor of Philosophy at the University of California, Santa Barbara (*The Self in Transformation*, Basic Books, N.Y., 1963). In para. 171 the Professor says of the doctrine of "reincarnation" and karma: "... we may recall that it was not any self-evident spiritual superficiality but the historical accident of official Christian opposition which stamped it out as an important Greek and Roman doctrine, a doctrine profoundly meaningful to Plato as well as to the masses." Further on he writes: "I have tried to set the stage for detailed analysis by suggesting that karmic insight emerges in the situation of one who is driven by anxiety and suffering, who seeks self-awareness, and who is grappling in a highly personal and direct way with the fragmented, enslaving lives which he has lived, is living, and hopes to escape." Prof. Fingarette's plea is for an understanding of karma as a means to overcome suffering, and his approach is along much the same lines as that taken by Buddhism.

The second paper presents excerpts from *The Symbolic and the Real*, by Dr. Ira Progoff (Julian Press, N.Y., 1963). Dr. Progoff is Director of the Institute for Research in Depth Psychology at Drew University, and author of another book, *The Death and Rebirth of Psychology*. Dealing with Socrates and his doctrine of rebirth, Dr. Progoff writes: "Socrates' goal as a goad was to stir up men so that the traces of knowledge garnered through the timeless journey of the soul could come alive again. He sought to open a way for the true wisdom of which the oracle had spoken. His goal was to touch the depths in men, to evoke what was hidden and unremembered there, in order that it might serve as an inward source of truth. We can see at this point a striking similarity between the calling of Socrates and the trend of work emerging in modern depth psychology. Both proceed on the hypothesis that the resources of wisdom are hidden in the depths of the human being."

These two writers are not so much concerned with karma in relation to organic disease. Their interest in it comes from the light the doctrine throws upon abnormal mental conditions. It has a significant bearing on the fact that many psychological disorders are congenital. The tendency towards psychosis may remain latent until some unusual stress produces the overt symptoms by which they are recognized. They thus follow the karmic pattern, in which *vipāka* (result) has to await suitable supporting conditions for its ripening. If certain external or physical factors are not present as conditions (*atthi-paccaya*) a karmic tendency remains suspended, when it is known as "stored-up" karma (*kaṭattā-kamma*).

A very good example of this is found in war neuroses. Dr. Roy R. Grinker, Director of the Institute for Psychosomatic and Psychiatric Research and Training, Michael Reese Hospital, Chicago, and the author of *Psychosomatic Case Book, War Neuroses,* and other works on neurology, writes: "Individuals previously psychoneurotic, the psychologically immature, the withdrawn asocial person, and the overcompensated tough psychopath succumb more quickly and develop more severe neuroses than do the relatively stable" under the strain of active military service. "A few latently psychotic soldiers," he adds, "develop a full-blown malignant psychosis such as schizophrenia," and although "very few malignant and permanent psychoses develop, ... many depressions result from a feeling of failure...."

Here there is a promising field for the study of karma bearing its fruit under favourable conditions. There is still no certainty as to the cause of the group of personality disorders that come under the heading of schizophrenia, but it is generally agreed that in most cases the origin goes back to early infancy and may be present at birth. The strain which brings it out as a form of war neurosis is only a contributing factor, acting upon a latent tendency already present.

Formerly these neuroses were known as shell-shock, but the term was found to be completely inappropriate and now survives only in popular usage. As Prof. James Drever writes in his *Dictionary of Psychology*, shell-shock was "the name formerly given, but now discontinued, to temporary or prolonged nervous disorders, manifesting a variety of symptoms, developed through experience of war conditions in the field, and of a functional character." It is now known that there is, properly speaking, no such condition as "shell-shock." The more accurate term "war neurosis" denotes a state brought about by prolonged exposure to the strain of war in the field; it is not a condition that can be produced by explosions or bursts of gunfire, but the cumulative effect of anxiety, fatigue, hard physical conditions, and the sight of the dead and wounded, over a fairly long period. Here again a multiplicity of causes comes into operation.

When one considers that large civilian populations, comprising persons of both sexes and all ages, were exposed to regular aerial bombardments during the second World War without developing war neurosis, one is bound to conclude that another factor is involved in the situation. I feel that we are justified in believing that factor to be the karma of the individual.

The scientific mind might be less prepared to admit the possibility of karma being a factor in organic disease. Nevertheless, although the seeds of a specific disease may not be present from birth or early infancy, we see that there are parallels between the development of a psychosis and of a cancer. Many of the contributory causes of both are known, but not all of them, and it is far from certain what causes should be regarded as decisive. The time may well be at hand when research will take a new direction, and the study of parapsychology will open the way to a better understanding of the moral laws that operate in the life of all beings. By denying the law of karma and its fruit which the Buddha proclaimed 2,500 years ago, the West crippled its progress along these lines. Now at long last it is awakening to the fact that its scientific field is extremely narrow and exclusive, the result of the violent reaction of reason against supernaturalism. There are signs that the pendulum is now swinging back. Materialism as a philosophy and a basis for scientific disciplines has contributed much to human knowledge, but its limitations are being increasingly recognized. In course of time the world must come to Buddhism; and for the advancement of knowledge, to say nothing of the perpetuation and further progress of our civilization, the sooner it does so the better.

(March, 1967)

54

VIII

The Karmic Force in the Rebirth Process
Questions and Answers

THE QUESTIONS

According to Buddhism man is a congeries of physical and mental energies
without a self or anything belonging to a self. At death the psychical energies
leave the body. Assuming the next rebirth is on the human plane, what
happens next? The male sperm and the female ovum provide the physical
basis for the psychical energies.

Now my question is this: Under what conditions do these psychical
energies become associated with ovum-perm combination?

(a) Are the psychical energies only attracted by the *pure physical* basis of
the ovum-sperm combination?

(b) Are they also (or only) attracted by the mental or spiritual level of
the parents?

(c) Are the psychical energies attracted by the psychical energies which
may be present in the ovum and the sperm and consequently in their
combination?

(d) Are the psychical energies attracted by both the physical and the
psychical composition of the ovum-sperm combination?

In my opinion, case (b) seems to be improbable because conception can
take place without the presence of the father (artificial insemination).
Moreover, if I am not mistaken, an Italian professor seems to have succeeded
in producing conception by means of a sperm and an ovum without their
owners being present.

Another question: I sometimes read in Buddhist books that congenital
malformations, blindness, etc., are the result of "bad karma." In my opinion,
this is not always the case: the foetus could have been damaged by the
mother taking, for example, a wrong medicine.... My question is: Do

---

These questions, submitted to the Buddhist Publication Society, had been referred to
Mr. Francis Story for reply. — Ed.

Buddhists always consider physical malformation the result of bad karma or do they consider it simply a result conditioned by a number of causes and conditions?

THE ANSWERS (by Francis Story)

(a) It would seem that the karmic force (or psychic energy) is primarily attracted by the physical basis at the time of conception, and that it operates upon the foetus during its formative intra-uterine period, but

(b) the nature of the parents also plays some part in the process, in that the karmic force (or psychic energy) is drawn to a combination which will provide it with a suitable genetic and hereditary background for its development as a psychophysical entity along lines laid down potentially by its previous personalities. Thus, one who has developed a great devotion to music is likely to be reborn of parents who are themselves musical, and so on.

This principle is not at all affected by the fact of artificial insemination or even the approaching possibility of babies being engendered in test tubes. Wherever the genetic factors are present, together with the necessary environmental conditions, karmic force from a deceased personality can take over and mould a new psychophysical organism. The hereditary factors carried by the genes will also come into play as part of the personality structure.

If, as already seems possible, the correct protein structures can be synthesized for the production of human-type cells, it may happen that ultimately karmic force of human type will utilize the artificial product in the same way that it normally utilizes the sperm and ovum combination. But this is still very much in the realm of conjecture.

Regarding the second question the Buddha said: "If anyone says that a man must necessarily reap according to all his deeds, in that case no religious striving is possible, nor is there an opportunity to end suffering." The corollary to this is the fact that not all events or experiences are due to past karma. More than one cause is needed to produce a given effect. External agencies also influence phenomena, and it is usually impossible to decide which factor is predominant, a past-karmic-result (*vipāka*), or an effect of causes in the external world, because both occur in combination. A karma has to wait for its ripening until the external conditions are favourable for it, and all beings have a supply of such unexpended karma-potential, both

56

good and bad. Hence it is quite possible that physical malformations in an embryo are the result of bad karma which the use of some harmful drug on the part of the mother has allowed to take effect upon the personality undergoing rebirth. In that case it is conceivable that the karmic force of a deceased person who had no such evil potentiality would not be drawn to such a genetic situation, or, alternatively, if it had been drawn to it, would not continue to develop but would seek rebirth elsewhere, resulting in a stillborn child.

A similar situation to this is seen in the case of many persons losing their lives or suffering injury in a common disaster. It may be that all the persons so affected in the disaster had suspended karma that was due to bear some such fruit, and that its results struck them down when the external causes (the causes of the disaster) were also present for each of them at the same time. It is due to the multiplicity of contributing causes in the production of any given result that the operations of karma are classed as "unthinkables" (*acinteyya*), one of the subjects that are beyond the reach of thought, and if unwisely pondered over lead to "unhinging of the mind and disorganization of the personality."

(1968)

IX

The Buddhist Doctrine of Rebirth in Subhuman Realms

A Reply to Dr. Willem B. Roos

The question of whether a human being after death can take rebirth on a lower biological level has been debated for many years by Western Buddhists, particularly by those whose approach to Buddhism has been via Theosophy, and whose interpretation of it has remained syncretic in spirit. The latest contribution to the subject is an article by Dr. Willem B. Roos of Sacramento, California, entitled "Is Rebirth in a Subhuman Kingdom Possible?" (*The Maha Bodhi*, July 1967).

Dr. Roos begins by quoting His Holiness the 14th Dalai Lama, who in Appendix I of his book *My Land and My People* makes the following statements:

> Meritorious karma causes beings to take rebirth in the realms of gods, demi-gods, and men. Demeritorious karma causes rebirth in the lower realms of animals, *pretas*, and hells. Thirdly, *acala karma*, invariable karma, causes beings to take rebirth in the upper worlds, *rūpa* and *arūpa dhātu*, a world of form and a formless world.

The first comment Dr. Roos makes is that "these statements, short as they are, can be interpreted in different ways and it is not possible to know ... what His Holiness exactly meant to convey. It will be noted that he does not specify the term 'beings,' and also that he speaks of rebirth in different *realms* but not of rebirth in the different classes of beings themselves. The term "realms" could mean *states of consciousness*, though it is also possible that His Holiness wanted to express the popular beliefs of the Tibetans, that a *human* being could be reborn on *earth* in an *animal* body. This popular belief can be traced back to some of the Jātaka tales...."

Now the word "realm" is standard Buddhist terminology to express the meaning of the Pāli and Sanskrit words *loka* (world or sphere) and *yoni* (literally, "womb"). In the Pāli and Buddhist Sanskrit texts the animal realm is called *tiracchāna-yoni*, signifying, literally, (birth in the) animal womb.

But the same idea is sometimes expressed without the use of the word *yoni*, as in *tiracchāna-gāminī paṭipadā*, a phrase used to denote karma "leading to rebirth as an animal." A being that is reborn in an animal womb will naturally have an animal body.

In the Aṅguttara Nikāya (III, 415) the Buddha is recorded as saying: "There is karma, O monks, that ripens in hell ... Karma that ripens in the animal realm Karma that ripens in the realm of ghosts ... Karma that ripens in the world of men ... Karma that ripens in heavenly realms."

Here, the ripening of karma is again Buddhist terminology, its meaning being simply the fruition of karma which causes renewed existence as an inhabitant of one or other of the realms in question: as a being in a realm of torment, as an animal, as a human being, or as a deva or brahmā. Each of these realms has its own distinct life forms, which the reborn being assumes upon entering it. That, of course, is expressing the situation in conventional terms (*vohāra-kathā*); a more exact description of what happens would be to say that the karma of the human being who has died produces another form, appropriate to its particular realm, to carry on the world-line of cause and effect belonging to that specific current of existence (*bhavaṅga-sota*).

Again, it is said: "Greed, O monks, is a condition for the arising of karma ... Hatred ... Delusion is a condition for the arising of karma," and regarding the miserable destinies resulting from bad karma, the Buddha in the same discourse says: "Killing ... stealing... unlawful intercourse with the other sex ... lying ... slandering ... rude speech ... foolish babble, practised, carried on, and frequently cultivated, leads to rebirth in hell, or amongst the animals, or amongst the *pretas* (unhappy ghosts)" (Aṅguttara, III, 339).

Another discourse of the Aṅguttara Nikāya (IV, 459) states: "There are five courses of existence: hell, the animal realm, the ghost realm, the human world, and the heavenly world." A similar statement is made in the Dīgha Nikāya, Sutta 33.

Allusions to rebirth in the animal realm are also found in the Dīgha Nikāya, I,228; III,234; Saṃyutta, I,34; III,225; IV,168, 307; Petavatthu, IV, 11; and other canonical texts, as well as in the *Visuddhimagga* (XIII,93; XIV,207; XVII,154).

In all of these references, rebirth in the animal realm is treated in exactly the same way as rebirth in the human or any other world: it means rebirth as a being belonging to one of those realms. There is thus no ambiguity in the Dalai Lama's use of the word "realm" and his statement is fully in accordance with the Pāli texts of the Theravāda. Rebirth *as an animal* in consequence of demeritorious karma is one of the "unhappy destinies" (*duggati*). Its meaning is precisely that of "rebirth in the different classes of beings according to their nature."

Dr. Roos' comment that the term "realms" could mean "*states of consciousness*" is worthy of remark. In the Buddhist view, every state of being is primarily a state of consciousness. The world in which the animal lives is a world of apperception conditioned by its characteristic sensory equipment, just as the human world is the world *as it is perceived* by a human being. The same principle applies to all other states of existence, from lowest to highest: they are all states of consciousness. The animal inhabits the same external world as we do, but its perception of that world is different from ours to the extent that its sensory (and in Buddhism sensory includes "mental") organization differs from the human. It is precisely because the animal has a different kind of *body* that its world is not the same as ours although it exists on the same physical plane. The Buddha's use of the term "world" (in this case saṃsāra, the round of existences and their locale) is shown in his words: "Within this fathom-long body, equipped with mental faculties, O monks, I declare to you is the world, the arising of the world, its cessation, and the way to its cessation" (Aṅguttara Nikāya, II, 48). The world is therefore the individual's own state of consciousness, the particular interpretation he places upon the objects and events presented to his senses, and his reactions to them.

Mme. Alexandra David-Neel, in *Les enseignements secrets dans les sectes Bouddhistes Tibetaines*, describes a meditational exercise by which novices are trained to create around themselves, mentally, an environment which is very different from that considered to be real in the usual sense. Seated in his chamber, the meditator evokes a forest and experiences all the sensations of one who is walking among trees. "The utility attributed to this kind of exercise," she writes, "is to lead the novice to realize the superficial nature of our sensations and perceptions, since they can be provoked by objects whose character of reality we deny. According to the secret teachings we are perhaps wrong in denying their reality, for every mental creation possesses a kind of reality which is proper to itself, since it is capable of showing itself efficient."

Whatever presents itself to the consciousness of a sentient being, and is efficient in that it produces reactions and stimulates activities, must be considered real; but not in any absolute sense. Its reality is that of a certain state of consciousness at a certain time, its specific nature being derived from the sum of awarenesses possible on the level at which the being's consciousness functions. It must be remembered that the only world an individual knows is the world of his own consciousness. The Buddha said:

> "What, bhikkhus, is everything? The eye and forms, the ear and sounds, the nose and smells, the tongue and tastes, the body and touch, the mind and objects of mind. This, bhikkhus, is called everything. And, bhikkhus, whosoever should say: 'Rejecting this everything, I will proclaim another everything'—that would be mere talk on his part, and when questioned he could not make good his boast, and further, would come to a sorry pass. Why so? Because, bhikkhus, it would be beyond his capacity to do so."
>
> (Saṃyutta Nikāya, IV,15)

There is no reason to suppose that this must lead to solipsism. The external world has a real existence *on one particular level*, although it is not altogether what it appears to us through our senses. It is constituted of events that are common experiences to men and animals; but a human being and an animal may see the same object differently, may interpret it differently or, as is most often the case, simply respond to it differently.

Neither should the conceptual view of the world be confused with epiphenomenalism. Although consciousness is conditioned by the senses it is not created by them or absolutely determined by them. In the words of the Dhammapada, "Mind is the forerunner of all states (*dhamma*)." The word used here for mind (*mano*) implies volition (*cetanā*) as one of its functions. But it is in this respect that the animal differs most characteristically from the human being, for the animal's responses and the entire realm of its activities are to a far greater extent dominated by its physical organization. We shall return to this point when dealing with one of Dr. Roos' later arguments.

It is not my purpose in this article to prove that rebirth as an animal is possible, but to state the logic of the Buddhist position in the debate. For this it will be necessary to examine each of Dr. Roos' points in the order in which he presents them. Referring to the Tittira Jātaka, the story of the four virtuous animals, in which the Buddha identified himself with the partridge, Sāriputta with the hare, Maudgalyāyana (Moggallāna) with the monkey, and Ānanda with the elephant, Dr. Roos says:

It would be an error to use this Jātaka tale as a proof that the Buddha taught the possibility of rebirth on earth in a subhuman kingdom. It was obviously intended to illustrate the effect of the fivefold vow. Because otherwise the question would arise: "If rebirth as an animal body is the outcome of demeritorious karma, what evil deeds were done by the Buddha and his companions previous to being born as a partridge, etc.?", which would show the unsuitability of the Jātaka tales as a support for the thesis of rebirth into an animal to expiate sins.

It is generally acknowledged today that many, if not all, of the Jātakas were in existence as folk tales before the time of the Buddha. The suggestion has been made that the Buddha used them as popular forms of teaching by way of parable. This may be so, but they are in no way inconsistent with the general principles he taught. He does not figure in the Jātakas as a Buddha, but as a bodhisattva, and moreover a bodhisattva at different stages of development. The characters in which he is portrayed are therefore not always ideal; in one Jātaka, for example he figures as a robber chief. In both Theravāda and Mahāyāna the bodhisattva is acknowledged to be still in the state of a *puthujjana*, or "worldling" as distinct from any of the four classes of *ariya-puggala*. By reason of his vows he cannot even attain the state of *sotāpanna*, the first stage of sainthood, for if he did so his career as a bodhisattva would be curtailed. He has elected to remain in saṃsāra for an indefinite period of many aeons in order to benefit other beings, and in any of the lower stages (*bhūmi*) of his progress, which is very gradual, he may fall away from his attainment. So while a Buddha could not commit evil deeds that would cause him to be reborn in the animal world, a bodhisattva may do so. It is in fact believed that a bodhisattva does not take rebirth as an animal smaller than a quail or larger than an elephant.

This is the Theravāda interpretation; Mahāyāna adds the belief that a bodhisattva may deliberately choose to be born in the animal realm as part of his total identification in sympathy with all forms of life. Whichever view may be taken, his appearance in lower forms in the Jātakas is easily accounted for.

Dr. Roos goes on to say:

> The six realms mentioned by the Dalai Lama are always depicted between the spokes of the Wheel of Life ... The wheel's broad tire is divided into twelve parts, representing the twelve *nidānas*, known as Dependent Origination, *pratītya samutpāda* ... but there is no obvious

relationship between these twelve *nidānas* and the six realms. It is important to note that only two of the six realms could possibly refer to an objective existence on earth, viz., the realms of men and animals. The other four cannot be interpreted as localities of *physical* existence, and "rebirth" in these realms does not mean, therefore, reincarnation in the sense of a return to life on earth. Since logic and reason compel us to give a consistent interpretation to all six realms we must conclude that "rebirth in the realm of animals" does not refer to a physical existence in an animal body.

This is a good example of the need to differentiate between rebirth and "reincarnation," with its decidedly physical implications. Any continuation of the current of becoming, be it in a material, fine-material, or immaterial realm, is rebirth in the Buddhist sense. The earth on which we live is just one of many *bhūmis* (planes), and the fact that it happens to accommodate both the human and animal states of existence does not in any way distinguish it from other planes as a possible milieu for sentient life. In fact, besides humans and animals it harbours various classes of *devas* (deities), *pretas* (spirits), and other non-human beings. The twelve *nidānas* refer specifically to the current of interdependent causal and conditioning factors in *human* life; but the relationship between the *nidānas* and the six realms lies in the fact that at the stage of *jāti* (arising, or rebirth) the karma of the individual can produce rebirth in any one of them as well as in the human world. The interpretation of the Wheel of Life is therefore logical, reasonable, and consistent. The conclusion that rebirth in the realm of animals does not refer to a physical existence in an animal body has no justification. It is contrary to all that the pictorial representation of *pratītya samutpāda* is designed to teach.

The discussion next turns to "the important question: 'Is reincarnation in a subhuman kingdom possible?' and more specifically: 'Can a human Ego return to life on earth in an animal body?'."

This is stating the problem in terms which seem to require that it shall be solved in one particular way and not any other. Before following Dr. Roos further it should be noted that he again uses the word "reincarnation", and makes it the basic assumption of his next question, "Can a human Ego return to life ... in an animal body?" It has often been pointed out that the Buddhist doctrine of *anatta* disallows any persisting entity that can be called an ego or soul. But the animistic concept of an ego being reincarnated brings us right back to the impassioned speech in *The Merchant of Venice*:

63

"Almost thou mak'st me waver in my faith
To hold opinion with Pythagoras
That souls of animals infuse themselves
Into the bodies of men ..."

In thus being coerced into holding opinion with Pythagoras we are tricked into accepting reincarnation, transmigration, and metempsychosis (if not actual metamorphosis) all welded into a single, obviously impossible, hybrid of the imagination. If there were indeed a human ego that could never be anything but an ego, i.e., an unchanging entity with all human characteristics, the answer to Dr. Roos' question would have to be "No." It would not be going too far, indeed, to say that in such a case any kind of rebirth would be impossible. Because clearly the ego of, let us say, an elderly university professor could not be the ego of a newborn child, whimpering in its cradle. But what Buddhism most emphatically does *not* claim is that the ego of a dead university professor passes into the body of a helpless infant, or that the ego of an executed criminal passes into the body of an animal, even though the latter may be no more inconceivable than the former.

Yet, from a subjectivist point of view, we are entitled to ask ourselves: "Are there not times when the consciousness of an elderly man, however intellectual he may be, is temporarily that of a child? And is not the consciousness of a man given up to bestial desires sometimes on the same level as that of an animal?" And if the answer is "Yes," as I think it is bound to be, we are faced with facts concerning the supposed "ego" which are highly disconcerting. The truth is that the stream of consciousness which is human personality is not an entity with stable characteristics; it can touch the heights of divinity and it can sink to depths below the amoral level of the beast. In either of these its continuity can be resumed after death as well as on the human plane. It cannot be too often stated that the Buddhist doctrine is simply this: that as the result of a man's actions another being comes into existence after the dissolution of his phenomenal personality—a being which is "not the same, yet not another" (*na ca so, na ca añño*). The new being, be it man, deva, or animal, is the inheritor of the past being's karma; it carries on the world-line of identity to which he and all his predecessors belonged; it is the product of his thoughts, intentions, and desires, and most particularly the direct result of his final thought-moment before death. Instead of an ego, Buddhism speaks of a current of becoming (*bhava*), which can turn in any direction and give rise to any and every kind of formed or formless being. The reason why the Buddha laid such repeated emphasis on the *anattā* doctrine is because his Dhamma cannot be understood, even on the most elementary level, so long as there is a mental clinging to the concept of a persisting ego entity. In the list of the ten fetters (*saṃyojana*), the first to be broken is the erroneous belief in an essence of selfhood (*sakkāyadiṭṭhi*). Phenomenal personality exists— phenomenally—but it has no abiding essence.

As a preliminary to discussing the "technical" aspects of the two questions quoted above, Dr. Roos mentions a short article by Mrs. Rhys Davids, "Animal Rebirth," in *Wayfarer's Words* (Vol. III, pp. 1093/1096), in which she writes:

> Very significant for me is the silence of the Pāli Sutta on rebirth as an animal as compared with the Jātaka chatter about the dog of the Pāli Commentary. It is a silence almost total, that runs throughout the Piṭakas, once we omit the later Jātaka Commentary....[12]

Dr. Roos approves of this, commenting that it is her best argument, her approach otherwise being "rather emotional, without any sustained attempt at proving her point."

Now it is a fact, demonstrable from her writings, that Mrs. Rhys Davids' interpretation of Buddhism, especially of all aspects of it concerned with *anattā* and questions touching upon human survival, underwent a significant change after the death of her husband and son. The psychological causes of such a change need hardly be discussed here: we are more concerned with Dr. Roos' verdict that the passage quoted is her "best argument."

It is hardly possible to agree with this. In the first place, if what Mrs. Rhys Davids wrote at that time is true, it raises the question: "How did a doctrine so unattractive, so wounding to human pride, come to be adopted by the early Buddhists if it had no more support than an 'almost total silence' on the part of the Master?" People are inclined to believe what they wish to believe, and can be persuaded to accept unpleasant truths only with the greatest difficulty, if at all. Secondly, if the belief existed before the time of the Buddha, and he considered it to be false, he would surely have spoken against it, as he did against other errors, rather than preserve even a partial silence, much less a total one.

But the fact is that where Mrs. Rhys Davids professed to find almost total silence, an objective scrutiny of the Sutta Piṭaka discloses references to animal rebirth wherever the courses of future existence open to a human being are mentioned. The passages quoted above do not by any means exhaust the list. Aṅguttara Nikāya V, 208–9 records the Buddha as saying:

"Owners of their deeds (*kamma*) are the beings, heirs of their deeds, their deeds are the womb from which they spring, with their deeds they are bound up, their deeds are their refuge ....

"There is one who destroys living beings, takes what belongs to others, has unlawful intercourse with the other sex, speaks untruth ... is covetous, cruel-minded, follows evil views. And he is creeping in his actions by body, speech, and mind. Hidden are his works, words, and thoughts, hidden his ways and objects. But I tell you: whoever pursues hidden ways and objects, will have to expect one of these two results: either the torments of hell, or birth amongst the creeping animals."

In case there should be any doubt as to the literal meaning of this, the formula explaining what is meant by "rebirth" given in the exposition of dependent origination is as follows:

"But what, O monks, is rebirth? The birth of beings belonging to this or that order of beings, their being born, their conception and springing into existence, the manifestation of the groups of existence (the five *khandhas*), the arising of sense activity: this is called rebirth."

This formulation is found in the Saṃyutta Nikāya (II, 3), and is repeated again and again in other suttas. It leaves no margin for doubt that what is meant is literally the birth of living organisms of every kind according to their nature.

Turning to Mahāyāna we find an equal abundance of references to the five (or six) courses of existence (*gati*). A typical example is in the description of the Buddha Amitāyus given in the *Amitāyur-Dhyāna Sūtra*: "Within the circle of light emanating from his whole body, appear illuminated the various forms and marks of all beings that live in the five paths of existence."[13]

In *A Manual of Buddhist Philosophy* (Vol I, 73), William Montgomery McGovern writes as follows:

The Five or Six Gatis. This is the most important of all Buddhist classifications of sentient beings, and is the basis of the various Buddhist wheels of life or charts of existence. The fivefold division is made by most branches of Hīnayāna, the sixfold division by a few branches of Hīnayāna and most branches of Mahāyāna. The five *gatis* are:

1. The inhabitants of the *Narakas* or hells.
2. *Pretas*, ghosts, goblins, or demons.
3. Animals.
4. Mankind.
5. *Devas* or gods.

Where a sixth *gati* is added, it consists of the *Asuras*—titanic, demoniac monsters ...

It might be argued that all these allusions to animal rebirth in Theravāda and Mahāyāna texts are spurious interpolations. But if they are, it is difficult to conceive how they could have become so closely interwoven with the entire fabric of Buddhist thought, with the total Buddhist picture of the world, and with the pattern of moral causality embracing all sentient life that it presents, as we see them to be. It has become something of a fashion to decry the Pāli Commentaries for what Mrs. Rhys Davids called their "chatter," in spite of the fact that they contain much valuable material and that without them the correct meaning of many Buddhist technical terms would have remained in doubt. But in this instance it is not later exegetical literature, suspect or not, that we are dealing with. The question concerns the oldest Buddhist texts available to us, the sole source of our knowledge of what the Buddha taught. Moreover, it is a question of the integrity of the Buddhist world-view that is involved: that is to say, the place in the scheme allotted to every form of life, and the validity of its existence within the framework of a cosmic moral order. To this we shall return later, when discussing Dr. Roos' principal arguments.

The next authority to be introduced is Dr. W.Y. Evans-Wentz, with a passage from Ch. X, "The Rebirth Doctrine," of his Introduction to *Tibetan Book of the Dead*, which in Dr. Roos' abridgment is quoted thus:

> . . . . the esoteric interpretation may be stated ... as follows: The human form (but not the divine nature in man) is a direct inheritance from the sub-human kingdoms; ... the psychical seed of the life-flux which the eye cannot see—if of a human being it cannot incarnate in, or overshadow, or be intimately bound up with a body foreign to its evolved characteristics, either in this world, in *Bardo*, or in any realm or world of *sangsāric* existence.
>
> For a human life-flux to flow into the physical form of a dog or fowl, or insect, or worm is, therefore, held to be as impossible as putting into the bed of the Ganges River the waters of the Indian Ocean.

Dr. Roos writes with justice that he does not think the approaches of Mrs. Rhys Davids and of Dr. Evans-Wentz are wholly convincing, and that therefore he will "attempt to discuss the subject by using an entirely different approach." But before following him any further, the concepts and the terminology employed by Evans-Wentz should be examined in the light of what has already been said regarding *anattā* and the rebirth-continuum. In the quotation given above, Evans-Wentz speaks of "the divine nature in man" in just the same way as might a Christian theologian or a Vedantist. This "divine nature" has, it seems, the peculiar property of being able to incarnate in human bodies or in higher forms, but not to take any other direction. It can evolve, but cannot regress, so that its nature is capable of only one kind of change, which means, in effect, that its upward progress is inevitable. If the human sphere is a testing ground of moral worth, it is then like an examination in which the candidate cannot fail. This may be a very comforting view, but it postulates a principle of evolution that is contrary to any of the natural laws known to us: an irreversible process which can only go from good to better, and from better to some unguessable "best." But this is not the Buddhist view. In Buddhism, the divine nature of man is a *potentiality*, something not yet realized, and which can be achieved only by strenuous effort, with dangers of retrogression all along the way. What Evans-Wentz calls the "human life-flux" is really human only so long as it is associated with a humanpsycho physical organism. It has no unchanging characteristic, human, divine, or otherwise, but is wholly a transforming process, capable of giving rise to any kind of organic manifestation according to its karmic propensities. And each phenomenal manifestation altogether ceases to be when its immediate successor arises. The teaching of the so-called esoteric school of Northern Buddhism is in this respect no different from that of Theravāda. As Mme. David-Neel writes:

> In truth, the perpetual flow alone exists, at once continuous (it never halts) and discontinuous (it consists of distinct moments) of bursts of energy: causes and effects are engendered without the generating cause ever being able to know its progeniture-effect, since it disappears when the latter arises; or, rather, it is the disappearance itself which constitutes its effect—the new phenomenon.

Evans-Wentz wrote a great deal on the subject of rebirth, in which he was a firm believer. His first important contribution to the study of it was a book, published in Ceylon, called *The Science of Rebirth*. Later, in collaboration with the Ven. Lama Kazi Dawa Samdup he produced a translation of the

Bardo Thodol, The Tibetan Book of the Dead, from which Dr. Roos' quotation is taken. In *The Science of Rebirth* Evans-Wentz wrote: "I have no doubt that plants and trees have souls and are subject to the Law of Re-embodiment" (p.210). But he rejected the idea that a human being could be reborn as an animal through the effect of bad karma. "To me," he wrote, "it is neither reasonable nor logical, nor in accord with evolution, to believe that … a human being may descend from the human plane to that of the lowest animal, worm, or even insect" (p.82).[14]

In support of this view he appealed to what he called the "little known School of Esoteric Buddhism in Tibet" in which, according to him when "a man is said to be born as a cock, for example, the meaning intended is not that the man shall be born as a cock in reality, but that he shall be reborn as a man full of lust, since the cock, in the symbolism of the Wheel of Life, of the Mahāyāna School, in Sikkim and in Tibet, represents lust" (p.82).

"Esoteric Buddhism"

At this point it is necessary to take a glance at the widely held belief that there is an "esoteric" and an "exoteric" Buddhism. The "esoteric" form is supposed to be found in Mahāyāna, while the Theravāda is exclusively "exoteric." Whether any such distinction ever existed outside the syncretic beliefs of those whose approach to Buddhism has been via Vedanta and Theosophy is extremely doubtful, and in any case it seems to be based upon a confusion of thought. The term "Mahāyāna" embraces a vast complex of schools some of them diverging from others in several important respects, while the Theravāda has remained a homogeneous body of teaching. The Mahāyāna schools, however, have one characteristic in common with one another: in most of them it is possible to discern the features that usually appear when the need has been felt to institutionalize a religion in order to bring it within the scope and understanding of the masses. In the religions which have undergone this process of popularization we usually find an emphasis on ritualism, the establishment of a formal church hierarchy, a marked increase of the supernatural element, and, most significant as an indication of the wish to appeal to the average man and woman, the introduction of doctrines promising salvation by faith.

All of these items are present to some degree in Mahāyāna, the outstanding example being the faith doctrine of the Pure Land (Sukhāvati) school, wherein the recitation of *mantras* takes the place of self-purification by personal effort.[15] The same tendency is also evident in the more world-regarding

69

doctrines which substitute the bodhisattva ideal for that of the arahat and erase the distinction the Buddha made between Nirvāna and saṃsāra. These articles of faith, if not consciously designed to modify the teaching of renunciation taught by the Buddha, had the result, whether calculated or not, of making Buddhism easier for the ordinary man who was not ready to relinquish his hold on the world or loosen its hold upon him. Historical evidence as well as present observation seems to be the basis of the view expressed by Dr. André Migot who, writing of the Northern schools, says that some centuries after the Buddha there came to birth "a new Buddhism, the Mahāyāna, which had already been founded in North India under Kanishka, the inheritor of the primitive mentality closer to the people."[16] It can scarcely be denied that there is a dual aspect to Mahāyāna: the religion of the masses and the transcendental philosophy of the instructed. But apart from such metaphysical doctrines as those of the Trikāya, the Dhyāni Buddhas, the Ādi-Buddha, and the Shakti cults derived from the Tantras, the inner aspect of Mahāyāna does not contain anything that is not overtly present in Theravāda or that is not an essential factor in the Buddhist view of life.

If there is a teaching which may be called too subtle for the generality of mankind to understand, it is precisely the doctrine of *anattā* (*anātman*). This teaching is the common property of both Theravāda and Mahāyāna, but is more consistently held in the Pāli tradition than in the popular forms of Mahāyāna. A comparison of the two schools leaves little room for doubt that if either of them should be classified as "exoteric" it is the Mahāyāna, if only by reason of its infinity of gods and minor deities, its modes of worship, its docetic and supernatural view of the Buddha, and its teaching that Nirvāna and saṃsāra are one—a formulation clearly intended to shift the ultimate goal from the state beyond all conditioned phenomena, where Theravāda places it, back to the familiar world.

This is not to say that Theravāda is "esoteric"; it is nothing of the sort. Its teachings are open to all, as the Buddha intended them to be. With solemn emphasis he told his disciples, on the eve of his passing away, that he had never had the closed fist of a teacher who held some things back. He taught his doctrine of deliverance without making any distinction between "esoteric" and "exoteric" form, and with no discrimination as to persons.[17] To lay claim to a secret doctrine in the face of that clear statement would be to betray the Buddha's intention, and never at any time has the Theravāda done so.

On what grounds, then, has a secret tradition of teaching been attributed to Mahāyāna? It may well have arisen because of the manifest difference between the popular Buddhism of the masses, especially where Mahāyāna has been corrupted by admixture with indigenous beliefs, and the highly metaphysical teachings of Nāgārjuna, Vasubandhu, Asanga, and other founders of schools within the main body. But in this connection it should be remembered that the systems they erected are in actual fact reinterpretations and elaborations of the essential doctrines found in Theravāda, namely *anattā* and *suññatā* (voidness). To the Theravāda these ideas are not "esoteric" but are treated as truths available to all, the understanding of them being limited only by the capacity of the hearer. To the Lamaism of Tibet, in which they appear in the trappings of imagery and personification, the *Prajñāpāramitā* teachings may have taken on the character of a secret instruction, but the *Śūnyatā* concept which underlies them is only an extremely idealized form of the world-view that can be traced back to the *anattā* and *suññatā* of Theravāda.

The chief difference between the historical Buddha Gotama, and e.g., the Madhyamika philosophers who spoke in his name, is that the Buddha eschewed metaphysical constructions which lead nowhere but to the annihilation of logic (as they did with Nāgārjuna), and preferred to teach a direct and practical method of truth-realization. The Buddha made use of philosophy just to the extent that was necessary to communicate in words the basic principles he had discovered. Beyond that, knowing that there is a point at which all logical constructs become self-contradictory and all verbal communication fails, he preserved the ariyan silence, leaving the disciple to make the final breakthrough in the only way possible, by his own effort.

Evens-Wentz admits, in the *Tibetan Book of the Dead* (p.42), that "without any doubt, the *Bardo Thodol, if read literally*," (my italics) conveys "the exoteric interpretation." In this he is being no more than just: there is nothing whatever in the text to suggest that it is meant to be read symbolically. The same may certainly be said of the canonical references to the *tiracchāna-yoni* quoted above. The Pāli texts are notable, among the religious books of the world, for their literal and even prosaic character in the presentation of doctrine. It is a feature that has made them seem uninteresting to many people who expect to find in sacred teachings a cloudy mysticism clothed in allegory and poetic hyperbole. When the suttas do resort to simile and imagery it is expressly stated that a simile or an image is being used. This is so often the case that it practically constitutes a rule, with a set form of words— "*Seyyathā pi bhikkhave ... evam eva kho bhikkhave*"—"Just as, O bhikkhus ... even so, O bhikkhus"—being used. The Buddha seems to have had a profound distrust of language that could be misunderstood, and to have deliberately curbed all tendency to express himself oracularly. The texts themselves, apart from pseudo-biographical matter which has no bearing upon doctrine, for the most part follow his lead, and a sober, matter-of-fact tone prevails. That being so, it is permissible to ask: "If the situation is as Evans-Wentz represents it, why should a doctrine that can be stated clearly and simply be hidden in a symbolism that was certain to be misunderstood?" Such a course is completely foreign to the Buddha's method of teaching. Symbolism may legitimately be used when attempting to express the inexpressible, but never for the sake of mere mystification. Secrecy, the Buddha declared, is the characteristic of priests (the Brahmanical teachers) and certain other classes of people; for his own part he did not practise it.

Before leaving this side of the question I feel it necessary to point out that the indiscriminate reduction of ancient religious teachings to symbolism is one that can have no end, once it is started. To interpret symbolically statements which the ancients meant to be taken simply and literally is the last refuge of a theology driven to desperation. There is at least one of the great world religions which has had to be interpreted symbolically to the point where in fact nothing remains of it but the name. In contrast to this extreme case, the allegories and symbols of Buddhism, where they are found, belong to a later date than the original teaching of the Buddha, and add nothing to it of any value. They are interesting as products of the mythopoeic mind, but nothing more. A Buddha whose feet never touched the ground does not help us at all to realize the truths of Buddhism, which are securely grounded in human experience.

I shall not attempt to launch a full-scale inquiry into the origin of the belief in an esoteric school of Northern Buddhism, since to do so would necessitate delving into the obscurity that surrounds the origin of Buddhist and Hindu Tantra. But it is pertinent to say a few words concerning its influence on the thought and writings of Evans-Wentz if only because his arguments lean so heavily upon it. Where did he get the idea that there is an "esoteric" school which teaches that rebirth as an animal is to be taken symbolically? The answer is given in his own words in the *Tibetan Book of the Dead* (p.42), where he states that he had it "on the authority of the various philosophers, both Hindu and Buddhist," from whom he received his instruction. Unfortunately, the only authority directly named is the Ven.

Kazi Dawa-Samdup. On p.44 of the same work the Lama is quoted thus:

> The doctrine of the transmigration of the human to the sub-human may apply solely to the lower or purely brutish constituents of the human principle of consciousness: for the knower itself neither incarnates nor re-incarnates—it is the Spectator.

Now this statement, whether one accepts it as truth or not, is simply not Buddhism, either Mahāyāna or Theravāda. The "Knower" or "Spectator" is the Ātman of Vedanta, the same "immutable, unchanging soul" which all schools of Buddhism deny. What, then, is the explanation of such a statement coming from a Tibetan Lama?

It is not difficult to find, I think. The Venerable Lama Dawa-Samdup was anything but a typical member of the Tibetan priesthood. He was English-educated and had been exposed to the syncretic influences of Indian and Western philosophy. If we add to that the amiable characteristic of wishing to please the person to whom one is speaking, it needs no great effort of the imagination to understand how ready he was to accommodate himself to the ideas of his distinguished friend and collaborator. Two instances of this among many in my own experience come to my mind. In one, a Buddhist monk wrote to a foreign inquirer who had previously made it clear that he refused to believe in rebirth, telling him that the Buddha taught no such doctrine, and that it was a "popular misconception." The other case concerned a European who did not wish to believe in human free will. The Buddhist monk with whom he was in correspondence obligingly told him that there is no free will in Buddhism. This kindly readiness to fall in with other people's opinions—by which, incidentally, Asian Buddhists sometimes hope to make the Dhamma acceptable to Westerners—is quite sufficient to explain the encouragement that Evans-Wentz encountered in his efforts to inject the Vedantic Ātman and theosophical modifications into "esoteric" Buddhism. All that need be added on this score is that if such an esoteric school really exists, it appears that His Holiness the 14th Dalai Lama does not belong to it.

But before taking final leave of Dr. Evans-Wentz, the use he made of science in his debates is worthy of notice. In *The Science of Rebirth* (p. 312) he wrote as follows:

> Men of science see no possibility of accepting the Doctrine of the Resurrection of the physical body ... but the Doctrine is the exoteric interpretation of a long-hidden esoteric truth, namely, that the "soul"

may be resurrected in a newly-constituted physical body ... and this is scientifically possible. On the contrary, any form of a doctrine of the transmigration of a human "soul" or of any of the human *skandha* (*khandhà*) to the body of a sub-human creature, animal or plant, is scientifically impossible.

In passing it may be observed that it is the doctrine of rebirth itself which here becomes "esoteric." One can only wish that all scientists were as prepared to admit the scientific possibility of rebirth as Dr. Evans-Wentz naively supposed them to be forty years ago. But whether they would even then claim that rebirth as an animal is less possible "scientifically" than rebirth as a human being, is open to serious doubt. There might well be some who would consider that the homocentric idea of a "soul" that can reincarnate only in a human body was less scientific than the Buddhist concept of an impersonal life-continuum which is capable of giving rise to different kinds of organism according to the direction in which it has been channelled. The tendency of science today is to see even less difference between the human and sub-human species than Buddhism itself admits. But much depends, as the late Prof. C.E.M. Joad might have said, on what one means by "science."

The Kingdoms of Nature

It is something of a relief to turn from these loosely formulated and not very coherent ideas to the arguments of Dr. Roos, which we shall now take up again.

To begin with, he points out that "the various kingdoms of nature differ principally in the kind and extent of their powers and their knowledge. The higher kingdoms appear as compounds of the lower kingdoms, in the sense that the members, say of the animal kingdom, are *co-operative organizations* of members of the vegetable and mineral kingdoms." The power of cohesion enables plants to form roots, stems, leaves, and other organs for a variety of specialized functions, just as in the mineral kingdom it produces a great variety of crystals. "As a result, plants have a wider range of perception, hence a greater degree of consciousness than the individual members of the mineral kingdom of which they are composed. At the same time there is for each plant an animating something which keeps the various parts functioning together in harmony, to achieve a common aim, viz., the preservation of the individual plant in the first instance, and the propagation of the species as the next important aim."

This is perfectly true: the compounded (*saṅkhata*) nature of all phenomena is a consistent principle that runs throughout the universe, every higher and more complex organism being composed of aggregates drawn from the lower and simpler structures. The "animating something" is *jīvitindriya*, the life force, which is sometimes, and rather misleadingly, shortened to *jīva*, when in popular usage it takes the place of "soul."[18]

But Dr. Roos continues: "This 'animating something' could be called the 'soul of the plant' for lack of a better term." It is here that we encounter some difficulties. The first concerns the idea of purposeful organization which seems to be implicit in the argument. Biologists in the main are reluctant to admit any kind of entelechy in their picture of the life-process, and theories of a teleological kind are looked upon with suspicion. Only in the Vitalism of Hans Driesch do we find any strong scientific support for the theory of purpose in living structures. Buddhism, however, maintains that there is such a purpose although it is not fully realized as a conscious one. Rather, it is an unconscious drive that is inherent in natural processes themselves. It is not drawn from any external source nor is it projected into them from a higher level of their own being. It is the blind urge towards the gratification of sensory desires, which on the plant level is a purely mechanical functioning. This more or less cybernetic response to stimuli shows itself as phototropism and the tendency of creeping plants to wind their tendrils around any object with which they come into contact. In Buddhism plants are classified as "one-facultied" (*ekindriya*), and the one faculty they possess is that of life. Again the question of a "soul" does not enter the picture.

Another and more formidable obstacle is the seeming impossibility of attributing an individual *ens* to organisms which propagate, or survive, by division. Not only plants but various forms of animal life, such as the flatworm, multiply in this way, thus presenting a challenge to the accepted concept of individuality. When the parts of an organism can become detached from the parent body and each continue to live on as a separate animal, to become themselves the progenitors of more offshoots in their turn, they confront us with this problem in its most acute form. It is a difficulty which can be resolved only by discarding the notion of an individual entity and taking an altogether different view of what it is that survives in these prolifications. If we equate "identity" with serial continuity *alone*, we are not driven to conclude, with the zoologist Weisman, that organisms such as the protozoa are immortal. Dr. Roos therefore is well advised to qualify his use of the word "soul" by offering it only for lack of a better term. Unfortunately its implications are such, and are so inseparably bound up with the word itself, apart from its theological overtones, that it cannot fail to infect any process of reasoning in which it features as an essential point of reference. To talk of the "soul" of a plant at once exposes the weakness of the theory.

Going a step higher in the evolutionary scale, Dr. Roos observes that the members of the animal kingdom "have a still wider range of powers than that possessed by plants. With the power of locomotion added to the increased powers of sense perception an even greater demand for cooperation between the separate parts of an animal is required. Its 'soul' has to make a wide variety of decisions during the course of the animal's existence. But these decisions are not based upon reasoning processes nor upon reflective thinking, but solely upon impulses in accordance with its innate character. This means that the actions of an animal are determined by *desire* and *fear*, both of which are stimulated by the power of memory. In the higher animals this power is greatly developed, though it can *only* be activated by *association* with sense perceptions, while in the human kingdom memory is also activated by mental processes, wherefore a man can deliberately recall events of the past and consult his store of knowledge, which animals cannot do."

This brings us on to highly debatable ground. The behaviourists would say that man is also an organism activated by conditioned responses, and that the difference between his performance in relation to external stimuli and that of the lower animals is only in the possession of a wider range of possible reflexes. On the other hand, many naturalists have not hesitated to credit the higher animals with feelings of affection and impulses of self-sacrifice that go far beyond the mere gratification of the pleasure principle and the instinct of self-preservation. In man himself it is chiefly these two urges that motivate action, as Buddhism and modern psychology both recognize. Dr. Roos, moreover, is inclined to overstress the difference between humans and animals in the matter of memory. All organisms, at whatever level of consciousness, learn by remembering, and there is even a kind of memory in inorganic life. In many situations the higher animals show that they are capable of making the transition from remembering to reasoning, as has been proved by experiments with chimpanzees. The more our knowledge of human and animal psychology advances the more difficult

76

it becomes to draw any firm line of demarcation between them.

Again, Dr. Roos makes a distinction not recognized in Buddhist psychology when he asserts that in animals memory can only be activated by association with sense perceptions, while in the human kingdom it is also activated by mental processes. In Buddhist psychology the mind itself is classed as the sixth sense, and every kind of memory is associated with sense perceptions. Thus a specific memory may be provoked by an event in the external world entering consciousness through one of the five physical sense channels, or it may present itself spontaneously at the mind-door (*manodvāra*) as an idea. Ideas themselves are considered as being the sense objects of the mind, whether they arise in dream or in the waking state. That animals dream has been proved by tracing the activity of their brain cells while sleeping, so that it is clear that they share with human beings the faculty of ideation, together with its concomitants, memory and a form of mental activity independent of immediate external stimuli.

Dr. Roos continues: "The animal, therefore, is not responsible for its actions, since it has no choice but to follow the dictates of its nature. This means that an animal can neither make nor dissipate individual karma, i.e., there is no merit nor demerit possible in the subhuman kingdoms."

In general this is true; but there are possible exceptions among the higher animals. To give just one example of many, the English national newspapers of January 1960 reported the case of a blind man and his mongrel dog, both found dead in a burnt-out bungalow in Laindon, Essex. "The man, who lived alone with his dog," the report states, "had apparently collapsed as he tried to escape and his dog refused to leave him in spite of the intense heat and smoke."

This was simply the result of conditioning, of course; any disciple of Pavlov knows that perfectly well. And in that case, so also is the behaviour of a soldier who stays to help a wounded comrade under heavy gunfire. If we are going to accept the behaviourist explanation it would be better to do so in *toto*, and at least be able to claim the merit of consistency. If a choice had to be made between the theories of the scientific materialist and those of the believer in a personal "soul" or "ego principle," any clear-thinking person would choose the former without hesitation. Fortunately, the choice is not so limited.

However, as I have discussed the question of merit and demerit in animal behaviour elsewhere,[19] we will follow the remainder of Dr. Roos' argument. He proceeds: "This brings up the question how, in a Universe where Karma is supposed to provide JUSTICE for all beings, it is possible for animals to suffer physical pain, as they obviously do. To answer this question let us first have a close look at the nature of pain. Starting with physical pain, we see that this is merely a message telling the sufferer that something is wrong at the location where the message originated. It is intended to stimulate, or force, the sufferer to take the necessary steps to counteract whatever caused the pain. This shows that PAIN is beneficial, like a fire alarm, and that its purpose is to teach the sufferer certain important facts necessary to cope with the problems of physical life. Though all suffering is subject to the law of Causality, this does not mean that it is always a retribution as the outcome of a demeritorious act."[20]

This is perfectly true; suffering (*dukkha*) is an inseparable part of life, and there are some forms of pain which are merely the consequence of having been born, irrespective of past demeritorious action. Pain is a necessary part of the response of a living organism to undesirable features of its environment. But it is questionable whether a pain that cannot be remedied is beneficial, either to an animal or a human being. At the most it can be said to inform the sufferer that something is wrong, though the knowledge may not be of any help to him.

To do full justice to Dr. Roos' line of reasoning it is necessary to continue quoting him in full. He goes on to say:

> The members of the subhuman kingdoms suffer only as a result of physical circumstances and only so much as is useful to them for acquiring the skill necessary to avoid future suffering. There is no *mental* suffering in animals, and this fact alone should tell us that no comparison is possible between the sufferings of animals and men. The two belong to completely different orders of experience if we except the suffering of young children, of idiots, of lunatics, and of certain savages. Both orders of suffering serve useful though very different purposes because it is a corollary of the law of Karma that NO SUFFERING IS IN VAIN.

These are rather large statements. In actual fact, we know very little about the mental aspect of an animal's experience of pain. Some facts, however, are clear from common observation: for example, we see that animals can remember pain, for if they could not, they would not be capable of learning to avoid its causes. We also know that domesticated animals can pine and even die in the absence of their masters. They are also capable of suffering *in expectation of pain*, as a dog when it knows it is going to be beaten. But Dr. Roos has already weakened his own argument in advance

78

by bracketing the suffering of animals with that of "young children, of idiots, of lunatics, and of certain savages," because if pain is to be interpreted either as serving a useful purpose biologically, or as a result of karma, it is evident that these are classes of human beings to whom the interpretation has exactly the same applicability, and in the same degree, as it has to animals. In this view, if "an animal can neither make nor dissipate individual karma" and therefore "there is no merit nor demerit possible in the subhuman kingdoms," the same must be true of the idiot and the lunatic, since they too are not morally responsible individuals.

This point anticipates Dr. Roos' next argument, which is as follows: "In man this kind of suffering is in the mind and is produced by the *knowledge* of *undesirable events*, which have already occurred or which are now happening or are threatening to take place. The fact that these events are undesirable means that they are in conflict with his desires and therefore produce painful images in his mind which are the direct cause of his suffering. And since there is no useless suffering we must expect something good to result from it. It stands to reason that the reaction of this class of suffering tends to produce a disgust for the desires which were frustrated by the 'undesirable events.' This disgust will have a weakening effect upon the corresponding desires and may gradually lead to their destruction, and eventually to liberation from the wheel of saṃsāra."

This should indeed be so, but in practice it seldom happens that people learn from the experience of suffering alone; if they did, they would not have been revolving for countless world-cycles in saṃsāra. The individual may be perfectly aware of the direct cause of his present suffering, and may hope by using the knowledge to avoid it in the future. What he does not know is the basic cause of it, which is the craving that has brought him to birth. But the yogin who has cultivated the *jhānas* and is able to review his previous existences remembers the distress he experienced not only in human births but in his lives as various animals. He recalls the suffering, together with the karma that caused it, and in this way the experience of pain in the subhuman realms becomes of benefit to him. It contributes very powerfully to his feeling of disgust for conditioned existence, and hence to his liberation from it.

For the ordinary person, however, just as for the animal, there is much pain that is completely useless and unproductive because its cause has not yet been discerned. It is simply not true to say that "no suffering is in vain." All saṃsaric suffering is in vain until it is understood in its true nature by analytical knowledge. The universe observes its own laws of causality, which are not devised for man's particular benefit or with the intention of teaching him wisdom. "Empty phenomena roll on," as Buddhaghosa aptly says, regardless of whether man comprehends them or not.

From what he has said up to this point, Dr. Roos concludes that "animals cannot have emotional *suffering* because they are not ensouled 'mind-beings.' What to a human being would be an emotional disturbance, such as anger, fear, etc., would be a *natural* activity in an animal and could not be a source of suffering followed by a destruction of desires, as this would be the end of the animal itself."

Here Dr. Roos opposes a *"natural* activity" to "emotional disturbance," but on what grounds he does so is far from clear. It savours rather of the theistic religious idea of placing man outside of nature as a special creation; the Buddhist view is that all activities, emotional or otherwise, are natural. If by the phrase "not ensouled mind-beings" he means that animals have no mental life, he is taking a narrower view of what constitutes mental activity than does Buddhism or science, insofar as the latter admits of mind at all. In the Buddhist analysis, mind exists wherever there is conscious mental response, although such mental activity may vary widely in extent and quality between one form of life and another. Science, which studies psychology through the behaviour of both humans and animals, does not make any such sharp distinction between them as Dr. Roos evidently wishes to do. It is not easy to distinguish between anger, fear, etc., as "emotional disturbances" in a human being and "natural activities" in an animal. Surely they are equally "natural" reactions in both cases. If, in the case of human beings, one wishes to dignify them by calling them "emotions" the distinction is one of terminology more than anything else. The experience that makes a man angry may not excite a dog, but when the dog is infuriated its physiological reactions are much the same, and even the outward manifestations of its feelings are not very different from those of a man.

It is therefore not at all clear what metaphysical distinction Dr. Roos means to indicate by placing "emotional disturbances" and "natural activities" in opposition, or by characterizing animals as not being "mind-ensouled" beings. No one would deny, least of all a Buddhist, that the human mind is vastly richer, incalculably wider in scope, and capable of producing a far greater variety of thoughts and activities than that of an animal—and this we can assert with safety even though we know so little about the subjective life of animals that we cannot even be sure whether they experience colour perception in the same way as we do. But it seems that there is simply a difference in the *quality* and *range* of the mental activity, while the basic processes and even the fundamental motivations are the same. Put in another way, we might say that the difference between the consciousness and responses of an animal and those of a human being is rather like the difference between a child's toy piano of one diatonic octave and a concert grand. Basically, they both produce sound by percussion.

The Western mind is deeply imbued with the idea that man is, if not a special creation, at least a being in some unique way distinguished from the rest of nature. This notion of his special place in the cosmos has persisted as a relic of anthropocentric thinking despite the fact that it receives no support from biology or any other branch of knowledge. Even though the behaviour patterns of a human infant and of a baby chimpanzee may be identical through several stages of their development, the human child has to be regarded as a "mind-ensouled" being, animated by a human "ego-principle," which could not have "entered" the body of the chimpanzee. Even though the mind of a congenital idiot may be less capable of dealing with situations in the external world than that of a well-trained sheepdog, still it has to be considered a *human* mind, the seat of a human "soul," a metaphysical entity of some sort that could not have "reincarnated" in any lower form of life. On the other hand, a dog may show more faithfulness, courage, and devotion than many men are capable of, but being an animal it is not worthy to harbour that mysterious and sublime entity, a human "soul."

This is one of the extreme views that the Buddha deplored. At the other end of the scale we have the materialist who believes that man's superiority is nothing but the result of possessing an opposable thumb. If we point out to him that the apes also have opposable thumbs but this has not enabled them to paint Rembrandt's pictures or think out Spinoza's philosophy, his faith in his theory—which is no more than a reaction against supernaturalism—remains unshaken. Human superiority, for him, lies solely in the development of mental activity stimulated by the ability to manipulate objects. It is somewhere between these two extremes that we have to seek the truth.

The realms of existence are not clearly defined areas separated by impassable barriers; they impinge upon one another and their borders are as indefinite and fluid as the political divisions on a map of Europe. The human and the subhuman worlds exist side by side physically, and there are

81

points where they touch one another on the psychic level. But there is a pride in being human which may prevent us from acknowledging this, just as in some people there is pride in belonging to a particular nation or race, or having a skin of a different colour from that of other human beings. Under the influence of this pride, which is often quite unconscious, we tend to exaggerate the differences that we perceive and add to them totally imaginary ones. Man, the intelligent ape who has not yet succeeded in working out a plan for living without war, persecution, exploitation, and oppression, wants to feel that there is an essential and unchanging difference in kind between himself and other creatures. And even when he asserts in capital letters that ALL LIFE IS ONE, he is not willing to believe that if a man through his own moral failure loses his human status his karmic force can produce a being on a lower level more appropriate to it.

But as a Thai bhikkhu, to whom I put this question for his personal opinion just after writing the above, said: "There are times when a man is an animal in his mind. If his thoughts are again and again on that low level, and if his last thought-moment at death is of the same kind, why should not its product in the new arising be an animal?" This sums up the Buddhist position better than many volumes of scholarly argument.

For we see that there are great differences between men, which can be understood without the need of symbolism: between the mind of the great creative genius and the idiot the distance is great, as is that between the idiot and the ape. Where, then, is the barrier that cannot be crossed? Heinrich Heine wrote: "... the disproportion between body and soul torments me somewhat ... and metempsychosis often is the subject of my meditation. Who may know in what tailor now dwells the soul of Plato; in what schoolmaster the soul of Caesar! Who knows! Possibly the soul of Pythagoras occupies the poor candidate who failed in the examination due to his inability to prove the Pythagorean theory."[21]

This difficulty of the nature of a "soul" in relation to the total personality is one that cannot be resolved. The Upanishads attempt to dispose of it by asserting that the Ātman is completely independent of the phenomenal being, a something that remains unchanged and unaffected by all the thoughts, activities, and transformations of the continuing process that we know as personality. But just how unsatisfactory this is becomes apparent when we ask ourselves: "If that is the case, what ontological function does the 'soul' perform; or alternatively, what significance has the phenomenal personality in the order of moral values?" A something that exists apart from my own existence, a "Knower" or "Spectator" that does not form any part of my personality complex or participate in any of its vicissitudes or achievements, has simply no connection with me at all. If it exists, it does so as part of the world that is not-me, and to call it "*my* soul" is like calling somebody else's head my own. A statement of that kind can be made, but it carries no meaning. The Vedantic view is therefore subject to the same philosophical objection as Plato's theory of Transcendence and Immanence: that it postulates a real world (of soul) utterly remote and aloof from the familiar world (of phenomenal personality), so that existence falls into two halves between which there is not, and cannot ever be, any connection.

But Dr. Roos continues:

> "This great and fundamental difference between the members of the human and animal kingdoms makes it *impossible* that an animal body could be occupied by a human soul, i.e., a mind-being, even if the latter were heavily loaded with the karmic effect (*vāsanā*)²² of a long series of lives dedicated to evil actions. Reincarnations are governed by the need for *dissipating* the karmic *vāsanās*, which are stored in the mind (*ālaya-vijñāna*), and it is the force of attraction exercised by all the *vāsanās* that selects a suitable vehicle for the next rebirth, a vehicle through which the greatest possible amount of karmic debts will be paid off and karmic credits will be collected. At the point in the rebirth cycle where the return to life on Earth becomes imperative the human Ego will be attracted to a family most suitable from the point of view of the karma of the Ego as well as of the future parents. But there would be no attraction between the Ego and members of a subhuman kingdom because there would not be a possibility for the elimination of *vāsanās*, which can only take place under laws and conditions similar to those under which *vāsanās* are deposited in the *ālaya-vijñāna*. Therefore the fruits of acts committed in a human existence on earth must be harvested in a human existence on earth. This, then, is the principal factor why rebirth into subhuman kingdoms does not take place.

To put this line of reasoning into its proper perspective it is necessary to observe, first of all, that the law of *kamma* (as cause) and *vipāka* (effect) is the statement of a purely automatic process. In the psycho-ethical order of events it is the equivalent of physical laws such as that of thermodynamics, gravitation, and all the other principles which operate automatically in the material universe as essentials of its structure. It is not a law designed by a benevolent but punitive Providence for the purpose of *teaching* mankind, any more than is the law of gravity. It belongs to the order of cosmic necessity and exists in itself, whether there are minds that can understand it and profit by it or not, or whether some are able to do so, while others cannot. Therefore the argument that the suffering of animals does not serve any useful purpose from the standpoint of *kamma-vipāka*, because they cannot learn from it at the time of experiencing its action, is quite irrelevant. If the argument had the cogency that Dr. Roos attributes to it, it would be equally applicable to mentally defective human beings, placing them also outside the realm in which karma and its results are meaningful.

In the second place, and as a direct consequence of this, we have to recognize that some lives are, to employ the terminology of human values, merely "expiatory" and nothing more. The animal, like the morally irresponsible human being, is simply a passive experiencer of the results of bad karma: it can neither learn from the experience nor can it originate fresh good karma, except perhaps in some of the rare cases among the higher animals that I have mentioned earlier. Even this slender possibility of originating fresh good karma does not exist for beings reborn in the realms of extreme suffering, the *nirayas*. And since the law of "as above, so below" is also valid, we see that at the other end of the scale the beings reborn in the *deva-* or *brahma-lokas* are simply enjoying the kind of happiness that results from their particular good karmas, without being able to originate any fresh karma so long as they remain in those realms. In fact, the human sphere is the only one in which it is possible to act karmically, because it is in this world alone that beings have moral responsibility and moral choice. Just as an animal is unaware that it is suffering the results of past *akusala-kamma*, so the deva or Brahmā may not be conscious that he is enjoying his exalted state because of his past good actions. In the Brahmajāla Sutta (Dīgha Nikāya, 1) it is related that Mahā Brahmā himself was not aware that he had arisen spontaneously in that state as the result of actions done in a previous life. And since he was the first to arise spontaneously (*opapātika*) at the beginning of the new world-cycle, he believed himself to be the creator of all who arose in it subsequently, a false theory which the other beings adopted in their turn. It was thus that ignorance of rebirth and of the law of *kamma-vipāka* led to the belief in a personal creator.

The Buddhist analysis of karma divides it into the following classes:

1. Weighty (*garuka*) karma.

2. Habitual (*ācinnaka*) karma. Both of these produce their results earlier than does karma of lesser moral significance or karma that is more rarely performed.

3. Death-proximate (*maranāsanna*) karma, which controls the last thought-moment at death and produces the reflex of some past good or bad karma, giving way immediately to its result, the rebirth-linking consciousness (*patisandhi-viññāna*) of the next life.

4. Stored-up (*katattā*) karma, which is an unexpended potential made up of good or bad karma in a state of suspension, awaiting a favourable opportunity to produce its result. This is karma which has been so far prevented from ripening by some weighty or habitual karma that has taken precedence over it.

Every being possesses a residue of stored-up karma, which will come into effect and duly bear its results in the absence of any fresh karma. It is thus that a being whose last existence has been in the animal realm can, when the bad karma producing that existence has become exhausted, take birth again in the human world. Rebirth as a human being once more does not depend upon the karma of the animal, but upon the stored-up good karma of a previous human life, the ripening of which has been arrested by some weighty evil karma which must have taken effect at the last thought-moment of a human life and produced an animal rebirth.

Let us assume that a human being of mixed good and bad karma has a last thought-moment in which unwholesome karma predominates, because it is either weighty or habitual karma. As the result of this, his rebirth-linking consciousness arises in an animal womb, as being the most appropriate level for its manifestation. What happens thereafter is that the resultant current of consciousness is carried on in the subhuman form until the karmic impulse that has been generated is exhausted. We will also assume that the animal is totally incapable of producing karma, either good or bad, but that it is passively working out the results of the human being's bad karma, and nothing more. For it must be granted that if the animal's lack of moral sense prevents it from originating good karma, its acts of killing, for food and for self-protection, must also be karmically neutral.[23] If at the animal's death its sufferings have measured up to the karmic requirements, the debt has been paid, and the unexpended potential of stored-up good karma will bring about another rebirth in human form.

There is another Buddhist classification of karma *according to function*, which helps us to understand this. It is as follows:

1. Regenerative (*janaka*) karma. This is the karma which produces the mental and corporeal aggregates at rebirth and keeps on producing them during the life-continuity.

2. Supportive (*upatthambhaka*) karma. This is karma which is not reproductive, but sustains karma-results (*vipāka*) which have already been produced.

3. Counteractive (*upapīlaka*) karma. This is karma which has the power to counteract or inhibit the results of other karma.

4. Destructive (*upacchedaka*) karma This is karma which takes complete ascendancy over weaker karma, nullifying it and substituting its own results instead.

These classifications taken together show how a weighty karma may function as destructive or counteractive karma in relation to weaker karmic impulses, and how it may furnish the regenerative karma for the rebirth. By this means it may produce a being on a lower or higher level than the human, until such time as its *vipāka* is expended, when, if no new karma has been produced, the stored-up karma comes into operation. Throughout this process there is no "being" that transmigrates; instead, there is a series of mind-body aggregations which arise as the result of karma in now one, now another of the thirty-one abodes which comprise the five (or six) realms of rebirth.

The metaphysical teachers of Mahāyāna were extremely careful to preserve the voidness doctrine of *Śūnyatā* which distinguishes Buddhism from the Vedanta of the Upanishads. This is most evident in their treatment of the *ālaya-vijñāna*, which must on no account be interpreted as a static entity. When they speak of *vāsanas* being deposited in the *ālaya-vijñāna*, the intention is always to give an account of memory, not to provide an equivalent for the "soul." The usual rendering of *ālaya-vijñāna* is "storehouse of consciousness," but 'storehouse-consciousness' is closer to the meaning of the Sanskrit term. There is no entity in which consciousness is "stored," but there is a mode of consciousness which makes memories accessible, and it is this that can be described as consciousness *acting* as a "storehouse." The *Śūnyatā* of Mahāyāna was at first identical with the *suññatā* of the Theravāda texts; it is that aspect of *anattā* which is summed up in the stanza.

No "doer" of the deeds is found,
No one who ever reaps their fruits;
Empty phenomena roll on
This view alone is right and true.

Visuddhimagga, XIX, 20

The *Mahāyānasaṃgraha* of Asaṅga (1.133b 28) says: "The consciousness receptacle profound and subtle, like a violent current, proceeds with all its germs (*sarvabījo*). Fearing that fools (*bālāna*) should imagine it to be a 'soul' (*ātmā*), I have not revealed it to them."[24] To which the commentary adds: "*I have not revealed it to fools*: I have not revealed it to those who embrace the view of 'self' (*ātmadrishti*)."[25] But in the same work it is stated that "In the Vehicle of the Srāvakas, equally, the consciousness-receptacle is mentioned under synonyms (*paryāya*)."[26] The commentary explains: "In the school (*nikāya*) of the Ārya Sthavira they also call that consciousness by the name of *bhavaṅga*. It is by reason, be it of the *bhavaṅga*, be it of the retrospective thought, that they (the six consciousnesses) die." Prof. Etienne Lamotte comments on this: "I understand: When the six consciousnesses die, it is by reason of the *bhavaṅga* into which they subside, or of the retrospective thought which makes them subside into it."

In Theravāda the *bhavaṅga* is the subconscious life-continuum, of which Nyanatiloka Thera writes: "*Bhavaṅga* (*bhava-aṅga*) is in Abhidhamma commentaries explained as the foundation or condition (*kāraṇa*) of existence (*bhava*), as the *sine qua non* of life, and that in the form of a process, lit. a 'flux' or 'stream' (*sota*), in which since time immemorial all impressions and experiences are as it were stored up, or better said functioning, but as such concealed to full consciousness, from where however they as subconscious phenomena occasionally emerge and approach the threshold of full consciousness, or crossing it become fully conscious. This so-called (subconscious life stream) or undercurrent of life, is that by which might be explained the faculty of memory, etc."[27]

The *ālaya-vijñāna*, therefore, is nothing but the *bhavaṅga* of the Theravāda Abhidhamma, and it is precisely in the same sense that it is understood by the philosophical schools of Mahāyāna, as we learn from no less an authority than Asaṅga. It is in popular Mahāyāna Buddhism, to which *anātman* is an "esoteric" teaching, that this interpretation of *bhavaṅga* under the name of *ālaya-vijñāna* has become practically indistinguishable from the concept of "self" or "soul," a misunderstanding that has not taken root in Theravāda.

So much for what Dr. Roos hopefully describes as "the principal factor why rebirth into subhuman kingdoms does not take place." To a true understanding of *anātman* the factor does not exist. It is a chimerical product of that universal obsession which Buddhism calls *sakkāya-diṭṭhi*, the Delusion of Self.

"It may still be useful," Dr. Roos continues, "to point out that rebirth into an animal body *would not be a punishment* for one who, during his human existence, had led a purely animal life, dedicated to pleasures of the senses, because such a rebirth would furnish uninhibited brutish enjoyments without any feeling of remorse. A punishment must have a *redeeming* feature, as otherwise it would be merely an act of revenge." This again underlines the basic misconception which distorts Dr. Roos' view. At every point his argument seeks to satisfy the human desire to find a system of rewards and punishments in the operations of karma and its fruits. There seems to be an unspoken assumption that the whole thing was designed by somebody "to improve man and correct his morals." No doubt, the results of karma assume, in human eyes, the form of prizes and retributions, but Buddhism does not assert that the system has been devised to that end. There is no Celestial Schoolmaster who doles out justice to a humanity he is committed to educating and reforming. The experiences produced by karma are the consequences of a purely automatic and impersonal law, which continues on its way whether men learn anything from it or not. Furthermore, a situation that in one set of circumstances appears to be a punishment could well seem, in another context, to be a reward. Man becomes what he desires to be, and if his desire is to live as an animal, and he obtains it, his basic ignorance (*avijjā*) could make it seem to him that he had been rewarded—that is, of course, if as an animal he were capable of thinking about his situation. The fact that an animal cannot look back on its previous life as a human being and congratulate itself upon being released from moral restrictions, but instead takes its present liberty for granted, surely removes the idea of reward from the situation as certainly as it does that of punishment. No man, however depraved, would wish to be an animal; but he might desire to enjoy an animal's licence *with a human consciousness*. Only then would it seem to him that he was being benefited.

Dr. Roos' line of thought also overlooks the important truth that "rewards" and "punishments" are relative concepts. Let us suppose, for example, that one were to see a man being mercilessly flogged. The natural conclusion would be that he was undergoing punishment for some grave crime. But in fact the supposed victim might be a masochist who had paid a substantial sum to obtain his peculiar form of enjoyment. The case of a man who derives pleasure from physical pain which a normal person would shrink from is not quite on all fours with that of the human being reborn as an animal, but at least it exposes the fallacy of thinking in terms of rewards and punishments where a law is concerned which is as indifferent to them as are the stars in their courses.

Therefore Buddhism speaks of painful results of unskilful actions (*akusala-kamma*) rather than of "punishments" for them. As I have indicated, the idea of punishment implies a punisher, the Celestial Schoolmaster, or a personal Judge, with whose justice a certain amount of vengeance must always be mixed. "Vengeance is mine, saith the Lord." Thus it can be seen that all Dr. Roos' assumptions spring from the same source: a conflict between the Buddhist doctrine of karma and unresolved theistic components which are alien to the structure of Buddhist thought.

The conclusion of his argument is an attempt to "interpret the occasional statements found in Buddhist and Sanskrit literature which seem to imply a rebirth in a subhuman entity." These, he says, "nearly always refer to the process of transmigration which should not be mistaken for reincarnation. Transmigration means the constant exchange of physical and psychic elements with the surrounding space ... All this material transmigrates incessantly among the members of the various kingdoms and particles proceeding from the animal part of our nature will easily find a lodging in a corresponding beast because of the law of affinities which governs the process of transmigration."

It would be pointless to reproduce all that Dr. Roos says on this subject, since it has no counterpart in any aspect of Buddhist philosophy or teaching. As part of a metaphysic of his own it may have some validity, but to connect it with Buddhism can only be misleading. Dr. Roos is entitled, as we all are, to work out his own system of thought. What none of us is entitled to do, however, is to attribute our own conjectures to great sages of the past who would be profoundly astonished by them. As I have pointed out elsewhere and often before, it is more honest (and less confusing to others) to disagree with the Buddha and his Teaching than to invent a system of one's own and call it Buddhism. This is in fact what the esoteric interpreters try to do in the matter of animal rebirth and the theory of transmigrating souls.

To wind up the discussion of Dr. Roos' article I only wish to repeat that it has not been my intention to try to prove that animal rebirth actually takes place. The question of whether it does or not lies in a different area of inquiry and calls for other terms of reference for debate. In the absence of any possibility of obtaining empirical evidence there could be no profit in pursuing it. What I have tried to show is that rebirth in subhuman forms of life is a part of Buddhist doctrine, and that Buddhism is not in any way inconsistent in holding it. If, incidentally, I have also shown that the idea of rebirth as an animal does not do violence to any genuinely philosophical view of human personality, I am content in having achieved rather more than I set out to do.

X

Did the Buddha Teach Rebirth?

Readers of English-language newspapers in Ceylon have recently been following with interest a controversy that has flared up in one of them, on the issue of whether the Buddha taught rebirth or not.

To a Buddhist it must be a matter of astonishment that such a dispute could arise—not because rebirth is a dogma of Buddhism but because without it Buddhism itself would have no meaning. The Buddha taught the Dhamma for the ending of suffering. If suffering automatically comes to an end with the dissolution of the physical body, it is pointless to commit oneself to a rigorous system of self-discipline and purification, such as Buddhism calls for, in order to free oneself from suffering. Such a course would serve no purpose but to add more suffering to life; for it is nonsense to pretend that the Buddhist way of purification—or any religious system of self-improvement—is an easy path to follow. Much easier is the way of the world, which is *not* the way to Nibbāna. An argument might be made out for the social utility of the Five Precepts regardless of karma, but who would wish to inflict upon himself the pains of the first attempts at meditation if there were no higher goal in sight?

If everything ends with death, the entire teaching of *kamma* and *vipāka*, or actions and results, goes by the board. It is a matter of common observation that evil deeds do not always bring their retribution in the present life, nor good ones their reward. This, in fact, is the chief argument of Buddhism (as it is of the rationalist) against the belief in a just and benevolent God.

It is precisely this teaching of a moral law operating from life to life which forms the greater part of the Buddha's instruction both to bhikkhus and laity. All the other doctrines of Buddhism revolve around it, even that of the means by which Nibbāna is attained. For what is Nibbāna but the cessation of the beginningless round of existence, linked with actions and their results?

Moreover, the Buddha again and again described in unmistakable terms the process which we call, for want of a better word, rebirth. This idea of rebirth, and of the necessity for bringing it to an end, is interwoven in the fabric of the Dhamma. It permeates the whole of Buddhism, from beginning to end. Thus, the *sotāpanna*, if he does not attain any higher stage in his current life, is assured of having no more than seven rebirths at the most, before gaining release. The *sakadāgāmi* returns but once to the five-sense world; the *anāgāmi* does not return at all, but passes into Nibbāna from the Brahma-world when his life span there is ended. The arahat at death passes straightaway into the Nibbāna in which no remnant of clinging remains.[28]

If the Buddha did not teach rebirth, what is the meaning of all this—to say nothing about all the other references to it scattered as thick as the renowned *siṃsapa* leaves, or the sands of the Ganges, throughout the Tipiṭaka?

To maintain that the Buddha did not teach rebirth is surely the most curious aberration that has ever made its appearance in Buddhism. It places upon one who holds it the burden of proof that most of the statements attributed to the Buddha were not made by him at all. Which is equivalent to saying that the major part of the Tipiṭaka is a fraud.

For a non-Buddhist to declare that he cannot believe in rebirth is, from his point of view, reasonable and honest. The Buddhist will concede that he is entitled to his opinion, be he an annihilationist (*ucchedavādī*) or an eternalist (*sassatavādī*). But for one claiming to be a Buddhist to maintain that the Buddha did not teach rebirth is an intellectual dishonesty of the worst kind. It would be better for such a person to state frankly, as the non-Buddhist does, that he believes the Buddha to have been mistaken. In so saying, the eternalist or annihilationist is at least being true to his own convictions, erroneous though they are, and some credit is due to him for that. Better is honest doubt or sheer disbelief than a perverse falsification of the Enlightened One's clear teaching. The sincere doubter is always open to conviction, but one who has willfully perverted the Buddha's words and meaning has a rather miserable future before him—the future of one who has deliberately cut himself off from truth. This is the case because even if the doctrine of rebirth were not true, *it is true that the Buddha taught it*. The denial of that fact constitutes the lie.

It is intellectual dishonesty of this kind which represents the greatest danger to Buddhism today. The Dhamma can stand up against any criticism from those of other religions or of none; but there is little defence against the calculated confusion of ideas which works destruction from within. This is the most subtle and effective form of anti-Buddhist propaganda. Unfortunately, little is being done to check it. Buddhism has no central authority for the preservation of doctrine, and anyone, be he in yellow robes or layman's dress, can put forward whatever travesty of the Dhamma he cares to propagate.

The present situation offers a curious paradox. At a time when more and more thinking people all over the world are beginning to take rebirth seriously as a possible explanation of life's enigmas—as evidenced by such books as *Reincarnation: An East-West Anthology*, and by the fact that even some Christian churches are beginning to pave the way towards an acceptance of rebirth as being not contrary to Christian doctrine—some self-styled "advanced" Buddhists are trying to discard it. To anyone who understands their mentality the explanation is quite plain: these advocates of what they consider a "modernized" Buddhism are simply out of date. They belong to the late nineteenth century, with which they have only just caught up. Their attitude pleases them for one of two reasons: either because it deludes them with a feeling of intellectual superiority, or else because it is part of their identification with the materialism which they fondly imagine to be the latest development of human thought. They could be dismissed as negligible cranks, but for the influence they unfortunately wield over immature minds.

What exactly are the facts in this matter? They are, first and foremost, that the Buddha rejected both extremes, *sassata-diṭṭhi*, belief that the self or soul is eternal, and *uccheda-diṭṭhi*, belief that there is no continuity of the life process after death.

Now "continuity of the life process" is not the same as postulating the transmigration of a soul. Only to the most naive thinker—one completely unacquainted with philosophical concepts—could it appear to be so. During life there is continuity of the life process but there is no persisting entity to be found in that process. Exactly as it is during life, so it is when the life-continuum projects itself into the future at the end of one life and the beginning of another. The world-line of "identity" is preserved as a purely causal continuum. It is thus that rebirth has to be understood. Far from the doctrine of *anattā* (non-soul) being incompatible with rebirth, it is the only way of regarding personality in which rebirth could be seen as possible. A persisting, unchanging "self" or "soul" could not be reborn. It would remain forever in a state of frozen immobility, incapable of progress in any direction. There is in fact no such entity anywhere in nature—least of all in the personality of living beings, where all is change and becoming.

Anattā teaches what the psychologist and physiologist now know perfectly well—namely, that there is no single item of the psychophysical process that endures for any length of time. This is accepted as a fact; yet still we know that the phenomenal personality continues through all the stages from infancy to old age and death. It is this that we mean when we speak, conventionally, of "I," "myself," and so on. It was this which the Buddha meant when he used these terms himself. Since it is an ideational necessity for practical purposes to think of personality, one's own and that of others, in this way, it becomes a linguistic necessity as well. Only the extremely dull-witted could fail to see this. It was explained centuries ago by Nāgasena in his conversations with King Milinda. And Milinda, being apparently more intelligent than some of our modern "intelligentsia," seems to have grasped it easily.

That which continues after death, then, is not a "soul," but a form of energy. That energy is generated by the craving and grasping (*taṇhā* and *upādāna*) of the being that existed previously. Craving itself is a mental force. It carries with it the karmic potential of a new life, a new psychophysical formation, another "personality." That personality is "not the same" as the previous one (*na ca so*), in the sense that there is not one single element in it, physical or mental, that was in the former one; at the same time it is not "different" (*na ca añño*), because it belongs to the same world-line of causality. Its "identity" with the previous personality is simply one of causal sequence. It exists because the former personality existed, and it inherits the karmic tendencies of that personality.

These karmic tendencies may be so strongly developed that the karmic force is capable of impressing certain characteristic patterns on the brain-substance of the developing embryo. Thus it is that we get, occasionally, children showing extraordinary talents which they have never acquired in their present life. History is full of such cases. In some other instances we find there are residual "memories" belonging to the previous personality which have been carried forward into the new life. It is then that we are justified in saying that the child remembers a previous life.

The entire universe consists of energy. Recognizing that fact helps us to understand that human personality is also energy. It is something that incessantly flows, the units of energy—in Buddhism, the thought-moments—arising and passing away, but even in their transience constituting the greatest force in the universe. It may be said that *because anattā* (non-soul) is true, rebirth is true. Today there is less excuse than ever before for thinking in animistic terms, or on the other hand for taking the view that because there is no "soul" there can be no rebirth. It is because people are still deluded by the idea of "soul" that they imagine rebirth cannot take place if there is no such entity. Annihilationism is nothing but eternalism turned upside-down.

***

From an unfinished article titled
'Rebirth in states of greater suffering' (1944)

Here an analogy may be useful. We say that the sun gives light, and everybody knows what we mean by the statement. But what actually happens is something that should be stated differently for it to be an accurate description. The sun generates an energy; that energy is projected into the void of space, where there is nothing physical to transmit it. Nevertheless it is transmitted over millions of miles of sheer emptiness, and that emptiness remains in black darkness. When, however, the sun's energy reaches the earth's atmosphere, its character undergoes a change. Diffused by the particles of gas constituting the atmosphere, it becomes discernible to our eyes and we call it light. Therefore we say "the sun gives light," but what it really gives is only energy, which does not become light until the right physical conditions, namely, something substantial to reflect it and physical organs and consciousness capable of receiving and interpreting it, are present.

In the same way, no ego-entity or "soul" is transmitted from one personality to a subsequent one in the process of rebirth. All that is transmitted is the effect of a prior cause, which corresponds to the invisible energy of the sun traversing empty space. That energy becomes a new "personality" when it is drawn to the physical constituents of embodied life, and in that new manifestation it bears the karmic characteristics that were generated in the past, just as the sun's energy becomes light on contact with solid objects capable of reflecting it.

XI

A Change of Heart

Does it mean a change of personality?

Articles by Mr. Abraham Kovoor, President of the Ceylon Rationalist Association, are a recurring feature of the Ceylon newspapers, and are usually stimulating. From the Western viewpoint there is nothing particularly new about them and at times they have a quaint period charm that recalls the rationalist fervours of the late nineteenth century; but by challenging accepted ideas in a way that has not been customary in Asian countries they cause people to take a closer look at some of their beliefs and to ask themselves just why certain cattle are sacred while others are not. Sometimes they are quite beneficial in pointing out the absurdity of superstitious practices that have nothing whatever to do with religion yet have somehow become mixed up with it in the popular mind.

Recently Mr. Kovoor has been much concerned about the doctrine of rebirth. His disinterested attitude makes his criticisms worthy of attention, but he is sometimes inclined to let his enthusiasm run away with him. One of this latest articles had reference to the first operation on a human being for the transplanting of a heart. Since the article was published, the patient, a Mr. Louis Washkansky, has unfortunately died. But his death appears to have been from causes other than the heart transplant, so that Mr. Kovoor's comments still have as much, or as little, relevance as when they were written. The point he raised was: How can rebirth be possible when parts of different people's bodies are made to be interchangeable; and would any part of the personality of the young woman whose heart was transferred to Mr. Washkansky after her death have survived in him? As well as affecting the Buddhist doctrine of rebirth, Mr. Kovoor appears to think that the transplanting of a heart from one person to another disposes altogether of the Christian belief in an immortal soul and the resurrection of the body.

It does not seem to me, however, that the transplanting of hearts affects either the Buddhist or the theistic positions any more than does the grafting of corneal tissue or any other addition to or subtraction from the body.

Revised version of an article first published in the *Ceylon Daily News* (Colombo), 12 January 1968.

According to almost universal ancient ideas, the transfusion of blood, the vital fluid, would have been considered a more serious matter. It is still regarded in that way, and as such forbidden, by certain Christian sects. So far as personal immortality and physical resurrection are concerned, the Christian beliefs rest altogether upon the supernatural and miraculous; and since the miraculous is by definition the impossible, they are as unassailable by science as they are opposed to experience. The Buddhist doctrine of rebirth, on the other hand, rests upon an entirely different foundation and can even be said to come within the scope of personal experience, although not that of everybody. An experience of any kind does not necessarily have to be common property in order to be valid.

The grafting of another person's brain, of course, would be a more radical substitution than the transplanting of a heart, since it would presumably involve a complete change of mental activity, memories, and character. Even this, however, would not seriously interfere with the Buddhist interpretation of personality as consisting of nothing more than an ever-changing flow, a stream of conditioned "becoming" that has no persisting substratum. We shall return to this point later on.

So far as Buddhist doctrine is concerned, the young woman whose heart was used in the operation had already been reborn when that organ was removed from her body. Rebirth is held to take place immediately after the last conscious or subconscious moment of the life-stream (*bhavaṅga-sota*) has been cut off. The rebirth is not necessarily in another human body, needless to say, but can be in one of the spontaneously arisen (*opapātika*) beings commonly called *petas* (spirits), *devatās* or, on a higher level, *Brahmās*.

As for the subject of the experiment, Mr. Washkansky, he would have continued to go on being the "same" Mr. Washkansky as before; i.e., his life-continuum would have persisted in carrying on the same stream of identity, its individual world-line of "becoming," until he died. Neither his character nor his consciousness of personality would have been in any way affected.

Here it should be mentioned that the belief that consciousness is located in a drop of blood in the heart, which was supposed to be of different colours according to temperament, is clearly a pre-Buddhistic idea. It has found its way into some Buddhist writings from the physiological pseudo-science of ancient days. It has its counterpart in the West, where formerly the heart was thought to be the seat of the emotional life. As the late Shwe Zan Aung pointed out (*Compendium of Philosophy*), the Buddha himself "was very careful not to commit himself to the cardiac theory (of consciousness), even by way of concession to the popular view." Where the "heart-base" (*hadaya-vatthu*) of consciousness might be expected on grounds of accepted terminology, the Paṭṭhāna formulation has: "*Yaṃ rūpaṃ nissāya manodhātu ca,* etc."—"*That material thing* on the basis of which apprehension and comprehension take place...." The commentators had to give a name to this *rūpa*, and they wrote "heart" in accordance with the popular theory. Essential Buddhist teaching, as given by the Buddha, does not suggest that the heart is anything more than an organ for regulating the blood stream.

By a curious reversal of the more likely order of events, modern surgery has made it possible to graft vital organs from one body to another before it is able to transplant arms and legs. Nevertheless, we already have to envisage a future in which a particular body may have had each and all of its separate parts exchanged for new ones, but will still have to be considered as belonging to the "same" personality as when it emerged from the womb. A close parallel to this is the case of an aeroplane which was built in 1945 and given a serial registration number. It subsequently had to be provided with a new engine, then a new fuselage, new wings, and so on at different times, until at last not a single screw or nut of the original fabric remained. It was bought by a certain internal airline and thereafter continued to operate as a freight plane under the same registration number as it originally had been given. Conventionally, it was considered to be the "same" aircraft although in fact the original plane had disappeared, not all at once but piece by piece. Its "life" ended only when it was finally relegated to the scrap heap. And even then, some of its newer parts may have been incorporated in another machine. Thus, parts of its *rūpa* were still extant when its *nāma*, the registration number, had passed away. Similarly, some parts of a human being's body may still be preserved after it has ceased to function as a personality factor. On the atomic level this has always been the case; after death the chemical changes that have been going on imperceptibly all through life continue in the form of disintegration.

The career of the aeroplane described above represents fairly well the course of events in the lifetime of a human being, as seen by Buddhism. The arms, legs, and internal organs of the body we die with are not the same those it had when it was born. Physical tissues and consciousness alike are arising and passing away all the time throughout the unbroken life span, yet we still refer to this process as being the "same" person throughout, calling him John Smith, or Aloysius Folliott Montague de Alwis

Samarabandake or whatever name he may have been blessed (or cursed) with at this naming ceremony.

If it ever becomes possible to transfer the brain of one person to another it will be interesting to see what line the identity-consciousness will take, and which of the two personalities will have to be considered as being the surviving one. The situation will doubtless give rise to legal as well as metaphysical problems, and like many of the vaunted advances in our technological way of life will probably produce more conflict and unhappiness in human relations. At present we can only speculate on what would happen if, say, the brain of A, a living person, were to be transferred to the cranial cavity of B, another living person, and vice versa, and if both A and B were to continue living after the operation. Since the brain is, if not the actual seat of consciousness, at least the organ which gives to consciousness its specific character, we can only assume that there would be a transposition of personalities, A becoming B, and B becoming A. Therefore personality A would die when the body of B, with which it had become associated, died; and vice versa. In that case rebirth, in the Buddhist sense, would still take place in the ordinary way. The kamma of A would produce another psychophysical compound (*nāma-rūpa*) which would be the "rebirth" of A. The personality B would die when the body of A, with which it had become associated, died. The kamma of B would then give rise to another *nāma-rūpa*, and that would be the "rebirth" of B.

In short, the situation does not present any difficulties to the Buddhist interpretation because personality is not identical with the body or any of its parts, nor with the consciousness or any of its parts. It is nothing but the stream of cause and effect, or *kamma* and *vipāka*, together with supporting and coincidental factors, which constitutes personal identity. The personality is the phenomenal aggregation of these parts, the five *khandhas*. All the parts are subject to perpetual transmutation, so that the term "identity" means only continuity in change (*santāna*).

Thus the problem is really one of semantics, and the Buddha solved it by pointing out the meaning of meaning, in a way that can be done only by making the necessary distinction between conventional speech and the speech of philosophical truth.

In the long sequence of different personalities which culminated in Gotama Buddha, and came to an end with his Parinibbāna (*lokiya-vohāra* or "conventional speech": "In the Buddha's previous births, etc."), there were some that were notable for scepticism. Honest doubt in itself is not a bad thing and the Buddha never condemned it. But it ought not to be deliberately cultivated until it takes complete possession of the mind; for while scepticism within bounds helps the development of wisdom which depends upon correct judgement, it is inclined to obstruct the higher insights. Unlike doubt, which can be resolved, scepticism tends to become an inveterate mental pattern, artificially creating reasons for disbelief where none exist. We should not go through life intentionally seeking for things to be sceptical about, for if we do we shall always find them, and finish up by making it impossible ever to arrive at certainty about anything. It was a previous history of scepticism which compelled the Buddha to struggle for six years in his last life to obtain Enlightenment, whereas it is said that other Bodhisattas obtained it without difficulty. But in the end, as he declared, he "overcame doubt" and thereby reached the fullness of insight.

Our present age is hag-ridden by a spirit of doubt and uncertainty which makes *vicikicchā* (sceptical doubt) perhaps the most difficult of the fetters to overcome. Many people today who are submerged in negative intellectual currents would be leading ethical and spiritually constructive lives if they could convince themselves that there is good reason for believing in a higher order of values. Yet with all this, the sceptical mind is inconsistent. It swallows blindly whatever is offered to it in the name of science, although it cannot verify scientific findings for itself and for the most part they are incomprehensible to it. It ignores the plain evidence that many items of knowledge derived from scientific disciplines are not final and complete revelations of truth but only working hypotheses, and as such, often have to be qualified or even discarded in favour of new ones as knowledge expands. It also credits science with a competence in certain directions which the real scientist is far from claiming. Science, in fact, has become the folk mythology of the new age and its holy writ is popular science fiction and the comic strip.

This is not to advocate a return to the age of credulity. The two extremes of scepticism and unreasoning faith lie on the periphery of a circle and to carry either of them too far is to make it unconsciously approach the other. The human mind cannot live in a vacuum of negation, and that is why modern man has become inclined to worship the mysteries of science rather than those of religious tradition. But we are not committed to a choice between the two extremes; there is a middle way, and it is that which Buddhism recommends. Rather than exchange one form of superstition for another it is better to examine all propositions with an unbiased mind and to cultivate genuine and reliable powers of discrimination. That is the true meaning of the Kālāma Sutta, not the licence to doubt everything and to go on doubting, which many people today are all too eager to read into it. Regarding the doctrine of rebirth *as it is taught in Buddhism*, the correct question to ask ourselves is not, "Can it be proved scientifically?" but: "Has science so far made any discovery which makes it impossible?" To that question the answer is most certainly, "No."

The intellect, if used in the right way, can never be an obstacle to Enlightenment. But if it is turned into a blind alley it cuts off all further progress, even along its own particular lines. The first thing of which the cultivated intelligence becomes aware, on strictly impartial scrutiny, is its own limitation. Having reached that point it becomes willing to grant that there must be an infinite range of possible knowledge beyond the bounds of perceptual and intellectual restrictions. I do not mean by this the vague "intuitions" that many people claim to have, and which may be nothing more than fantasies of the imagination or symptoms of a neurosis. Still less do I mean the abnormal conditions that can be artificially induced by hallucinogenic drugs. What is meant here are subjective, but real, experiences that are measurable by the attainments of others. Such are the insights of the arahat. They are not private worlds of disordered perception, but transcendental experiences shared and confirmed by those who have attained them in the same way, and whose lasting effects testify to a complete restructuring of the personality. That much we can infer from the Buddhist scriptures. It is in the lives of the Buddha and the arahats that we find evidence, if we need it, that such a transformation of the human into the divine is possible. And if any witnesses are worthy of credence, these surely are.

XII

A Question of Terminology

One of the major difficulties of writing on Buddhism in English is to express the meaning of the Pāli word *"punabbhava"* in a language which has no precise equivalent for it, or at least none that will convey to the ordinary reader the difference between "renewed becoming," which is what *"punabbhava"* really means, and the words "reincarnation" and "transmigration."

"Reincarnation," a word with which the West is more or less familiar, means the taking on again of a fleshly body (incarnation) by a spiritual entity. "Transmigration" means the passing from one physical body to another of an immortal "soul," and amounts to the same thing. Neither of these is suitable to express the Buddhist concept, in which there is no unchanging spiritual entity, no "soul" and in fact nothing that is not subject to arising, decay, and passing away.

We are left, then, with the word "rebirth," which is the one in general use (or should be) among Buddhist writers—excluding, of course, those who have adopted the new fashion of reducing Buddhism to crude materialism (and incidentally, to nonsense) by denying that the Buddha taught a doctrine of renewed existence after physical dissolution.

Although I have said that "rebirth" should be in general used to express the Buddhist idea, I have done so only because it is the nearest and least objectionable term. Any other substitute would be cumbersome and, to the general reader puzzling or meaningless. Yet I am fully aware that "rebirth" is not an entirely satisfactory word. The prefix "re" implies that there is a *something* which is born again; and in Buddhism this is definitely not the case. "Rebirth" must be understood as one of the class of terms known as *vohāra-vacana*, a term of common usage; it is a concept (*paññatti*) belonging to *sammuti-sacca*, or conventional truth. In *paramattha-sacca*, or actual truth, there is nothing that is born again.

This idea should not present any real difficulty to understanding. Such words as "self," "I," "me," and even "table" and "chair" also belong to the *vohāra-vacana* class. They stand for things which exist on the ordinary level of understanding, but which when analysed into their component parts are seen to be mere agglomerations of other things, all of which can be further reduced into separate elements. A table consists of pieces of wood cut into specific shapes which, when duly fixed together in a certain relationship, form what we know as a "table." But when we have reduced the table to wood we have still not quite finished with it; we can further reduce it to ashes by burning it, and after that we can remind ourselves that although we cannot see them, the wood itself consisted all along of nothing but atoms, the atoms of electrons, neutrons, positrons, and whatever other lesser elements science may have discovered by the time this article goes to press. In the final result, nothing is left of the table but energy. That is the physicist's view of a table, and of all other material objects in the universe. Yet it would clearly be absurd to say that because of this no such thing as a "table" exists. The table exists on one particular level of reality, the level on which we ordinarily cognize it through our senses. If our senses were differently organized, or functioned on a sufficiently smaller spatial scale, we should be able to see the protons, electrons, and so forth, but would not see the table. In that case we should talk of "atoms" instead of "tables"; but the atoms and their components would be no more and no less "real" than the table is to us at present. Table, wood, atoms are all "real" on their particular level of existence; they are not "real" in any ultimate sense. This is the meaning of *sammuti-sacca*, conventional or *relative* reality; the vocabulary we use to discuss it and to convey ideas about it is the vocabulary of conventional speech, *vohāra-desanā*.

What has been said about tables, chairs, and all other objects of the external world is equally applicable to human personality. Living beings are also physical organisms, but they differ from inanimate objects in possessing consciousness and other intangible factors. Human personality consists of five *khandhas*, or aggregates; namely, *rūpa* (form or body), *vedanā* (feeling), *saññā* (perception), *saṅkhārā* (volitional formations), and *viññāṇa* (consciousness). When all these exist together in mutual dependence the result is a psychophysical organism, in Pāli, *nāma-rūpa* (mind-body).

But the "existence" of this psychophysical organism is merely a series of events. It contains nothing whatever that is permanent. The cells of the body are continually perishing and being replaced by new ones, so that at any given moment there is not a single cell in it which was there seven years before. On the nuclear level, of course, the process of arising and passing away is even more rapid, for according to the present state of knowledge, there is nothing in an atom which can be said to be the "same" from one moment of its existence to another.

103

It is exactly the same with the psychic factors. Feeling, perception, volitional formations, and consciousness all exist merely as a continual flow of events. As one moment of consciousness passes away, another arises. Each moment represents a birth (*jāti*), a point of stasis (*thiti* – which is purely theoretical, like the change from rising to descent at the apex of a jump), and passing away (*bhaṅga*). The mental factors of personality, like everything else in the universe, are in a continual state of coming-to-be and passing away.

Yet despite this we say, in conventional speech, that we exist, that personality exists. And so it does; but its existence is simply a current of events linked together by the relationship of cause and effect from one momentary existence to another. Existence, properly understood, is simply a continuum, and personality is merely the world-line that the continuum traces in space-time.

This is the meaning of the *anattā* doctrine which is so often—and alas, too often willfully—misunderstood. "Because that (state) exists, this (state) comes to be"; the causal relationship links them, without any enduring entity passing from one state to another.

Now we are in a better position to understand what really happens when, as we say, a being dies and is "reborn." In reality no being is reborn, but when a person dies, another psychophysical organism arises as a consequence of the current of cause and effect the previous personality generated by his karma. It is the "same" being in one sense—the conventional sense in which we say, for example, that a man is the "same" person at the age of eighty as he was when he was eight; but in another sense, the sense of actual *identity*, it is not the same person just as the eighty-year-old man is certainly not the same person as the eight-year-old child that he once was. This is what the Buddha meant by saying that the person reborn is not the same, yet not different (*na ca so na ca añño*), from the one who died. The current of causality carries on, in its interminable sequence of *kamma-vipāka*, actions and results, and the different forms it gives rise to represent the world-line of existence, the sequence of events which we call personality.

XIII
From Life to Life

Do you remember having lived before?

That may seem a strange question, because as a rule it is only yogis who succeed in recalling their former lives. It is one of the results of practising *bhāvanā*, or meditation.

Sometimes, though, it happens to apparently quite ordinary children. There are a large number of very interesting cases of this kind in Ceylon, India, Burma, and Thailand—and, even more surprisingly, in Western countries as well. It may be, of course, that these children had practised meditation in a past life, and acquired the faculty in that way. But there may also be other causes, which at present we know nothing about, that enable the memories of one life to be carried over into another. Nobody knows just how memory works, not even the scientists, although sometimes it seems as though they know everything. Buddhism says that memory is preserved in the *ālaya-vijñāna*, just as the biological "memories" are stored in a seed. And that is the most likely scientific explanation up to date.

In Burma, a lady, the wife of a government officer, told how in childhood she had been able to recall several important events of her previous life. As soon as she began to talk she started telling the names of her former relatives, and was able to identify those who were still living. Her husband in the former life had been a gambler, and she was always short of money. But she had a strong desire to get her eldest son ordained as a bhikkhu, so over a long period she had been saving up small amounts, which she kept buried so that her husband should not find them. If he had done so, he would have gambled it all away. Not intending to deprive her of it, of course, but meaning to *double* it for her! The curse of gambling is that people always think they are going to win. Sometimes they do; but more often they lose, causing great distress to their families and themselves. How many people have brought disgrace and ruin upon themselves by taking money that did not belong to them, in the firm but groundless conviction that they would be able to double or triple it by gambling, and then pay the original sum back. In that way a man can become a thief, without ever intending to be one.

So this poor woman, whose husband was that kind of person, was saving up secretly for her son's admission into the Sangha. It was the dearest wish of her life, and she was looking forward with keen delight to the great day. But, as so often happens, death cheated her out of her happiness. She was taken ill, and in a very short time she had passed out of that existence.

Now Buddhism teaches that as soon as a being dies, rebirth takes place. The Burmese lady was reborn straightaway in the world of spirits. She then saw her own dead body, with the mourners all around, and wondered what they were weeping and wailing for. She herself felt quite happy, for in life she had always kept the Buddhist precepts faithfully—not merely repeating them like a trained parrot, as so many people do, but really acting upon them in her daily life—so she knew she had nothing to be afraid of now that she was "dead." On the contrary, she felt a great freedom, away from the old body which had started to worry her with unexpected pains here and there of late. It was pleasant, too, to feel herself free of all responsibilities and for the first time, as far as she could remember, able to do exactly as she liked.

The only thing that troubled her was that she wanted to tell her relatives about the money she had hidden, and ask them to have her son ordained with it. But when she tried to speak to them she found that they could neither see nor hear her. All their attention was fixed on the dead body, which seemed very silly to her. She had finished with that body, and felt no further concern for it. She was more interested in the living; and so ought we to be!

Her relatives were carrying out all kinds of ceremonies and making offerings, but none of it was of the slightest use to her. The only thing that could help was her own good karma, and as a Buddhist she knew that. Her relatives were supposed to know it, too, but they seemed to have temporarily forgotten all about the Buddha's teaching. If she had not felt so sorry for them, the sight of their foolishness would have made her vexed. "Why are they wasting so much money?" she asked herself. "I could have given a good feast to the poor in honour of my son's ordination, with all that money they are squandering." And she even thought, a little wistfully, that her husband and relatives had never spent so much on her when she was alive. But, being a good Burmese wife, she did not allow such ideas to take possession of her.

There was nothing she could do about it, so when the time of the funeral arrived she followed the procession out of the house. She found that she could move about freely anywhere she liked, and it was interesting to be a guest at her own funeral. It was quite a stately affair for a modest person like herself, and while she was following it she came to realize that funerals in general are more for the purpose of showing the family's importance than for honouring the dead. Maybe it was due to her good karma, or to the fact that she was relieved of all her usual preoccupations, but her mind seemed to be working more clearly now than it had done before.

After a time, the party came to the Salween river, and everybody got into boats to cross over, together with the coffin. But the lady had heard that spirits cannot cross running water; and as whatever we believe strongly enough is true for us, she was obliged to stay behind. She watched the boats cross the river, and followed the procession with her eyes until it vanished from sight on the other side.

For the first time, she began to feel rather sad and lost, not knowing what to do with herself next. All her life she had been kept busy, looking after her family, preparing the meals and keeping the house tidy, nursing her children when they were sick, and her feckless husband when he was well, and now there was a great emptiness in her life because she could do none of these things any longer. It was nice to have a rest, of course; but— well, part of the pleasure of resting is knowing that you will soon be at work again. She was beginning to feel bored already. It is the best side of a woman's nature that she finds her greatest happiness in serving those she loves. That is one of the reasons why it is more difficult for a woman than it is for a man to find peace and fulfilment in the monastic life.

She did not know how long she stayed by the river bank, for when there is no daily routine to be followed and nothing is happening it is difficult to keep track of time. At last, however, she saw a man on horseback approaching. As he came nearer she recognized him as a neighbour of hers, a man whom she knew slightly. He was taking the road back to the village, so quick as thought she jumped up behind him, and in that way she returned to her old neighbourhood.

After that she remembered nothing more until she found herself in the present life, a child of the man from whom, all unknown to him, she had got a lift back. She was about two years old when she began to speak, and as soon as she could form connected sentences she told the story. The people she named were identified and she was able to point out to her former husband the clothes she had worn in the previous life. But when she wanted to show him where the money for her son's ordination was hidden, there was an embarrassed silence. He had found it already; and of course had tried to double it.... He was able to tell her who had won it off him, but that did not console her very much.

In the case of this lady, it may have been her strong desire to have her son made a bhikkhu which enabled her to remember from one life to another. No one can estimate the power of a wish, when there is sufficient good karma to bring it about. But to make such a wish effective there must also be single-mindedness of purpose, and continual renewal of the idea. That is one reason why some people get what they wish for, while others do not; a very strong desire-force has to be generated. But that also has its dangers, for what we crave for is seldom the best thing for us; and when we get it we often no longer want it, but have already fixed our desires on something else. It is better far to be without desires, as the Buddha taught, or at least to keep our desires as few and as simple as possible. Craving can never bring anything but unhappiness in the long run.

From Burma comes another story of rebirth which illustrates the force of a wish often repeated. A poor village girl used to pass a fine house every day on her way to the paddy fields. Owned by a wealthy family, it was the best house for several miles around. Every time she came in sight of it the village girl was reminded of her own wretched little wooden house, with its thatched roof that was powerless to keep out the monsoon rains, its broken walls, and the single living room where the whole family crowded together at night. She used to gaze at the fine house of the wealthy family with longing, wishing that it were hers. Every time she went to the temple and lit candles and incense, and whenever she gave alms to the bhikkhus, she repeated the same wish, until she was quite obsessed with desire to own that particular house. To be its owner seemed to her the supreme happiness that life could offer.

While she was still young the girl died, and soon afterwards was reborn as the daughter of the owner of the grand house. She was able to remember her previous life, and told her parents all about the wish she had made. Eventually the house came into her possession, but long before she inherited it she had become so used to living in it and thinking of it as hers that it no longer held any novelty for her, and possessing it gave her no special pleasure. Her desires had fixed on something still bigger and better: she wanted to live in Rangoon, where there were more pleasures and everything was more exciting. She even wondered how she could ever have been so keen on the big, lonely old house surrounded by paddy fields.

And that is how it comes about that our desires always cheat us, for us soon as one craving is satisfied another takes its place. When we understand that truth, we understand the nature of saṃsāra.

Another interesting point in this rebirth story is that obviously the poor village girl could never become the owner of the big house. To get her wish she had to die and be reborn. And in being reborn she ceased to be precisely the same person that made the wish. She was not the same because she grew up in a new environment, in which the hardships of her previous life were unknown; she had different preoccupations and different thoughts. The only thing that identified her with the previous personality was her memory of it. As for the coveted house, it could never mean the same to the child who was born in it, and took it for granted, as it had meant to the same person when she was a poor village girl. Its value had changed because she herself had changed.

There we have two important Buddhist principles made clear: the doctrine of *anattā*, which teaches that there is no permanent, enduring self; and *anicca*, which tells us that all things are subject to change. Seen from one point of view, her background of poverty and want, the house had seemed all that was desirable, its possession the very apex of human happiness. Seen from another, it was a very ordinary thing, not a possession to get at all excited about. Yet it was the same house; it was the girl herself who had changed. If she had not been able to remember her previous life, as most of us cannot, she would have been absolutely ignorant of the fact that she had obtained her dearest wish.

Do you remember having lived before? Most probably you don't. But if you ever feel discontented with your present life, just think of some of the things that are really good in it, the things you perhaps take for granted but which many people have not got. *Maybe one of them is a thing you longed for above everything else, in a life when you were not so fortunate as now.*

II

Cases of
Rebirth Memories

In addition to the cases of recollected rebirths found in Part II, another two cases—those of Ah Nyo and the Karen houseboy—are discussed in Part III, "The Case for Rebirth".

Acknowledgements

Grateful acknowledgement is made to the following editors, publishers, and authors for their kind permission to reprint in this volume the articles indicated below:

Chapter XV: "The Case of Warnasiri Adikari," reprinted from *Journal of the American Society for Psychical Research*, Vol. 61, No. 2, April 1967; by permission of Mrs. Laura A. Dale, Editor JASPR, and Ian Stevenson, M.D., co-author, who reserve all other rights.

Chapter XVI: "The Case of Disna Samarasinghe," reprinted from *Journal of Asian and African Studies*, Vol. 5, No. 4, October 1970 (E.J. Brill, Leiden); by permission of Prof. K. Ishwaran, editor, and Ian Stevenson, co-author, who reserve all other rights.

The following four articles by Francis Story are reprinted by permission of the Editor, *FATE Magazine*, Highland Park, Illinois, U.S.A.:

Chapter XVII: "The Case of the Siamese Sergeant Thiang San Kla," from *FATE Magazine*, Issue No. 199, Vol. 19, No. 10, October 1966.

Chapter XVIII: "The Metamorphoses of a Mother: The Case of Win Win Nyunt," from *FATE Magazine*, Issue No. 209, Vol. 20, No. 8, August 1967.

Chapter XIX: "Rebirth or Possession: The Case of Phra Rajsutharn," from *FATE Magazine*, Issue No. 219, Vol. 21, No. 6, June 1968.

Chapter XX: "What Happens between Incarnations? The Cases of Private Keaw, Nang Tong Klub, and U Sobhana," from *FATE Magazine*, Issue No. 271, Vol. 25, No. 10, October 1972.

XIV
Types of Rebirth Cases

Evidence for rebirth comes from a variety of sources. The following are the main types of cases from which we can obtain such evidence.

I. *Recall of purported previous lives under hypnotic regression.*

There is already an extensive literature about these cases, which has led to much controversy. It has been shown that some cases of this kind are examples of cryptomnesia; others are fantasies constructed to carry out the instructions of the hypnotizer, who has told the subject to recall a previous life, or has previously told him that he is going to take him back under hypnosis to a period before he was born. The creation of fantasies can be controlled, and by the same token can be to a great extent reduced, if not eliminated. But it is only when objective proof that the statements made under hypnosis are correct can be obtained, that the alternative theory of fantasy can be entirely eliminated. Cases of lives reported in Atlantis or on other planets are naturally beyond the scope of such verification. In cases of fantasy another possibility is that the subject under hypnosis has had clairvoyant, telepathic, or even precognitive access to material either in writing or in the subconscious of another person. The only fully compulsive proof of the genuineness of these cases would be xenoglossy.[29] But cases of true xenoglossy are rare. It must not be confused with glossolalia[o] Hypnotic regression has its greatest usefulness in recovering more detailed memories of a factual kind in cases of spontaneous recall. Even then, many precautions must be taken to ensure that suggestion from the hypnotist has not influenced the material.

2. *Cases in which the subject's previous life/lives have been described by an ostensible spirit-communicator through a medium (sensitive).*

Under this heading come examples such as the life-readings of Edgar Cayce. Allan Kardec also has some examples ("The Spirits' Book"). These cases are by no means rare in spiritist literature today. These revelations of previous lives frequently go back to very remote times, and seldom give information of any precise or detailed kind by which their veracity could be established. They quite often also relate to purported lives in Atlantis, Lemuria, and on other planets, which cannot be verified. The reason for this is that the ostensible spirit-communicators are more concerned with explaining the karmic causes of present disabilities, and the way to remove them, than they are with trying to prove the truth of rebirth.

The most impressive feature of these cases is precisely this: the tracing of a karmic pattern which is often very convincing, and the often successful therapy, both psychological and physiological, which they provide. This feature is very marked in the Cayce life-readings. But if psychological or physiological treatment has been successful it may be said that the therapeutic measures taken have been successful on their own merits, and that their success does not necessarily prove, or even substantially support, the reincarnation hypothesis which goes along with them. Similarly, Ayurvedic medicine is often successful, although many theories of Ayurvedic are non-scientific, to say the least.

3. A wide spectrum of cases in which the subject vaguely feels that he has lived before, and may have characteristics which could plausibly be accounted for as being *saṃskāras* from a previous life or lives, but has no specific memories of these lives.

This is a quite interesting class of cases. It is extremely widespread and the most suggestive examples are those found in cultures that do not accept reincarnation or are even hostile to it. Probably most of the outstanding persons in the West who have subscribed to the belief in reincarnation held it because of some such personal experience. This seems at least to be the case with many of the writers, such as John Masefield and others, quoted by the compilers of the anthology *Reincarnation in World Thought* (eds. J. Head and S.L. Cranston; New York: The Julian Press, 1967).

4. Cases where the subject has had dreams, or hypnagogic[31] or fully-waking visions, which he believes to be memories of previous lives emerging from his unconscious (*ālaya-viññāṇa*).

Professor Ian Stevenson has collected a large number of such cases and I have read brief accounts of a few of them. It would appear that this type of experience tends to occur most frequently to people under stress, or with personality disorders. In stressful or dubious situations people become introspective, frequently asking themselves such questions as: "Why has this trouble come to me?" The answers may then seem to come to them in their visions with their corresponding emotions and some knowledge of events in a past life. These seem to the subject to have a bearing upon his present situation. The idea that these experiences come most often to people with personality disorders, or in need of help, may, however, be quite incorrect, being based solely upon a psychiatrist's case book. Many other people may have them, but it is only the psychiatric patient who normally speaks of them.

5. *The same as* (4) *above, experienced in the course of Buddhist or yogic meditation* (*trance states*).

It is not the express purpose of Buddhist meditation to recall previous lives, but this does occur at a certain stage of development, and the Buddha mentioned it as one of the accomplishments of an arahat. It comes about when the meditator is sufficiently advanced to benefit by the knowledge of his past deeds and experiences, instead of being injured by it. Professor Stevenson and I studied the case of a nun in southern Thailand who when practising *vipassanā* (insight) meditation at the age of about twenty, had unexpected images of events in the life and death of a three-month-old infant. The memories were verified as remarkably accurate. The infant had lived in a village about ninety kilometres from where the nun had had her "memories" and, so far as we could learn, she did not acquire information about the deceased infant by normal means.[32] Some of the children who spontaneously recall previous lives in Buddhist countries may have this ability because they had practised meditation in previous lives.

6. *Cases of spontaneous recall in early childhood.*
(Such cases are described in many of the following chapters. – Ed.)

XV

A Case of the Reincarnation Type in Ceylon

The Case of Warnasiri Adikari[33]

Introduction

We have studied cases of the reincarnation type in Asia separately and together for a number of years. I.S.[34] visited Asia on several occasions to study cases of this type and has published reports of a number of the Asian cases that he investigated (3). F.S., an Englishman by birth, has lived for the past twenty years in Southeast Asia, chiefly in Burma and Ceylon, with periods in India, Thailand, and elsewhere. As a student of Oriental religions and a writer and lecturer on Buddhist philosophy, he has had occasion to study a number of cases in which memories of a previous life have been claimed, most of them in Burma and Ceylon. In 1959 he gave a short account of some of these cases in a booklet dealing with the Buddhist doctrine of rebirth (4). The cases he mentioned were representative of those in which certain evidential items such as spontaneous recognitions of persons and places occur, and they included two which he had observed in Burma.

The majority of people in the West seem to be unaware of the number of such cases occurring in the Asian countries, and also of the fact that they are found, though with less frequency, in the West. Among those who have taken note of them, it is commonly supposed that the belief in reincarnation promotes the development and bringing forward of cases of this type. It is true that the belief itself is bound to favour the uninhibited expression of what appear to be prenatal memories in young children when they occur, and to encourage their retention over a longer period. But it is equally true that the cases also contribute to and strengthen the belief in reincarnation, for to those who observe them they usually appear to provide confirmation of this belief. We can evaluate the merits of such widespread convictions only by a careful study of the cases themselves, and preferably at first hand. For whatever final interpretation we put on the cases, a great number of them seem to provide evidence of some paranormal experience. Hitherto, the investigation of this type of case has been neglected—in the East because it is taken for granted, and in the West because it is less freely discussed than other kinds of paranormal experience.

In 1961 we collaborated in the investigation of three cases of the rebirth type in Ceylon (3). Since then we have been able to investigate some more cases both there and in Thailand. Of these, only the case of Warnasiri Adikari, here presented, has yielded material that justifies a separate report now. Other cases are still under investigation. Apart from the fact that this case shows various features similar to those we have found in other examples in Ceylon and elsewhere, thereby suggesting a common ground of experience, the case of Warnasiri deserves attention because F.S. was able to investigate it at a time when the main events relating to it had only recently occurred. Thus errors of memory due to lapse of time, which have left some other cases open to doubt on certain points, are likely to have distorted the testimony of the witnesses of this case very little. Care has been taken to check the reports of different witnesses against one another in order to eliminate individual errors of memory as far as possible.

Case Report

Brief History of the Case and its Investigation

Warnasiri Adikari was born on November 9, 1957, and lives at Kirikita, near Weliweriya, about twenty miles northeast of Colombo. When he was about four years old, Warnasiri began to talk to his father, Julis Adikari, about a previous life in the village of Kimbulgoda, some six miles away from Weliweriya. The boy's father knew nothing of the person Warnasiri claimed to be, but after some delay decided to take his son to Kimbulgoda. Before he could do this, however, word of the child's statements spread to the neighbouring community of Kimbulgoda. A resident of Kimbulgoda, Mrs. Emma Nona, had some relatives who lived in Weliweriya and she heard about the statements of Warnasiri and mentioned them to her sister, Mrs. T. Ranaweera. Mrs. Ranaweera recognized similarities between the statements of the boy and facts in the life of her son. This son, Ananda V. Mahipala, was born on October 26, 1926, and died suddenly on October 26, 1956. She visited Weliweriya in the spring of 1962 and met Julis Adikari, but not at that time his son, Warnasiri. The latter was then away, but he had said earlier that his former mother would visit him in three days' time—an accurate prediction of the visit and time interval. Her conversation with the boy's father increased her wish to meet Warnasiri and she invited him and his father to visit Kimbulgoda.

They returned her visit some two weeks later. Warnasiri had previously indicated the general location of the house of his claimed previous life in

117

Kimbulgoda. When Warnasiri and his father arrived at the village, the boy led the way to the site of the previous house, but it had been torn down. They then went to a neighbour's house. Amid a crowd of women who assembled there, Warnasiri recognized Mrs. Ranaweera as his mother of the previous life, despite attempts by other women in the crowd to draw him toward them. Warnasiri asked Mrs. Ranaweera about some of the former possessions of Mrs. Ranaweera's deceased son, correctly identifying several of them.

Shortly after this first meeting between Warnasiri and Mrs. Ranaweera, the case came to our attention and F.S. journeyed to the two villages on two occasions in July and August 1962 to investigate the case at first hand and to witness a test of Warnasiri's ability to recognize other members of the deceased man's family, chiefly his sisters. In this test, Warnasiri initially failed. At the time F.S. (and the crowd) was watching what Warnasiri would do when asked to recognize Ananda's sisters, he definitely did not do so. But in 1965, two of these sisters asserted that when the tension and attention abated and people were attending to other things, someone again asked Warnasiri if he could recognize his sisters. Thereupon he went to Irangani Mahipala and Vinitha, two of Ananda's sisters, and took their hands. F.S. did not see this episode. Irangani Mahipala, the informant about it, was satisfied that Warnasiri had, by his gesture and behaviour, recognized her.

Warnasiri met Mrs. Ranaweera on one other occasion in 1962 (before the first visit of F.S.) and at that time asked her about another of the possessions of the deceased Ananda. In 1965 F.S. returned to the area (with some different interpreters) to recheck the testimony and learn of developments in the case since his earlier visit. He learned that Warnasiri had made a few additional statements about the life of Ananda Mahipala and also some additional statements about another life in Kelaniya.

In July 1966 we again reviewed the case together during a visit of I.S. to Ceylon. We visited both the family of Warnasiri Adikari and the family of Ananda Mahipala, the deceased personality Warnasiri claims to have been. Prior to this review of the case, we had obtained a translation into Sinhala of an earlier draft of this report, including the list of statements and behaviour reported of Warnasiri with regard to the previous life. This list we give in the Tabulation to follow. We showed this translation to the two chief witnesses of the case, the father of Warnasiri and the mother of Ananda. They read the list, made a few minor changes of unimportant details, and signed it as according with what they remembered of the facts.

In 1966 a few further items were added to the testimony and some (usually minor) corrections of previous testimony made.

Warnasiri also claims to recall a brief life as the first baby of his mother, Mrs. B.A. Roslin Nona Adikari, which baby died an hour after birth. And he further claims to remember still another life anterior to the one in Kimbulgoda when he lived at Kelaniya, near Colombo, worked as a dental technician, and died in a boating accident. The few details of this life which Warnasiri has given are consonant with circumstances in Kelaniya, but because verification of some of these continues, we shall not list them in the tabular summary which we furnish of the declarations and recognitions of Warnasiri.

Relevant Facts of Geography and Possible Normal Means of Communication of Information to the Subject

As already mentioned, the two villages of Kirikita and Kimbulgoda lie about six miles apart. Access from one to the other is not difficult, although in Ceylon this does not mean that wide acquaintanceships occurred between persons in the two villages. Julis Adikari had visited Kimbulgoda on one or two occasions before the first visit with Warnasiri. However, he stated that he and his wife knew no one in Kimbulgoda and had never spoken to Warnasiri about the place prior to his declarations about his alleged previous life there. Mrs. Ranaweera similarly had known nothing of the family of Julis Adikari, and she knew no one connected with this family. She had been to Kirikita, but had no connections there and no interest in the village. As already mentioned, her elder sister had some relatives in Weliweriya from whom she first heard of Warnasiri's statements.

Persons Interviewed During Our Inquiries.

At Kirikita, we interviewed:

Warnasiri Adikari

Mr. Julis Adikari, father of Warnasiri

Mrs. B.A. Roslin Nona Adikari, mother of Warnasiri (interviewed only in 1965 and 1966)

Mrs. Isabella Kumarapelie, mother of Mr. Julis Adikari and grandmother of Warnasiri.

At Kimbulgoda, we interviewed:

Mrs. T. Ranaweera, mother of deceased Ananda V. Mahipala (this informant's correct married name is Mrs. T. Mahipala, but she is known in her community by her maiden name and so called Mrs. Ranaweera)

Mrs. Irangani Mahipala Pieris, sister of deceased Ananda V. Mahipala (interviewed only in 1965 and 1966)

Mrs. Swarna Jayawardena, sister of deceased Ananda V. Mahipala

Mrs. H. Albert Pieris, brother-in-law of deceased Ananda V. Mahipala (interviewed only in 1965)

Mr. D.A. Ranaweera, a relative of Mrs. Ranaweera, who witnessed Warnasiri's recognition of her

Mr. R.K. Dharmaratne, a neighbour.

When F.S. visited the Adikari family in 1962, Mrs. B.A. Roslin Nona Adikari, Warnasiri's mother, was extremely shy and withdrew from the room where he was talking with her husband. (Such behaviour is common among Oriental women in front of strangers, especially among rural women.) Her testimony was therefore not presented at that time. In 1965, however, she was less timid and F.S. was able to talk with her through interpreters. In 1966 she was even more affable and gave testimony freely. On the common points touched upon, her testimony corroborated that of her husband as to the statements and other behaviour of Warnasiri.

We present below in tabular form a summary of all the statements and recognitions made by Warnasiri with regard to his claim to be Ananda Mahipala reborn. The *Informants* column gives the names of witnesses to what Warnasiri did or said in relation to the previous life, while the *Verification* column lists the names of those who testify to the accuracy of what Warnasiri said or did with regard to the previous personality. We have listed at the end of the tabulation those statements and recognitions (items 22 through 29) which occurred after the first study of the case in 1962.

Relevant Reports and Observations of the Behavior of the People Concerned

Warnasiri exhibits, according to his father, a considerable identification with Ananda. He has repeatedly asked his father to take him to Kimbulgoda. He insists that his former mother loved him more than does his present one. After the first meeting with Mrs. Ranaweera, Warnasiri insisted on seeing her again and refused to eat until his father agreed to take him. Once when another boy said he would attack Warnasiri's "good mother" (i.e., Mrs. Ranaweera), Warnasiri became angry and attacked this boy. Mrs. Ranaweera

Summary of Statements and Recognitions Made by Warnasiri Adikari

Item	Informants	Verification	Comments
1. The mother of his previous life lived in Kimbugoda, but his father had died.	Julis Adikari, father of Warnasiri B.A. Roslin Nona, mother of Warnasiri	T. Ranaweera, mother of Ananda	Ananda's father, D.M.N. Mahipala, had died in 1953, three years before Ananda died.
2. The mother of his previous life was fairer and fatter than his present mother.	Julis Adikari B.A. Roslin Nona	Verified by our observations and comparisons of the two women.	
3. His former mother had more money than his present parents. Request to his father to buy a car	Julis Adikari	T. Ranaweera	Ananda himself had had a car. This was also verified by several persons who had known Ananda. Mrs. B.A. Roslin Nona confirmed that Warnasiri had asked his father to buy a car.
4. In his previous life he had stored some money in a drawer at home..	Julis Adikari	T. Ranaweera	Some money had been stored in a drawer at the time of Ananda's death as indicated by Warnasiri. According to Mrs. Ranaweera, however, the money was hers, not Ananda's.
5. The home of his former life was beside the main road near the school.	Julis Adikari	T. Ranaweera	This house had been taken down after the death of Ananda. The verifications therefore came from Mrs. Ranaweera only and we could not examine the house.
6. The house was blue, and had a tile roof.	Julis Adikari B.A. Roslin Nona	T. Ranaweera	
7. The house was a better one than the house of his present parents.	Julis Adikari B.A. Roslin Nona	T. Ranaweera	See comment for item 5. From our knowledge of Warnasiri's house and the description of the house that was torn down, we believe that this was an accurate statement.

Item	Informants	Verification	Comments
8. A guava tree grew in front of his previous house.	Julis Adikari	T. Ranaweera	See comment for item 5. The guava tree had been planted by Ananda and another boy. In 1965 Mrs. Ranaweera stated that Warnasiri still talked much of the guava tree.
9. The house was near a culvert.	Julis Adikari	T. Ranaweera	See comment for item 5. Also verified by F.S. when he visited the old site.
10. Recognition of the school in Kimbulgoda on his first visit there.	Julis Adikari	T. Ranaweera	Mrs. Ranaweera has taught at this school for many years. The school might be recognized for what it is from the road. It is, however, set well back from the road and does not look conspicuously like a school.
11. Recognition of the site of home in previous life.	Julis Adikari	T. Ranaweera	See comment for item 5. Passing the school, Warnasiri led his father on the way to the house another quarter of a mile and when they reached the site of the house, he said: "The house is not here."
12. Recognition of mother of previous life, Mrs. T. Ranaweera.	Julis Adikari	T. Ranaweera	Warnasiri picked her out of a crowd of women in response to the question whether his former mother was in the group. The only other comments or suggestions made consisted of efforts of other women present to draw him to them, saying, "Come here, I am your mother." All these he ignored, going straight to Mrs. Ranaweera. Mrs. Ranaweera and her deceased son had been extremely fond of each other. In 1962, Mr. D.A. Ranaweera said that he had witnessed the unprompted recognition by Warnasiri of Ananda's mother. In 1966, however, he denied that he had been present at this recognition. We cannot explain this change of testimony.

Item	Informants	Verification	Comments
13. Request to Mrs. Ranaweera for bicycle of previous life.	Julis Adikari	T. Ranaweera	Ananda had had a bicycle during his childhood. Mrs. Ranaweera had sold it subsequent to Ananda's death.
14. Request to Mrs. Ranaweera or almirah of previous life.	Julis Adikari	T. Ranaweera	An almirah is a wooden closet or cupboard used for keeping personal possessions. If used to keep a child's toys, it would, like a cupboard in the West, become an important place and source of memories for him. Mrs. Ranaweera had given the almirah to one of her daughters as a present. Mrs. B.A. Roslin Nona stated that Warnasiri had said he had had an almirah, but she was not a witness to this particular request of Warnasiri's to Mrs. Ranaweera.
15. In the previous life he had died from the effects of eating some "beautiful fruits."	Julis Adikari B.A. Roslin Nona	Unverified	Ananda died suddenly, and his death was attributed to heart failure.[34] Mrs. B.A. Roslin Nona said that Warnasiri had said he had died after eating "small fruits."
16. After eating the fruits, he had gone home, eaten breakfast, and died suddenly.	Julis Adikari	T. Ranaweera	Ananda did become ill after eating some food and died quickly. Ananda ate the meal in question about 10:00 A.M. It was in fact an early lunch rather than a breakfast, but Julis Adikari stated that Warnasiri had said he had died after eating breakfast.

34. The detail of some food taken or some food taken or some other seemingly unimportant event occurring just before death occurs quite often in the cases suggestive of reincarnation, for example, in the cases of Ravi Shankar and Parmod Sharma (3). Perhaps food taken or something done just before death becomes specially fixed in the memory because of the intensity of the experience of dying. Dostoevsky commented on the trivial details noted by men about to be shot of which he himself had personal experience. In the present case, a surviving Ananda, finding his body dead, might have cast around for a plausible explanation of such a sudden death and attributed this superstitiously to something he had recenty eaten. Such misplaced assignments of blame in illness and death occur commonly in the East, but also in the West. I.S. has drawn attention to incorrect or at least unsubstantiated assignments of causes of death by the present personalities in the cases of Swarnlata and Jasbir (3).

Item	Informants	Verification	Comments
17. His previous mother had had teeth.	T. Ranaweera	T. Ranaweera	Warnasiri said to Mrs. Ranaweera at their first meeting: "Where are your teeth, mother? You used to have teeth." Mrs. Ranaweera had had her teeth extracted after the death of Ananda.
18. Request for a toy drummer of the previous life.	T. Ranaweera Julis Adikari	T. Ranaweera B.A. Roslin Nona	Mrs. Ranaweera at first did not know what Warnasiri meant when he asked for the drummer, but on searching through some old things she found two clay toys that had belonged to Ananda, and one of these was the figure of a Kandyan drummer. According to Mrs. B.A. Roslin Nona, Warnasiri had kept the drummer among his toys and it was shown to us in 1965 and 1966.
19. In Kimbulgoda there is a person who sells gotukola and who is known as "Uncle Gotukola."	Julis Adikari	Julis Adikari	Gotukola is a local vegetable. A gotukola seller in Kimbulgoda was called "Uncle Gotukola." We were unable to verify this item independently. No informant in Kimbulgoda could in 1966 recall a person known as Uncle Gotukola, but Julis Adikari insisted that earlier Mrs. Ranaweera had verified the item to him. His wife, Mrs. B.A. Roslin Nona, also said it had been verified.
20. Initial failure to recognize sisters of Ananda when presented to him in a group of other young women. Later (1965) reported to have recognized two sisters of Ananda Mahipala.	Initial failure observed by F. S. on the occasion. Irangani Mahipala Pieris, informant for Warnasiri's correct (later) recognition of her and her sister, Vinitha.	T. Ranaweera	Initial failure possibly due to anxiety aroused in the child by the stilted, artificial manner of the participants and by a considerable crowd of persons who stared at the child. According to Mrs. I.M. Pieris, Warnasiri did later correctly recognize her and her sister after the initial tension of the staed event had abated. It seems, however, that Irangani asked Warnasiri a leading question, i.e. "Am I your sister?" to which Warnasiri said, "Yes."

124

21. After his death he was reborn as the first baby of his present mother, but died soon after birth and his body was placed in a cardboard box at the hospital.	Julis Adikari	Julis Adikari	Ananda died October 26, 1956. In the same month, Mrs. B.A. Roslin Nona did give birth to a baby boy whodied an hour after birth at the Government Hospital in Dompe. The infant was in the seventh month of the pregnancy. Warnasiri was bron a little more than a year later on November 9, 1957.[35]
22. He drove a Morris Minor car.	Warnasiri	H.A. Pieris Irangani Mahipala Pieris R.K. Dharmaratne	Testimony of 1965. Ananda had owned a car, but it was an Austin 40 model. His father, however, had owned a Morris car and Ananda had driven this car.
23. He had been in an automobile accident, running into a bus.	Julis Adikari		Testimony of 1965. Unverified. Mrs. Ranaweera said her son had never been in a serious automobile accident. She might not have known of a minor accident.
24. His names had been "Sudu Mahattaya" and "Ukung Mahattaya."	Julis Adikari Warnasiri	T. Ranaweera D.A. Ranaweera	Testimony of 1965 and 1966. These names were, in fact, nicknames by which Ananda had been called.
25. Failure to recognize a photograph of Ananda.	Julis Adikari		Testimony of 1965. Details of attempt to test recognition of photograph not given.

35. The hypothesis of reincarnation by itself implies nothing as to when a personality assumes occupancy of a new physical body. In most of the Asian cases now under study, the interval between the death of the previous personality and the birth of the body of the new personality is more than a year, although it is rarely more than ten years. But in a small number, the interval seems shorter so that conception and some embryonic development of the body of the second personality must have begun before the death of the first. In one (unpublished) case in India studied by I.S., the death ofthe first personality occured three days after the birth of the second personality, and in the case of Jasbir (3) the death of the previous personality occurred about three years after the birth of the present personality.

Item	Informants	Verification	Comments
26. Recognition of another photograph of Ananda.	F.S. witnessed this himself in 1965.		Testimony of 1965. A photograph of Ananda as a young man was shown to Warnasiri. He was asked: "Who is that?" and he at once said "That is myself." Witnesses of the two families said he had not been shown this photograph before.
27. Recognition of photograph of Ananda's sister, Padma Perera.	F.S. witnessed this himself in 1965.		Testimony of 1965. On being shown a photograph of Padma Perera as a child, Warnasiri said: "That is she," and pointed towards Padma Perera, who was present. Padma Perera had grown up and her features had changed considerably since this photograph was taken. F.S. would not himself have been able to identify Padma Perera from this photograph. Witnesses of the two families said that Warnasiri had not previously been shown this photograph of Padma Perera. We are certain that no person present told or hinted to Warnasiri (at the time) the identity of the persons in the photographs of items 26 and 27.
28. He had sisters at his home.	B.A. Roslin Nona	We met several of Ananda's sisters.	Testimony of 1966. This item was not given earlier, but Mrs. B.A. Roslin Nona indicated that it was among the statements Warnasiri had made before any verification had taken place. Ananda had had five sisters.
29. His former mother was school teacher.	B.A. Roslin Nona	T. Ranaweera	Testimony of 1966. See Comments to Items 10 and 28.

affirms that Warnasiri's personality closely resembles that of Ananda at the same age.

As already mentioned, Warnasiri said he could recall three previous lives anterior to his present one as Warnasiri. He believed that prior to his birth as Warnasiri, he incarnated briefly in the infant baby of his own mother, Mrs. Roslin Nona, in 1956; prior to that he lived as Ananda in Kimbulgoda, and prior to that he lived in Kelaniya and died in a boating accident. To his father, Warnasiri has several times expressed disgust with being reborn again and again and resolves to become a monk and make an end of it all.[35] For a time he had the habit of throwing rubbish into a well at his home. When questioned about this, he said that he wanted to fill up the well, build a house at that site for his new parents, and then leave them to become a monk. His father had great difficulty in checking this habit. Indeed, at one point he thought he could not do so and sent Warnasiri away to stay with relatives in the hope that this would break his habit of throwing things into the well. Mrs. B.A. Roslin Nona Adikari said in 1966 that Warnasiri still wanted to become a monk.

When F.S. saw Warnasiri in 1962 he appeared to be an extremely serious, shy, and indeed withdrawn child. He seemed at times to be abstracted from his surroundings, staring blankly into space. He spoke reluctantly and in single, disconnected words. But his father testified that he is quite intelligent. In 1965 and 1966 Warnasiri was happier and more communicative.

For her part, Mrs. Ranaweera believes fully that Warnasiri is her deceased son Ananda reborn, and she exhibited during interviews with her all the emotions to be expected in a woman talking of her beloved son.

In 1965 we learned that the affection of Warnasiri and Mrs. Ranaweera had continued, as had the visits of Warnasiri from time to time to Kimbulgoda. Warnasiri's family were somewhat reluctant to have him visit Mrs. Ranaweera often, but permitted occasional visits. Warnasiri's mother stated that he often asked to be taken to Kimbulgoda and "worried her" about this. In 1965 F.S. took Warnasiri with him to visit Mrs. Ranaweera again. On this occasion, the boy was eager to go and delighted with the visit. In Kimbulgoda he showed a very definite affection for Mrs. Ranaweera (which she returned) and during the visit he obviously much preferred her company to that of other persons present whom he largely ignored.

In 1966 we again took Warnasiri (and his father) with us to Kimbulgoda. On this occasion no strong emotion was shown by either Warnasiri or Mrs. Ranaweera, but they seemed to enjoy seeing each other.

Up to 1966 Warnasiri had also continued a lively interest in automobiles, a passion difficult to account for solely on the basis of opportunities in his own family, which owns no automobile. He seemed also to have some precocious knowledge (for a boy of eight as he was in 1965) of how to drive an automobile. Ananda, we were told, was skilled as a mechanic. As for other behavioural traits which might have been related to the previous life, we found no evidence of these. Warnasiri, according to his mother, showed no fear of water (related possibly to drowning in the life at Kelaniya) or of fruits (related possibly to his idea of the cause of his death as Ananda).

In 1966 we learned from Warnasiri's mother that he still spoke of the previous life when asked about it, but no longer spoke spontaneously as he had earlier. This fading of memories or at least of verbalizations occurs in most cases of the reincarnation type in children.

Comments on the Evidence of Paranormality in the Statements of Warnasiri

We have been unable to find any motives and opportunities for fraud on the part of the informants of the case. In 1965 the previous impression of their integrity was further strengthened when it was proposed to attempt hypnotic regression of Warnasiri. (This endeavour, which was conducted with interpreters, failed.) When F.S. explained and proposed this to his parents, they readily agreed. They understood the possible revelations of Warnasiri, if hypnotized, and would hardly have agreed to this procedure if they feared that some information unfavourable to themselves would emerge from the experiment. Furthermore, our two principal informants, Mr. Julis Adikari and Mrs. T. Ranaweera, signed after reading (in Sinhala) our tabulation of items (1–27) of the case recording their testimony to the facts as they remembered them.

Although Warnasiri's declarations of a previous life dwell on a more prosperous existence than his present one, we have found no evidence that he or his family have profited or can hope to profit from the narration of his apparent memories. If these represent only wish-fulfilling fantasies, they gain nothing for him by narration to others. But obviously he believes he has true memories of a previous life and frets against the restrictions of incarnated existence. Nor can we reasonably trace the impulse for Warnasiri's behaviour to his parents, who certainly do not wish their child to prefer other parents or to fill up the family well.

128

The detailed and intimate information possessed by Warnasiri about the life of Ananda V. Mahipala can hardly have been known totally to anyone but Mrs. T. Ranaweera. And yet, according to the witnesses, she was a total stranger to Warnasiri's family until after he began talking of the previous life. Many villagers of Kimbulgoda might know the details of the subsequently destroyed residence of Mrs. Ranaweera and her son. But knowledge of the possessions of Ananda would hardly lie in the public domain. Even Mrs. Ranaweera had forgotten about the existence of the toy drummer belonging to her son when Warnasiri first mentioned this. In any case, no other villager of Kimbulgoda knew the Adikari family. We could find no person who could have acted as a carrier of information to Warnasiri.

We must regard the recognition of Mrs. Ranaweera as inconclusive since, although some ladies tried to divert Warnasiri to themselves, he was asked to identify his mother and glances toward her may have guided him. This explanation does not, however, account adequately for the affectionate behaviour of Warnasiri towards Mrs. Ranaweera. The glances and even open encouragement of onlookers could hardly manufacture this behaviour on the spot or sustain it over several years.

Warnasiri's initial failure to recognize the deceased man's sisters may have arisen from anxiety rather than ignorance. For despite efforts at dissuasion, a considerable crowd of onlookers gathered at the time for the attempted test of recognitions and this, together with the stilted artificial behaviour of the principal participants, may well have made Warnasiri tense, as he seemed to be at the time, and inhibited the flow to consciousness of whatever information he had about the people there. This hypothesis of his initial failure is supported by the later testimony of one of Ananda's sisters, who said that after the initial failure Warnasiri did in fact recognize her and another sister. Unfortunately, we did not observe this episode and only heard about it three years later; and leading questions seem to have played a part. F.S. did, however, witness in 1965 Warnasiri's recognition of photographs of Ananda and one of his sisters.

Summary and Concluding Remarks

We have reported a case of the reincarnation type in Ceylon which we had an opportunity to investigate within a few months of the occurrence of the main events of the case. The case contains features commonly found in other cases of this type in different parts of the world. For example, the child concerned gave out information about his claimed previous life in different utterances spoken at different times; the apparent memories focused on persons and possessions of the previous life and on the details of the death of the previous personality; the subject showed a longing to return to the family of the previous life, although some discontent also with this "pull" which he felt; and he showed affectionate behaviour towards the mother of the previous personality appropriate for that personality, but most unusual in a small child meeting a strange older woman. He has, moreover, sustained this affectionate behaviour over a period of four years.

We have outlined our reasons for thinking that the child showed paranormally derived information about the previous personality. There are, it seems to us, three important rival hypotheses for explaining the facts of the case if we allow that the child did in fact acquire the information he had about the previous personality through some paranormal process. These hypotheses are: personation of a previous personality motivated by a desire to escape the present environment (acknowledged by the child to be less desirable than the previous one), making use of extrasensory perception and sanctioned by a culture favouring the idea of rebirth; possession of the child by a discarnate personality, presumably that of the previous personality; and reincarnation.

The first of these three theories is favoured by Chari (1) and by Murphy (2) as explanations of reincarnation type cases. I.S. (3) has argued elsewhere that this explanation may account for some cases of this type, but it fails, in our opinion, to account for several features of some of the cases, such as the strong and persisting claim of many of the subjects of a continuing identity linking the previous and the present personalities. If the behavioural features of these cases are to be accounted for by a combination of delusions of identity and paranormal processes, they certainly stand out from any other cases of delusions of identity whether in the East or the West. Obviously, no firm conclusion can be drawn from any single case and we do not propose to do so in the case of Warnasiri. But we can state that its features, so similar to those of many other cases observed, make us favour reincarnation as the most reasonable way of accounting for all its aspects and details. Further studies of these cases, which are urgently needed, may turn up new information which will make us favour some other explanation. In the meantime, it seems to us that reincarnation ought to be taken seriously as an explanatory principle for cases of this type.

A Case of the Reincarnation Type in Ceylon

References

1. Chari, C.T.K. "Paramnesia and Reincarnation." *Proc. S.P.R.*, Vol. 53, 1962, 264–86.
2. Murphy, Gardner. 'Body-Mind Theory as a Factor Guiding Survival Research." *Journal A.S.P.R.*, Vol. 59, April, 1965, 148–56.
3. Stevenson, Ian. "Twenty Cases Suggestive of Reincarnation." *Proc. A.S.P.R.*, Vol. 26, 1966, 1–362.
4. Story, Francis. *The Case for Rebirth*. Kandy, Ceylon: Buddhist Publication Society, 1959. (Revised edition, 1964). (Part Three of this volume.)

131

XVI

Another Case of the Reincarnation Type in Ceylon

The Case of Disna Samarasinghe [36]

Introduction

Cases suggestive of reincarnation occur in many different countries of the world. They are found in Europe and North America, and reports of European and North American cases are in preparation.[37] They are, however, found more abundantly in many countries of Asia. During the past seven years we have studied twenty-eight cases of the reincarnation type in Ceylon. We have already published four reports of cases of this type[38] and several other case reports are in preparation.[39] One of us has written an article summarizing the main features of cases of the reincarnation type in Ceylon[40] and in another article[41] the Ceylonese cases have been compared to those found in Turkey and among the Tlingit Indians of Alaska.[42]

 The present case report is presented here in order to bring a rather typical case of the kind to the attention of readers not familiar with the specialty literatures of parapsychology or Buddhism in which, up until now, all reports of Ceylonese cases suggestive of reincarnation have been published. We do not expect the present case—or, for that matter, any other single case—to compel any particular interpretation of the data presented, but we hope that readers will be sufficiently stimulated by this case report that they will wish to read other reports of similar cases published and in preparation.

Methods of Investigation

The methods used in the investigation of the present case followed those outlined in detail elsewhere[43] and we will therefore not describe them fully here. Suffice it to say that our practice is to interview as many witnesses as possible first in the village or town of the subject and then in the place where he (or she) claims to have lived. We make detailed notes of all the testimony as the witnesses talk. As much as possible, we try to interview informants separately so that they will not contaminate each other's memories or tend to harmonize their narrations falsely. We check the statements of one witness against those of others and against what he has said on another occasion if we interview him more than once. We then compare the statements and behaviour attributed to the subject (or expressed by him to us directly) with the corresponding events reported for the deceased personality the subject claims to have been. In short, our methods of investigation and of analysis are those of lawyers, historians, and psychiatrists who try to reconstruct as nearly as possible what happened during particular past events.

An important component of our data consists of observations of the nonverbal behaviour of the witnesses and particularly of the subjects of the cases as they talk about the various details. These nonverbal elements of behaviour give valuable clues both to the reliability of the witnesses and also to the emotions, often very strong ones, which these cases generate in the participants for various reasons. Cases of this kind consist not only of the attributed statements and recognitions of the child, but also of the evidences shown by the child of behaviour appropriate for the deceased personality.

We will give next a short summary of this case and of its investigation and in doing so will introduce the reader to its chief participants and witnesses.

Summary of the Case and Its Investigation

The subject of the present case is Disna N.K. Samarasinghe, who was born in the village of Udobagawa, near Galagedera (about 20 miles from Kandy) on April 26, 1959. Disna is the second living child and elder daughter in a family with four living children. Her father is Mr. A.S. Samarasinghe, a grocery merchant of Udobagawa and her mother is Mrs. Seelawathie Samarasinghe, a teacher in a nearby school at Minigamuwa.

Disna began to speak when she was about a year and a half old. When she was about three years old her mother was washing clothes one day when Disna suddenly said that she had washed clothes herself when she was at her home in Wettewa. When Disna's mother asked her where Wettewa was, she correctly indicated the direction of Wettewa which is a village about three and a half miles from Udobagawa. In response to further questions from her mother, Disna said that at Wettewa she had cooked alone, eaten alone, and lived alone. Then over the next weeks and months Disna gave additional details of the life she claimed to have lived in Wettewa. She said that at the house where she lived there was also one "mahatmaya" and a "woman." Disna used the Sinhalese word, "*amma*," which strictly means "mother." It turned out later that she was using the word in a contemptuous fashion to refer to "that mother" of her son's children, a person she did not approve of. "Mahatmaya" is a term of respect often given to older men, especially if they hold some supervisory position. The person referred to by Disna was later identified as R.M. Gardias, whose mother, Tilakarachige Babanona, died at the age of about 68 on January 15, 1958, thus fifteen months before the birth of Disna. The deceased woman, who was generally known as Babanona, in addressing R.M. Gardias regularly called him "*loku puta*," which means simply "elder son," a common form of address among the Sinhalese between persons related in this way. When, however, Babanona spoke of her son to other people she referred to him as "Mahatmaya" and other persons also regularly called him by this name. He is in fact an overseer for workers in the rubber plantations and secretary of the local cooperative of the area.

To resume Disna's statements, she continued to tell her mother details of the life she had led at Wettewa. Especially when she saw her mother doing some household chore, e.g., cooking or washing, she would comment on having done it herself, perhaps better! And indeed Disna showed a remarkable precocity about some such household chores to which we will return later. She also talked abut the children of "that woman," saying for example, "That woman has some children who are so black I wouldn't like to carry them in my arms."

Disna never expressed any desire to visit Wettewa and in fact said she did not wish to go there, alleging that Mahatmaya had mistreated her. According to Disna, Mahatmaya had favoured his wife over his mother. She said that he had given presents of cosmetics and perfumes to his wife, but had been restrictive and even cruel to her. Disna claimed that Mahatmaya had kept a cane with which he sometimes beat her if she did not do what he asked.

Disna's reluctance to visit the family of the previous life stands in contrast to the behaviour of many children in cases of this type who put mounting pressure on their parents to take them to the other family and sometimes threaten to run away or actually do so.[44] Eventually, however, curiosity in Disna's mother overcame Disna's reluctance to visit Wettewa. Disna finally agreed to go to Wettewa after being assured that her mother would not leave her there.

Disna and her mother, accompanied by three other persons, went on foot to Wettewa on April 24, 1964. Disna showed the way to a short-cut through paddy fields which cut about half a mile off the route following the main road. Disna's mother and other companions did not know where she was leading them except in a general way to Wettewa. As they came out of the paddy fields by this path Disna had selected, she pointed to a house and said, "That is the house." They had already passed several other houses on the way, so Disna did not just pick the first one they came to. The group went towards the house and as they approached they noticed a woman standing in the compound. Disna's mother asked Disna who that was and she replied, "That's the mother." They then approached the house and as Disna was thirsty they asked for some water. The woman invited the group into the house and they entered. Disna, it was noted, entered the house not by its main entrance, but by a side entrance. This side entrance was not visible from the road, but Disna seemed thoroughly familiar with it. (It turned out to be the entrance to the house regularly used by Babanona since it gave access to the areas she used for washing and she rarely went out on the main road.)

Inside the house the party introduced themselves to T.N. Alice Gardias. They learned that she was the wife of R.M. (Mahatmaya) Gardias. They told Alice Gardias why they had come and she supposed rather quickly that Disna was having memories related to the life of her mother-in-law, Babanona. She sent for her husband who shortly came and the group then engaged in a discussion of Disna's statements and their verification. Disna made various remarks about objects in the house and these, together with the statements made by Disna which her mother narrated to the Gardias family, convinced them that Disna was in fact Babanona reborn.

After this initial meeting between the two families, various members of Babanona's family and friends visited Disna to hear her talk about the previous life or perhaps be recognized by her. In fact, Disna clearly recognized only one of these people as described later. Disna also was taken to Medagoda, a neighbouring village where Babanona had lived before she moved to Wettewa.

The difficulty of analysing cases of this type is often increased by the uncertainty of knowing how much the two families have mingled their memories of what the child said before they met and what was learned about the other family after they met. There are a number of cases, most still unpublished, in which a written record has been made of the child's statements *before* the two families have met. The present case is not one of these, but Disna's mother did make (not later than June 1964) a rather detailed written report of Disna's main statements and of the events leading up to the first visit to Wettewa. This written record accorded very well with the testimony given during our later investigations.

Our first investigation of the case took place in May 1965, when F.S. visited the area of Galagedera and spent two full days in gathering testimony. Our investigation was then dropped until March 1968, when we together spent another two days working on the case. On this second occasion we interviewed again nearly all the witnesses previously interviewed by F.S. in 1965 and additionally took testimony from a number of new witnesses such as Babanona's daughter, R.M. Nonnohamy, who lives near the town of Rambukkana about 20 miles from Wettewa, and U.A. Bacho Hamy, a former neighbour of Babanona in the village of Medagoda.

We have also had available a translation of the written record made by Disna's mother and some other information gathered by Mr. P.K. Perera and Mr. H.S.S. Nissanka, who had earlier studied the case. Mr. Godwin Samararatne obtained some additional information about details on a visit to the area of the case in the summer of 1968.

Relevant Facts of Geography and Possible Normal Means of Communications between the Two Families

As already mentioned, Wettewa is a village about three and a half miles from Udobagawa where Disna and her family live. About a mile farther down the road away from Udobagawa is the village of Medagoda where both R.M. (Mahatmaya) Gardias and his brother R.M. Romanis[45] now live and where Babanona once lived before she moved to Wettewa to stay with her son there. This came about because R.M. Romanis moved to another village considerably farther away. Babanona, then an elderly person rather set in her habits, did not wish to move so far away. So she lived by herself for two years in Medagoda. Then she became somewhat infirm, and went to stay with her other (older) son in nearby Wettewa. She lived there with his family for six months before she died. The house occupied by Babanona in Medagoda figured in some of the statements and recognitions of Disna.

Babanona's body was buried on a slope behind the house in Medagoda, about half-way between this house and the house in Wettewa (of R.M. Gardias) in which she died. The burial site, which is near an anthill, is not visible from the site of the house in Wettewa.

The villages of the two principal families concerned in this case lie rather close together, the distance between them being less than the average distance for such villages in Ceylonese cases. The distances considered from the point of view of travel and communication are, however, considerably greater than they may seem to Western readers. Neither of the families concerned in this case possessed an automobile, but buses run along the main road between the villages. There would ordinarily be little intercourse between members of the different villages who were not related.

We questioned the principal informants about their knowledge of the other family before the development of the case and the first meeting of the two families. The testimony of different witnesses was quite concordant on the extent of the acquaintanceship between the families. They recognized each other on the road as they occasionally passed, but they did not know each other's names and had never had any social acquaintance, much less been in each other's houses. The plausibility of the denials of prior acquaintance between the two families is strengthened by the fact that the two families come from different castes, Disna's family being of a higher caste not at all likely to socialize with members of the caste of Babanona's family.[46]

We did learn of two acquaintances shared by the two families. One of these, the Ven. Ambanwelle Somasara, chief priest of the temple at Wettewa, had known Babanona well and had some acquaintance with the Samarasinghe family. We learned also that a customer of Mr. Samarasinghe's shop, William Kankanam, had lived in Walpolatenne before moving to Udobagawa. He had known the family of Babanona when she had lived in Walpolatenne and he was able to verify some of Disna's statements even before her mother took her to Wettewa. We found no evidence, however, that these two persons, or anyone else familiar with the facts of Babanona's life, had access to Disna in a way that would have permitted her to gather information from them about Babanona except by extrasensory perception.

Persons Interviewed during our Inquiries

In the investigation of this case, we interviewed seventeen informants altogether. The most important of these were Disna Samarasinghe and her parents and R.M. Gardias (son of Babanona) and his wife. We also talked with R.M. Romanis, another son of Babanona and his wife and two of his children, as well as with various other members and neighbours or friends of both families.

Statements and Recognitions attributed to Disna

Lack of space obliges us to omit a detailed list of all the statements and recognitions attributed to Disna by our informants. This list and some additional details of the case will be published elsewhere.[47] Disna was credited with thirty-four statements about facts related to the previous life. All but one of these were verified by informants acquainted with the facts of the life of Babanona. The unverified statement was Disna's claim that in the previous life her son (R.M. Gardias) had beaten her with a stick. R.M. Gradias denied this and we could find no confirmation of it from other informants. It seems probable that he had been somewhat severe with his mother at times, but improbable that he had actually struck her. He said that he had at times threatened to beat himself if his mother did not take her medicine and it is possible that Disna remembered such a scene in a distorted way; also her parents may have misunderstood what she said.

Many of Disna's statements referred to places where she had lived or visited (with names mentioned) or to specific events of the life she claimed to have lived. The details were so numerous and so specific in so many instances that there can be no doubt Disna was referring to the life of Babanona and no one else. In contrast to some cases we have studied, we feel quite confident about the identification of the related previous personality in this case. This is a fact independent of judgements about how Disna acquired the information she showed about the life of Babanona.

Disna's statements included references to details of the life of Babanona, such as that she (Babanona) had traveled by train and car to visit relatives at Rambukkana. She also referred to items that were known to only a very small number of persons in Babanona's family, for example, when she claimed to have hidden some money in a cigarette tin near a hearth in one of the houses she had lived in. This money had been found after Babanona's death. No one had known she had hidden it there when she was alive.

Disna also made several statements about experiences she claimed to remember after she died as Babanona and before she was born as Disna. She correctly stated that Babanona had been buried in a particular place and near an anthill. She gave a rather circumstantial account of experiences after the burial of her body and before her claimed rebirth.

In addition, Disna was credited by our informants with fifteen statements indicating recognition of people or places related to the life of Babanona. She was said to have been correct in all but one of these statements, and in that instance our informant was a second-hand reporter of the statement.

We have not included among the fifteen recognitions several other reports of recognitions made by Disna which she might have based on inference. It seems unlikely that she could have inferred the information on which she based the fifteen statements of recognition we have included. For example, the people accompanying her on the first visit to Wettewa did not know where Babanona had been in the habit of bathing, but Disna correctly indicated this place as they approached the house where Babanona had lived. And at the house, when the party had been invited to enter, Disna spontaneously went around the side of the house and entered by a door that was not even noticeable from the front. This door had been the habitual entrance used by Babanona. In the house Disna recognized a number of household objects which had belonged to Babanona or which she had used. In these latter instances subtle cues given unconsciously may have guided her. Disna recognized the wife of R.M. Gardias and she recognized a shopkeeper who had formerly sold rice to Babanona. She did not, however, recognize most members of Babanona's family when they visited her.

Relevant Reports of Observations of the Behaviour of the People concerned in the Case

Under this heading we shall describe our observations of the behaviour of the informants of the case, first with regard to the bearing of their behaviour on the authenticity of the case, and secondly with regard to the personation by Disna of Babanona.

In the present case the testimony of different witnesses was quite concordant with regard to the main facts of the case. There were discrepancies about details of the testimony such as one finds in nearly all cases of this kind, but in this case the number of discrepancies fell below the average. Furthermore, comparing the testimony recorded in the notebook of Disna's mother (June 1964), that of the first investigation of F.S. (May 1965), and that of our second investigation (March 1968), the testimony of the same witnesses was remarkably consistent. Some of the cases we have studied have included unsavoury events such as murders or lesser scandals and one sometimes understandably finds evasiveness connected with such events. The present case, apart from the allegations by Disna that her son had beaten her (as Babanona), was generally free of occasions for such evasiveness. We detected some hesitation and discrepant testimony around possessions and think that a fear Disna might reclaim property may have led the members of Babanona's family to be less than frank about some such items. Other than these items, however, we never found the slightest suspicion that the truth, so far as it could be remembered, was being concealed from us. On the contrary, the witnesses seemed open and eager to lay the details before us. And in the other direction of bias, we did not find any evidence that the case had been embellished by the addition of false details over the years. Here again, we have occasionally found some adornment of the facts by witnesses who wish to enhance their own role in a case or to strengthen, as they think, an otherwise weak point in a case.

All the principal informants of the case believe that Disna has given them satisfactory evidence of being Babanona reborn. Such admissions are often rather easily obtainable from grieving families in Ceylon who welcome the chance of believing that a deceased loved one has returned. (But it would be quite untrue to suppose that every claim to rebirth is uncritically accepted without careful examination of the statements made by the claimant.) For Disna's family, however, the acceptance of the identification of Disna with Babanona involves an acknowledgment of association with persons of a lower social and economic class, something not undertaken lightly in Ceylon.

As for Disna herself, she was reported as showing in several important respects definite character traits similar to those remembered in Babanona, or at least harmonious with what was stated about Babanona's situation and character. We will next describe some of these traits in detail.

First of all, there is Disna's strong antagonism towards Mahatmaya and her reluctance to visit Wettewa, features of behaviour in which she contrasts with most (but not all) other children of cases of this type. Disna complained that Mahatmaya had beaten her and had unfairly favoured his wife over her, and although we could not learn from any first-hand witness that R.M. Gardias had in fact beaten his mother, the consensus of witnesses (other than him and his wife) was that he had been restrictive and harsh towards her. He himself admitted to the Samarasinghes that he had kept a stick with which he sometimes threatened to beat himself (but not her) when she would not take her medicine properly. The combination of this stern conduct on the part of her son and the other evidence of "in-law" trouble which we learned about make it extremely likely that Babanona was unhappily domiciled with her son and daughter-in-law when she was with them in Wettewa for the last six months of her life.

Under the circumstances, it is appropriate for Disna to wish not to be reminded of the life in Wettewa and this is what her behaviour showed. Other children or her parents sometimes tease her by calling her "Babanona" and this upsets her. She beats her siblings if they tease her thus. When her father playfully called her "Babanona" in our presence in 1968 she burst into tears. At this time Disna was nine years old. Her mother said she was no longer talking spontaneously about the previous life, but would do so reluctantly if questioned. If they reminded her of the previous life, she would tell them not to recall it to her. Disna made it perfectly clear that she preferred her present existence immensely to the one she recalled having lived at Wettewa.

A second trait in which Disna's behaviour seems to resemble markedly that of Babanona is her religiousness. Babanona, at least in her later years, was a pious lady who practised meditation regularly and read (to the extent that she could do so) a Buddhist book of meditation. When she grew too weak to visit the temple in Wettewa she would listen to the Bana preaching[48] on the radio before which she would sit on the floor with her hands held together in the attitude of worship.

Disna showed an interest in religion at a very early age. When she was about two years old she listened with attention to the Bana preaching on the radio, sitting and folding her hands in the attitude of worship. Neither her parents nor the other children of the family do this and it is most unlikely that Disna could have seen anyone behave like this before she herself did so. Certainly there were no models for such behaviour in her immediate family. Disna stated that when she was an old woman she had listened to the Bana preaching on the radio. Disna has continued to show much more interest in religion than her three siblings. In 1968 she had a toy Buddhist shrine where she worshipped, lit a lamp, and offered flowers, as do Buddhists in regular temples. The other children tried to break up Disna's shrine, but she persisted with it. Her behaviour with regard to religious practices was altogether quite exceptional in the family.

Thirdly, Disna showed a remarkable precocity with regard to competence in certain household tasks. She was particularly skillful at a very early age in cooking. She played at cooking with small pots and pans. She criticized her mother's cooking of rice and her father said that she did so with some justification, since Disna could cook better than his wife! Disna talked a good deal about cooking also and evidently found it a topic of very great interest. In 1968 Disna's mother said she was still playing at cooking with small pots and pans. In connection with Disna's interest in cooking and precocious competence at it, we may note that Babanona was exceptionally good at cooking and she cooked for herself as long as she could do so and until shortly before her death.

Disna also exhibited an untaught ability to weave coconut leaves about the time she first began to speak of the previous life, namely, at about three years of age. She said that she had done this in her previous life. Disna's mother was quite certain that Disna had not seen anyone in their family or otherwise weave coconut leaves. The Samarasinghes, being fairly prosperous, do not have coconut leaves on the roof of their house which is made of tiles and sheets of corrugated iron. But the houses of Babanona's family were so covered as we observed ourselves. And Babanona, according to her son R.M. Romains, was a skillful weaver of coconut leaves.

Fourthly, Disna shows a noteworthy possessiveness with regard to her belongings. She does not believe in sharing and is inclined to take more than she receives from others. She may grumble if not given adequate gifts. She puts money she receives in a box kept for this purpose. This trait accords with the noticeable parsimoniousness of Babanona. (The consensus of the witnesses was that Babanona was not particularly possessive except about money.) Babanona was inclined to hoard and hide her money, ostensibly to avoid solicitation of loans from persons who never repaid her. We have already mentioned one cache of money made by Babanona. When the family found this money they suspected that Babanona had hidden it. The hoarding and hiding of money are not uncommon in elderly persons of Ceylon, who often feel insecure vis-à-vis the younger persons with whom they live. But the possessiveness of Disna at an early age was a trait which struck her parents as being unusual among their children.

A fifth trait in which Disna's behaviour is concordant with that of Babanona consists of her habit of tying a knot in her mother's sari whenever she can. (Disna herself still wears only short dresses, not saris.) Babanona had the habit of tying a knot in her saris and there keeping some of her money.

Still another similarity between Disna and Babanona occurs in the attention both gave to cleanliness. Babanona was preoccupied with cleanliness and bathed regularly and lengthily at the same time every morning. Disna stands out from her siblings in her concern about cleanliness and has a preference for bathing in the morning.

In two respects Disna's reported behaviour differed from that of Babanona. The latter had a morbid fear of burglars and used to be much concerned about having all doors of the house locked. Disna does not show any such concern. Babanona was very fond of milk, but Disna had only an average fondness for it.

Disna showed a definite embarrassment about the circumstances of the marriage she claimed to have contracted as Babanona. The latter had married a person of lower caste and from the "low country."[49] During our investigation in 1968 Disna would not discuss her marriage in the presence of her father or of a group that had gathered in her father's store during our interviews there. She insisted on taking her mother and our interpreter into a back room where she confided to them that she had married against her parents' approval. Incidentally, Babanona herself disapproved of her son's marriage to a dark-skinned woman. After her son R.M. Gardias married against his mother's (Babanona's) wishes, she did not visit him and his wife for a year, conduct which must surely have contributed to the "in-law" trouble which darkened the last months of her life. Babanona scorned the dark-skinned children of this marriage, her own grandchildren, and would not carry them in her arms. Disna, in recalling these grandchildren of Babanona, declared them repulsive because of their dark skins and said she remembered that she had not been willing to carry them in her arms.

In narrating memories of the previous life she claimed to have lived, Disna did not complain of being in a small body as have some of the children of the cases we have studied.[50] She did, however, refer to events as having occurred "when I was an old woman," evidently experiencing the feeling of a body image appropriate to an old woman. One can also discern apparent memories of the infirmities of an old woman in Disna's remarks about losing her teeth and using a stick for walking. Disna said that without the stick for walking she would have fallen. She referred also on numerous occasions to wearing clothes which "extended up to her wrists," i.e., the long-sleeved jackets commonly worn by elderly ladies such as Babanona was, but not by small girls.

A gradual fading of the apparent memories as the child grows older is the rule in cases of this kind. Usually the child at first ceases to speak spontaneously of the previous life, but may still talk about it if questioned. Later the child may forget everything or nearly everything.[51] A few children seem to preserve the memories apparently intact into adulthood. In 1968 Disna's mother told us that Disna had stopped speaking spontaneously about the previous life, but her memories remained quite vivid. Disna still responded, sometimes passionately, when questioned or teased about the previous life as we ourselves observed.

Discussion

Elsewhere one of us has published a lengthy discussion of the principal hypotheses which must be considered when confronting a case of the reincarnation type.[52] We shall therefore here only summarize some of the main points to be considered with reference to the present case.

Before considering the main rival hypotheses we will first comment on the different weights we assign to the three main types of evidence suggestive of some paranormal process on the part of Disna and other subjects of similar cases. These are: (a) the statements about the previous life attributed to the child; (b) the child's reported recognitions of people, places, and objects; and (c) the behaviour of the child which is reported as being consonant with that reported of the previous personality.

Of these three types of evidence we attach least importance to the recognitions. In cases of this type tests of recognition are rarely conducted by the persons concerned with anything like the kind of control one would like to see.[53] There are usually many opportunities for the (perhaps quite unconscious) passing of information or cues to the child. Also the recognitions occur quickly and are usually immediately confirmed or refuted by the bystanders. Some witnesses may not hear or may mishear what the child said and this may account for the greater frequency of discrepancies in the testimony concerning recognitions than in that concerning the child's statements at other times.

Despite these deficiencies of the reported recognitions, we are not prepared to discount all reports of recognitions by such children as Disna, especially those in which the child is reported as having quite spontaneously pointed to a person or object and identified him or it before anyone else present had drawn attention to the person or object identified. Disna seems to have made a number of spontaneous recognitions of this type.

We also do not attach great weight to the report of personation of Disna as corresponding *specifically* to the behaviour of Babanona. But the personation by the child has this importance, that the child is clearly behaving, if we are to credit the parents, as if there was in her personality a strong mixture of *some* other personality. In short, the child is distinguished by her conduct from the other persons of the family and acts in ways that are not appropriate for an ordinary child, but which are in many respects appropriate for a much older person, whoever that may be. And this abnormal behaviour must be explained, or explained away, by anyone attempting a full clarification of the case.

Turning now to the different hypotheses to be considered and, if possible, eliminated, we will take up the possibilities for fraud first. We have heard of fraudulent cases of the reincarnation type, although we have not yet had the opportunity of studying one which in our opinion was fraudulent. In the present case, fraud seems extremely improbable. We found no evidence whatever that, with the minor exceptions noted, facts had been withheld or their report modified consciously. Nor could we learn of any motive for fraud on the part of Disna or her family. The past life claimed for Disna was definitely that of a person in a lower economic and social class than that of her family. The house, really only a cottage, in Wettewa was far inferior to the Samarasinghe's house. This case, incidentally, forms an exception to the majority of cases in Ceylon and India in which the subject claims to remember a previous life in a higher caste.[54]

More plausible than fraud as an explanation of the case is the hypothesis which supposes that Disna somehow learned about the life of Babanona from some friend or relative who visited her home and narrated the events of the life of Babanona in Disna's hearing. Disna herself would certainly not have been able to go to Wettewa by herself before she began to talk of the previous life. She would have to have heard of this from some visitor. But the visitor would have had to be primed with a very considerable amount of detailed material from the life of Babanona. He would have had to have known about such intimate family matters as the existence of the anthill near Babanona's grave, the money which Babanona had hidden in the hearth at the house in Medagoda, Babanona's use of a side door at the house in Wettewa, and who was present when Babanona died. It is most improbable that anyone could have acquired all this information and then have narrated it in Disna's presence without her parents being aware of such a visitor and afterwards remembering him. The theory of cryptomnesia seems to ask for too much to be forgotten by Disna's parents.

One person who knew Babanona well and who had some acquaintance with the Samarasinghes was the Venerable Ambanwelle Somasara, chief monk of the Wettewa Temple. But A.S. Samarasinghe said that, so far as he could remember, the monk had not been in their home between Disna's birth and the time of Disna's first visit to Wettewa five years later, on which occasion she recognized him. It seems certain also that Disna had not known the monk elsewhere before this occasion.

Even supposing, however, that Disna has somehow acquired normally all the information about the life of Babanona which she showed, we should still have to account for the very strong behavioural features of the case. For, as already mentioned, Disna did not merely recall details in the life of Babanona; she personated an older woman like Babanona, that is, she showed traits similar to those which Babanona was known to have exhibited or could be thought likely to have shown. As already mentioned, these traits exhibited by Disna are certainly not specific for Babanona. They could be found in any number of elderly, devout Buddhist ladies of Ceylon. But they were unusual for a child of Disna's age and situation. In short, there was an expression in Disna of odd behaviour, which behaviour was not by itself accounted for by her having simply heard about the life of Babanona and which was appropriate for the character of Babanona. Also if Disna was going to identify strongly with an adult one would have expected her to select one within the orbit of her everyday life such as a parent or older neighbour.

One plausible hypothesis is that which supposes that Disna acquired the correct information she possessed about Babanona through extrasensory perception and then utilized this information in the manufacture of a secondary personality having the behavioural features of Babanona. There are, however, several important obstacles to this theory. First Disna's parents had observed absolutely no evidence that Disna had any capacity for extrasensory perception other than the knowledge of Babanona's life if it was derived by extrasensory perception. (In a small number of cases of this type the parents have observed some slight evidences of extrasensory perception in the children of these cases.[55] Whether such slight amounts of extrasensory perception as these few children manifest can account for the details of the rebirth cases in which they figure is another question.) Secondly, if Disna gained her knowledge through extrasensory perception she must have done so in a selective way, picking out knowledge only related to Babanona's life and omitting or not expressing other knowledge gained in this way. Finally, we should have to ask what motive Disna would have for identifying herself with a life which was, according to her, quite unhappy and one of which she said she did not wish to be reminded. Is it to be supposed that subconsciously she relished the idea of a previous life as an infirm old woman maltreated by her son, while consciously insisting that she found the memories repugnant?

If one eliminates the foregoing hypotheses, one comes to others which suppose some kind of survival of human personality after death. The two commonest of these are possession and reincarnation. The theory of possession supposes that the deceased Babanona, persisting as a discarnate personality, has somehow influenced Disna and imposed her memories and her behaviour on Disna so that Disna claims she is Babanona reborn. The theory of reincarnation simply supposes that Disna's personality is somehow continuous with that of Babanona which, after an interval, became reborn in a new terrestrial body and was given the name of Disna.[56] A clear distinction between possession and reincarnation as hypotheses for cases ostensibly of the reincarnation type cannot be made in cases such as that of Disna. In our opinion such distinctions can be made for certain other cases, notably those in which birthmarks occur.[57] Space does not permit a full discussion of these points of distinction in this place. Nor do we claim that hypotheses other than possession or reincarnation can be firmly excluded in the present case. In our own judgement, however, the case calls for some explanation including paranormal cognition on the part of Disna. Reincarnation is in many respects the simplest explanation for the case. It involves less complicated explanations than does the combination of extrasensory personation and secondary personality. But it is not the most plausible explanation for the average Westerner unaccustomed to considering that the idea of survival of human personality after death might be supported by empirical evidence. In any case, it is not our purpose to press our own interpretation of this case, but to present it for the purpose of drawing attention to the potential importance of such cases and the need for their much more intensive study.

XVII

The Case of the Siamese Sergeant Thiang San Kla

The Siamese army sergeant was a small, wiry man with rugged features and nothing remarkable about him except the large disfiguring birthmark, a capillary naevus, which spread from above his left ear towards the base of the skull. The dark red, puckered skin, on which no hair grew, looked like clotted blood.

I met him at the Military Camp at Surin, central Thailand, in 1963, when I was investigating the case of a Buddhist monk who was said to remember his previous life. The sergeant, Thiang San Kla, was sent to me by his company commander, Capt. Nit Vallasiri, as another example of a man who remembered his former life.

Cases of persons who believe that they can remember having lived before are not unknown in the West, but in the East they are much more common. This is to be expected, for ordinarily we recall most easily the things we are predisposed to remember, and the influence of Buddhism and Hinduism creates a favourable atmosphere for this kind of memory. In Western societies, children who create so-called fantasy worlds usually are discouraged at the outset. But in Asia a child's mental creations are taken seriously as possible memories of a former life, particularly if they seem to contain material outside the child's normal range of knowledge. Recently some of these claims have been investigated by Western parapsychologists.

During the past eighteen years, which I have spent in various Asian countries, I have come across a number of such spontaneous cases, mostly in India, Burma, Thailand, and Ceylon. They seemed to me worth methodical investigation, but only recently, thanks to financial backing from the Parapsychology Research Fund of the University of Virginia, have I been able to make detailed on-the-spot studies of them.

The case of Sgt. Thiang belongs to a most interesting category, that in which birthmarks or congenital deformities correspond to injuries remembered to have been sustained in the previous life. Briefly, this is his story:

Born in October 1924 at Ru Sai village, Surin Province, he had marks resembling tattooing on both hands and feet, in addition to the birthmark on his head. Also, his right big toe was slightly deformed, with a thickened nail and skin puckered like scar tissue.

At the age of about four he told his parents, in halting, childish speech, that he was his father's brother reborn, and that he remembered perfectly his previous life and death. He insisted that his real name was "Mr. Phoh," and became angry when people addressed him as "A-pong" (Baby). Phoh had been the name of his father's brother, who had died in July 1924, three months before Thiang's birth. As soon as he could talk, Thiang related to his parents all the most important incidents of Phoh's life. He had been wrongly suspected of cattle stealing and was set upon by some villagers. One of them threw a knife at close range and it penetrated his skull, causing almost instantaneous death. The stabbing was at the exact spot where Thiang's capillary naevus is situated and its position corresponds to the downward motion of the blade as it struck.

For several months before his death, Phoh had been suffering from a suppurating wound on his right big toe, and he had "protective" tattooings (magical symbols believed to give immunity from weapons) on both hands and feet, in the same places as the congenital markings now appear on the hands and feet of Thiang.

Thiang remembered seeing his own body lying on the ground, and wanting to return to it. But it was surrounded by people, and he was afraid to approach. He saw the blood oozing from the wound. His description of this part of his after-death experience is reminiscent of the accounts given by people who have had experiences of being "out of the body" while under anaesthetics or at the critical point of an illness.

In his disembodied form he then visited all his relations and friends, but felt grieved that they could not see him. He thought of his brother with affection, and wanted to be with him. At once he found himself in his brother's house.

There he felt in some way drawn to his brother's wife, who was having her breakfast. She was pregnant, and in Thiang's own words he felt himself irresistibly impelled to enter her body. During the remaining months of her pregnancy he retained his consciousness, being aware sometimes of being outside her body. Later when he told his mother this, she remembered that before his birth she had a dream in which her husband's brother, Phoh, appeared to her saying that he wanted to be reborn as her child.

Thiang's father died about two months after the child began to talk, but he had heard enough to convince him that the little boy was indeed his brother returned from the grave. Not only had he related events of Phoh's life which were known to them but had related things they did not know but had been able to verify from others. He knew the names of all the members of both families, and was able to recognize and identify the deceased Phoh's friends.

When he was about fifteen, Thiang's mother died. He was then placed in the care of an uncle, who ordered him not to talk about his previous life. When the boy disobeyed him he punished him by inflicting burns on his chest. Opening his shirt, Sgt. Thiang showed two scars where he had been burned in this way.

The late Mr. Phoh, who had been about forty at the time of his murder, had a wife, Pai, who died in 1962 at the age of 76. When Thiang was about five years old she came from her home in the village of Ar Vud, where Phoh had been living and where he had met his death, to find out whether the stories she had heard of Thiang being her husband reborn were true. Ar Vud is approximately 25 km from Thiang's birthplace, Ru Sai, and even today there is not much communication between the two places. She brought with her a number of articles that had belonged to her late husband, mixed up with other things. Thiang easily identified the objects that had belonged to him when he was Phoh; he also proved his identity to her by relating intimate matters of their family life. When Pai became convinced that her husband indeed was reborn she became a Buddhist nun. She felt that as she was not a married woman, yet could not consider herself a widow, she had no alternative. Thiang showed me a photograph of her in nun's robes which he evidently cherished.

Two witnesses to the story, which was well known all over the neighbourhood, had come along with Sgt. Thiang to see me. One was Sgt. Manoon Rungreung, of the same army division. He said that he had been familiar with this story of Phoh and his rebirth from childhood, and was convinced of its truth. Physically there was no resemblance between Phoh and Thiang, he said; Phoh had been "tall, fair, and handsome," whereas Thiang is the reverse.

The second witness was a man of 72, Nai Pramaun, of the Municipality Office, Surin. He had been formerly Assistant District Officer, and was a young man at the time of Phoh's murder. He had known the late Phoh, and had known Thiang from childhood. He told me Phoh actually was a cattle-thief and a notorious character in his lifetime. Nai Pramaun had investigated the case of the cattle theft and the murder in the course of his duties. On hearing the rumours concerning the rebirth of Phoh he had gone to see the child who was then between four and five years old. Thiang had recognized him and had addressed him by his name. He also had given correctly all the names of the people concerned in the affair. Nai Pramaun had examined the birthmarks and found they corresponded exactly with Phoh's death wound and with the other marks he had had on his body. He found also that Thiang remembered the man who had killed him, a villager named Chang, and wanted to take revenge. Fortunately, Thiang never met Chang, who died while he was still a boy. Nai Pramaun confirmed all the other facts of the case as being precisely as Thiang had related them. He added that the story is well known throughout the district and nobody doubts it.

The interesting feature of the man's evidence was that it completely demolished poor Thiang's attempt to whitewash the character of his previous personality, who according to his version had been "wrongly suspected" of cattle stealing. Nai Pramaun, despite his age, appeared to be vigorous and alert, with a clear memory. He gave his evidence with assurance, replying promptly to all my questions. He was obviously a good type of old-time provincial government officer, a man thoroughly reliable and accustomed to responsibility.

The day following my interview with Sgt. Thiang, I had a visit from Capt. Nit Vallasiri, Company Commander, C Company, Military Camp, Surin. He had come to volunteer further information and to learn my opinion of the case. He said that he had long been familiar with the story of Sgt. Thiang's previous life and confirmed everything I had already been told. He added that some years ago Sgt. Thiang had laid claim to some land adjacent to the army camp, on the grounds that it had belonged to him in his previous life as Phoh. He gave up the claim only on being assured that no court would uphold it. This incident had earned Thiang the army nickname of "The Landlord," by which he is known to everyone. It appears that he had recognized the land as having belonged to him when he was Phoh, without being informed of this fact and, in making his claim to it, he had given correctly the circumstances in which Phoh had acquired it.

Asked about Thiang's character and intelligence, Capt. Nit Vallasiri said he was emotionally stable, a good soldier, and had shown a high level of intelligence in army tests. His ambition and intent were to take his discharge from the Royal Thai Army and take up the post of headman of his village.

I investigated this case on January 22–24, 1963, at Changwad Surin, and my interpreter was Dr. Thavil Soon Tharaksa, Provincial Health Officer of Surin District. Two American Peace Corps workers then stationed in the locality were present during the interviews by my invitation. This very pleasant young couple afterwards confessed that Thailand had given them a new and utterly unexpected experience.

The transference of physical marks from one body to another in the process of rebirth—or rather their reproduction in a new body—is a recurring feature of many of these cases. It can be explained, I think, only on the assumption that there is a psychosomatic interaction brought about by a strong mental impression during the previous life or at the time of death. It seems to belong to the same order of mind-body relationships that can cause a weal to appear on the arm of a hypnotized person who, being told he is going to be burned, then is touched with a cold object. Thus, apart from the question of survival, the scientific study of cases of persons who claim to remember previous lives suggests the alluring possibility that by this means we may be able to throw more light on a subject of great importance in the treatment of disease—the connection between the psychic and physical aspects of personality.

XVIII
The Metamorphoses of a Mother
The Case of Win Win Nyunt

Professor Ian Stevenson of the Department of Neurology and Psychiatry of the University of Virginia has collected upwards of 600 cases suggestive of reincarnation from various parts of the world. Their geographical distribution, ranging from North Africa to Alaska, shows that they occur among peoples of diverse cultural backgrounds and even in cultures where religion gives no sanction to the belief in rebirth. A comparative study of these cases reveals that they have certain features in common which seem independent of conditioning factors in the subjects' mental environment. A case of apparent reincarnation is usually regarded as a scandal when it comes to light in a community where religious orthodoxy is entrenched against the belief. It is impossible to estimate, of course, how many such cases are suppressed for this reason.

In the cases in Asia which I have studied personally inhibiting social influences do not play a large part. Sometimes there are familial complications which prevent prolonged study and controlled tests of the case. The parents of a child who claims to remember a previous life and who has identified certain living persons as his former father and mother usually wish to break the child's attachment to these claimed parents rather than encourage it by fostering his memories. In several cases known to me the present parents have shown a definite fear that the family of the past life would alienate their child's affections or even attempt to take him from them. This, while it makes study of the case more difficult, is at the same time strong evidence for its genuineness or at least of the sincerity of the persons concerned.

A general survey seems to indicate that rebirth tends to take place in the same locality and social group, often in the same family, as that of the previous life. This is one of the common features to which I have alluded and is easily understandable on the basis of attachment and emotional pull. It is in fact exactly what might be expected. The principle is well illustrated by the case of a little girl, Win Win Nyunt, which came to my attention in Burma some years ago.

Win Win Nyunt's father, U Khin Nyunt, was Military Administrator and Sub-Divisional Officer of Pyinmana, Upper Burma, in 1948 when Communist insurgents were harrassing the district. When other rebel forces, the Karens, drove them out, U Khin Nyunt and his wife Daw Mu Mu were taken prisoner and conveyed to Thandaung in Toungoo District. U Khin Nyunt's mother, aged 67, was then in Rangoon and all communication between them was cut off. One night U Khin Nyunt dreamed that his mother was ill and yearning to see him. Later he dreamed that he was at her bedside and she was trying to tell him something which he could not understand.

While they were still at Thandaung, U Khin Nyunt's wife became pregnant and about that same time he had another dream in which he saw his mother lying dead. She was fully dressed, as if for cremation, in accordance with Burmese custom. The dream was so realistic that he was able to take precise note of the clothes she was wearing. And then his wife also had a dream in which she saw his mother who said that she was coming to live with them. In Daw Mu Mu's dream the mother got into the bed and lay down between U Khin Nyunt and his wife. This dream occurred early in Daw Mu Mu's pregnancy and in fact it was only after the dream that she realized she was pregnant. They had been married for six years but did not wish to have any children on account of the difficult and dangerous position they were in.

In due course the child was born; it was a boy and they named him Maung Maung Lay. About three months after his birth U Khin Nyunt had another dream of a very disturbing nature. He dreamed that his son was dead and that his heart, liver, and other organs were scattered around in a glass case.

Soon after this dream an opportunity came for them to escape but U Khin Nyunt had to take a different route from that taken by his wife and the baby. On reaching Rangoon he learned that his mother had died. For some time before her death she had been weeping and asking for him. On receiving the news he told his relatives about his dreams concerning his mother and it appeared that the date on which the last one had occurred corresponded with the date of his mother's death. When he described the clothes he had seen her wearing in his dream he was told that they tallied exactly with those in which her body had been laid out for cremation. They were new clothes which he never had seen her wear in life.

In Rangoon U Khin Nyunt was reunited with his wife and child but soon afterward the baby's health began to give them anxiety. They obtained the best medical advice available but his condition did not respond to treatment. In this troubled situation U Khin Nyunt's mother-in-law advised them to take him to a well-known Buddhist monk at Gyogon, to the late Yagyaw Sayadaw who was known to be clairvoyant. This they did. As soon as the old Sayadaw[58] saw the boy he said, "Your son is only a visitor here."

U Khin Nyunt was deeply perturbed by these words and even angry at the fatal prophecy they implied. Refusing to speak to the Sayadaw, he left abruptly. In Burma, Buddhist monks are held in the highest veneration and his behaviour toward the Sayadaw shows the measure of U Khin Nyunt's distress.

In April 1953, the little boy, then five years old, fell seriously ill with what was diagnosed as acute anemia. Just before this the father had another dream in which a frightful-looking personage in black was trying to pull his son away from him. With great difficulty he resisted but he awoke deeply troubled. And he could not shake off the feeling of depression left by the nightmare. It had been more like a waking vision than a dream experience.

The child was then taken to a WHO (World Health Organization) specialist who, after a thorough examination, sent a specimen of his blood to America for a report. When it came the diagnosis was leukemia—cancer of the blood for which there is as yet no known cure.

There followed another vivid and realistic dream. U Khin Nyunt and his wife both dreamed they saw his mother leaving their room and going downstairs. She was dressed as in the death dream and did not look at them nor speak. Still dreaming, U Khin Nyunt turned to his wife and said, "Just look at my mother! She didn't even speak to us!"

Two months after that Maung Maung Lay died.

During his final illness the little boy had wanted desperately to stay alive. He repeatedly said, "Can't you help me? Can't you save me from death?" About half an hour before the end he looked up at his parents and cried out, "I shall be coming back!"

After this loss the parents were inconsolable. They wondered very much about the dreams and the dying child's last words to them. What was the connection between U Khin Nyunt's mother and the little son who had left them so tragically? What was the meaning of those last words uttered with all his remaining strength? Would he really come to them again? In an attempt to resolve their doubts a sister took them to consult a reputed seer in Henzada. He said, "Your child will come back to you after three years.

155

But as a daughter, not a son."

Sure enough, three years later Daw Mu Mu became pregnant again. She dreamed she saw her little son come back. At about the same time one of their servants, who did not know the mistress was expecting another child, also dreamed that she saw the little boy enter the compound of the house wearing the clothes he had worn on his deathbed. When the servant asked him where he was going he replied that he was returning to the house. She told this dream to the master and mistress but they did not inform her of the pregnancy.

On March 22, 1957, a girl was born whom they named Win Win Nyunt. On her left ankle the baby had a rectangular birthmark, paler in colour than the rest of her skin and looking exactly like a mark left by adhesive tape. It was precisely in this spot that the WHO specialist, Dr. Perabo, had given a blood transfusion to their son during the three days preceding his death.

In U Khin Nyunt's employ there was a driver who had been very fond of the little boy. This man had been deeply grieved at the child's death and whenever he passed the cemetery used to call out, "Maung Maung Lay— come back!" When the little girl was shown to this driver the first thing he did was turn the baby over on her stomach. Then he pointed triumphantly to a dark patch on her buttock. "That is the mark I made!" he said.

The parents, not knowing what he was talking about, were surprised. He then told them that just before Maung Maung Lay's burial he had made a mark with charcoal on the dead child's buttock. The mark borne by the new baby was identical with the one he had made on Maung Maung Lay, he said.

When the little girl Win Win Nyunt was able to speak connectedly she claimed that she was not only the former Maung Maung Lay but also Daw U Shwe, the mother of U Khin Nyunt. By mentioning the names of persons she could not have known in this life and referring to incidents in the lives of Daw U Shwe and Maung Maung Lay, she convinced both U Khin Nyunt and his wife that they were indeed her former personalities. She sometimes forgot herself and addressed her father as if he were her son. In Burma where, as in most Asian countries, distinct forms of address are used to denote seniority and status within the family, this in itself was unusual enough to excite comment. Even without the use of the words "father," "mother," or "son," it can be known whether an elder or younger relative is being addressed.

While this history was being related to me by U Khin Nyunt and his wife at their pleasant home in Campbell Road, Rangoon, Win Win Nyunt was present. The conversation was in English but whenever the name Daw U Shwe was mentioned the little girl exclaimed, "That's me!" Like most of the children who claim to remember previous lives she seemed a precocious child. Several times she said in Burmese, smiling happily, "Daw U Shwe—that's nobody else but me!"

In Burma it is a custom to mark children who have died or are expected to die in the hope that they will be reborn in the same family and be identifiable by a birthmark on the same spot. The practice is noted by H. Fielding Hall in his book *The Soul of a People* and also in *A Burmese Family* written by a Burmese author in recent times.[59] In most of the cases of children believed to have been identified in this way the marks correspond to those made on the previous child by the parents, which are consequently known to them. This gives rise to the possibility that the mark may be reproduced by a prenatal suggestion coming from the mind of the mother, which in some unexplained manner acts on the embryo during its formative period. However, there is nothing in genetics to support the theory that a mother's ideas can affect her unborn child in this way and in fact most geneticists would flatly deny that it could happen. Nevertheless, this hypothesis has been put forward to account for such cases. But in the case I have recorded above it can be ruled out so far as the mark on the infant's buttock is concerned because the only person who knew that the body of Maung Maung Lay had been marked after death was the driver who did it. Both parents were unaware of his action which was prompted by his own affection for the boy. This makes the case one of special significance, apart from its other remarkable features.

It can be objected that the parents' desire for the return of the same child together with their belief in its possibility created a mental atmosphere in which they projected their wish onto the personality of the child who thereupon "acted up" to it. Possibly in such a situation this could happen; but it would not account for the child's knowledge of people and events connected with the previous personalities. And even if the parents' wishful thinking were sufficient to establish a fictitious connection between the boy Maung Maung Lay and the new baby there is no reason to suppose they were predisposed to see in Maung Maung Lay the reincarnation of U Khin Nyunt's mother. Neither does the theory explain the series of dreams in this particular case. Had the dreams concerning Daw U Shwe been experienced only by her son they could be dismissed as coincidences; but he and his wife both had similar dreams and at a time when they had no reason to think that Daw U Shwe might be dying.

There remains one other possible theory: Win Win Nyunt acquired her information telepathically from her parents and adopted the knowledge thus gained as her own memories. This, however, would be to stretch the potentialities of telepathic communication far beyond the limits of what has been demonstrated as possible by any experiments so far conducted. There is not, insofar as I know, any instance of telepathically acquired knowledge being absorbed into the personality as a permanent part of its structure. If all the children who have given proof of possessing knowledge of the lives of people no longer living have acquired it in this way, telepathy must be a much more common extrasensory faculty than controlled experiments have indicated. Moreover it must be capable of passing on information more detailed and exact than that received in any verified telepathic tests. It is a far cry from telepathically reproducing simple line drawings and calling Zener cards to relating incidents from the lives of other persons and identifying those persons and the places they had known, as these children have done. Sensitives, it is true, have obtained such information by psychometry but here again the impressions they receive always remain distinct from the contents of their own minds and do not result in any confusion between their own personality and those of others. Suppose that Win Win Nyunt was psychometrically sensitive—she must have handled objects belonging to many other persons in the household besides those of her dead grandmother and brother and there seems no valid reason for her acquiring information connected with them alone.

This interesting case brings into sharp focus the problems attached to the concept of personality. To what extent does a "transmigrating" entity remain the "same" entity—in any generally accepted sense? The components of personality commonly regarded as fundamental to its structure (such as sexually determined attitudes, characteristics formed by past experience, environment, acquired knowledge, and even personality patterns governed by the action of the endocrine glands), if they survive death at all, must undergo complete transformation in the process of rebirth when an entirely new physical basis and environmental situation comes into being. There then remains only the possibility of memory, of recalling the past, to maintain a connection between the present personality and previous personalities.

Actually the same difficulty exists if we choose to confront it in our idea of a man of seventy being the "same" person that he was as a boy of seven. If he suffers total loss of memory there remains no connection between himself and the child he once was. All that can be said is that he is the indirect *result* of that child in the same world-line of existence. In Buddhism the difficulty is overcome by holding that personality is purely an idea. The term merely signifies a current of cause and effect in which no enduring entity is to be found. At death all that we consider to be personality passes away, leaving only the potential of the past karma (actions) to produce a new psychophysical aggregation, a new "personality." One personality is linked with a former personality and with all those personalities that have gone before by the fact of belonging to the same individual stream of cause and effect in the psychic order. This is said to be the sole form of "identity" existing between one life-manifestation and another in the sequence. Mahāyāna Buddhism accounts for the recollection of previous lives by postulating a "reservoir of consciousness" (Sanskrit: *ālayavijñāna*) peculiar to each life-stream which may be tapped under appropriate conditions.

It may be this hurdle of the destruction of personality that rebirth entails that makes the doctrine unacceptable to many people. There are those who would prefer to be annihilated altogether rather than become another person as it seems to them they would in being reborn. We think of ourselves as personalities in terms of our past memories, our present consciousness and character, and all the mental furniture we have acquired, including the knowledge of our relationships with others from our earliest years. With all this gone and being cast into an entirely new environment, what remains of the individual I call *me*? The only answer is that each of us is the product of an individual stream of "becoming," a process in which nothing is constant except the cause-effect continuum.

Yet there is no need to take a nihilistic view of rebirth merely because it excludes a *total* survival of the personality. Where characteristic traits are strongly developed they reappear in the new life, often markedly enough to demonstrate a recognizable relationship between the two personalities. Special aptitudes that have been acquired in previous lives can be carried forward if they have been cultivated with sufficient determination and singleness of purpose. The child prodigy in music or any other sphere probably is not the recipient of an unearned gift. Change is the basic principle of growth and it is idle to ask whether the 300-year-old oak is the "same" plant as the acorn from which it sprang.

When a distinctive personality appears again and again in the same family, skipping one or more generations, it well may be that a factor other than heredity is involved; it may demonstrate a psychic heredity which is the individual's own property. The biological laws themselves would help to make it possible for the same ancestor to be born repeatedly in the line of his genetic descendants. In this connection the force of attachment to her relatives, which seems to have been operative in the case of Daw U Shwe, and the gravitational pull toward the family group displayed in many other rebirth cases, provides an explanation of what may be called the recurring family type, a phenomenon often enough observed in the lineage of families noted in history. By a logical extension of this principle a prolonged conditioning through a series of rebirths within the same ethno-psychological group would tend to produce those racial and national types which, although they have been grossly caricatured in literature and propaganda, undoubtedly do exist. A systematic study of the subject might throw light on the nature and origin of racial memories. The collective unconscious of Jung may be nothing after all but the submerged memories of previous lives and the subliminal impulses associated with them.

Honoré de Balzac characterized the process of "becoming" through a series of lives when he wrote in *Seraphita*: "The virtues we acquire, which develop slowly within us, are the invisible links which bind each one of our existences to the others—existences which the spirit alone remembers, for matter has no memory for spiritual things. Thought alone holds the tradition of the bygone life. The endless legacy of the past to the present is the secret source of human genius."

Perhaps he was right and it is this legacy of the virtues and skills we have striven for that constitutes our true personality, not the ephemeral and adventitious contents of our minds at any particular moment. I believe that to understand this is to have a true notion of what it means to say, "I exist."

Before closing this brief discussion of the case of Daw U Shwe something should be said about her change of sex in the intermediate life. It is possible that Daw U Shwe was born as a boy because her anxiety to be reunited with her son caused her to remanifest in a body that had been conceived before her death and was of the wrong sex. Unfortunately I was not able to obtain the exact date of the beginning of Daw Mu Mu's pregnancy but if my assumption is correct the child's early death would be explicable on the ground that Daw U Shwe's karma was not the kind to sustain a male personality. The situation could then be adjusted only by the transfer of her karmic life-potential to a new birth as a female. This does not mean that a change of sex in rebirth always must lead to such a result. On the contrary, there are a number of cases of sex change on record and their various degrees of sexual identification and adjustment are the subject of a special study. But in all or most of them there appears to have been predisposing factors in the former life that made the transition from one sex to another more or less appropriate. In the case of Daw U Shwe her strong maternal instinct makes the assumption that such factors were not present a valid one. Her brief life as a boy may have been nothing but a mistake on her part, one that nature quickly rectified.

This is my own interpretation of the case; others who read the facts may come to different conclusions. Whatever the finally correct interpretation may be, a case containing so many diverse elements of paranormal experience would be difficult to explain away without recourse to the doctrine of rebirth. Rather than strain beyond reasonable bounds the possible scope of telepathy, psychometry, clairvoyance, precognition, and other ESP phenomena, I find it easier to believe that Win Win Nyunt is precisely whats he claims to be—Daw U Shwe and Maung Maung Lay reborn.

XIX

Rebirth or Possession?

The Case of Phra Rajsuthajarn

Thailand (Siam) is a country fairly rich in cases of people purporting to have memories of previous lives. The evidential value of the Thai cases is not less than that of those I have studied in other parts of Asia and they have, in addition, a distinctive feature rarely met with elsewhere. A number of them include what are claimed as being distinct memories of the intermediate state of consciousness between one human life and another. In some of these cases long sequences of events, more vivid than those of a dream, are described in great detail. If these accounts relate to real psychic experiences they throw an interesting light on the states of consciousness possible in a disembodied existence, or rather in a state of being associated with a body of a different substance from that of earthly life. Matter, being merely a form of energy, may be capable of manifesting in states that normally are imperceptible to human senses yet are nonetheless physical on their own plane of being. This would certainly appear to be the case if the post-mortem experiences are veridical and not simply fragments of "what dreams may come when we have shuffled off this mortal coil."

The period to which these ostensible memories refer appears to be that immediately following upon the transitional phase described in the *Bardo Thodol*, the classic Northern Buddhist text published in an English translation by Dr. W.Y. Evans-Wentz; or it may be that they are part of that phase. In the Buddhist view the stream of consciousness continues unbroken between death and rebirth, so that every state it passes through has to be considered as a rebirth, no matter how short or how long its duration or on what plane of existence it occurs. To put the case briefly, where a Western statement would be that at death the spirit passes from the body, the Buddhist would say that after death rebirth as a spirit may take place. This is because Buddhism regards the entire life-continuum as an uninterrupted succession of deaths and rebirths taking place from moment to moment. This difference in viewpoint is important in order to understand what such experiences mean to those who claim to have had them if the subjects are Siamese, Burmese, or Sinhalese Buddhists. Actually it is only a more philosophical way of interpreting the theory of survival held by spiritualists.

A rather typical case of this kind is that of the Venerable Phra Rajsuthajarn, a Buddhist monk of Pa Yodhaprasiddhi Monastery, Changwad Surin, Thailand. He was born on October 12, 1908 at Nabua Village, City District, Surin Province. I interviewed him in January 1963, first in Bangkok and later in Surin, where I also questioned members of his present family and the family of the man he claimed to have been in his previous life. I also spoke with a number of local witnesses not connected with either family.

According to his own account, as an infant Phra Rajsuthajarn remembered his previous life before he was able to talk. In that existence he had been a farmer named Leng, living about 200 meters from his present birthplace. Leng, who had four sisters and two brothers, died of an undiagnosed fever at the age of 45 on October 14, 1908. He left three daughters named Pah, Poh, and Pi, who were still living in 1963, aged 74, 67, and 65 respectively.

Phra Rajsuthajarn stated that after dying as Leng he was reborn as the child of Leng's younger sister, Rian, but that the rebirth did not occur in the usual way. The personality of Leng passed into the body of the baby which had been born to his sister a day before his death. The woman who was formerly his sister thus became his mother in this present life.

His account of the brief interlude between Leng's death and rebirth is vivid. It appeared that after his death he saw his body laid out on a mat on the verandah, then he witnessed his cremation, saw the remaining bones brought back to the house, as is customary, and was present while Buddhist monks chanted the usual funeral scriptures. Describing his state of consciousness at that time he said he had the impression of being able to see in all directions.

While the funeral rites were in progress he remembered that one of his younger sisters had given birth to a boy the day before he died. As soon as he thought of her he found himself beside her where she lay with her baby. At the sight Leng felt a sudden surge of affection for both of them. He had a strong urge to touch the child, but was afraid of disturbing it. Apparently the mother saw his spirit form, for she addressed him telling him that he was dead and ought to go to his own place.

He went away but continued to watch from outside, and when he thought his sister was asleep he approached again. Once more she saw him and told him to leave her. He went away a second time, but the force of attraction was too strong for him. At the moment when he decided that he really ought to leave the place and was turning to go, he felt himself spinning around and lost consciousness. His last impression was of falling.

Next he was aware of being a young baby lying in a crib. He felt that he was still the same personality, Leng, and tried to recall his past life. His new situation was very unpleasant to him, for he felt frustrated at being unable to speak or to get up or to walk. At this stage he was not able to recognize anyone and his ideas were confused; but he then found that when he changed his position and lay on his stomach he could call to mind all the people he had known in his previous life and wanted to see them again. He first remembered the names, appearance, and characteristics of his relatives, then of his friends and neighbours, and he wished to see them again.

Phra Rajsuthajarn's mother had died some years prior to 1963, but I was able to interview the three daughters of the previous personality, Leng. They said that when Phra Rajsuthajarn was a child and his grandmother visited him he insisted upon calling her "Mother"—the relationship she had borne to Leng. He started talking about his previous life as soon as he could speak and without prompting gave the names of Leng's relatives correctly, including those of his sisters and brothers and of his mother, Ma Chama, and his father, Wa Sawa, who were now his grandparents.

As a farmer, it had been Leng's custom to go with a cart trading in other provinces at certain seasons. In this way he became familiar with the Laotian language. Although Laotian is not spoken in Phra Rajsuthajarn's community and nobody there has any knowledge of it, he was able to understand and speak that language when some Laotians visited the area. He was still a child at that time, and this ability to converse in an unknown language with strangers astonished the villagers.

Another curious incident occurred when Phra Rajsuthajarn was a boy of about 13. He had taken some cows to pasture a long distance from home and recognized a certain stretch of road, although he had not been there before. He suddenly recalled seeing a woman giving birth to a child by the roadside there and following a widespread custom, a fire had been lit to assist the birth. On his return home the boy related this apparent memory to his mother, describing the scene with the fire blazing brightly and the woman lying beside it. His mother at once remembered that she and her brother, Leng, had seen such a sight on a certain occasion at precisely the spot her son indicated. They had been returning from the paddy field together at the time. "That happened when I was 14 and you were 15," she told her son.

At the age of 16 Leng had entered the Buddhist monastic order (Sangha) as a novice and he remained in it until he was 25. Phra Rajsuthajarn also

164

became a novice at 16, and found that his religious studies came very easily to him. The Pali Buddhist manuscripts from which the monks study are written in Cambodian characters, which differ in several respects from the Siamese. Hearing a monk reading aloud from such a manuscript one day, the young novice took some scriptures to his room and started trying to decipher them. He was able to read in Thai but so far had not received any instruction in the Cambodian alphabet. Nevertheless, on his first attempt, he found that he could read the Cambodian characters with ease. He had learned them in his previous life when he was a monk.

The witnesses I interviewed in this case were the three daughters of Leng, then living at Kraton Village, Surin, and several neighbours who had known Phra Rajsuthajarn's parents and had witnessed his identifications. The first daughter, Mrs. Pah, said that she was about 22 when her father, Leng, died. When Phra Rajsuthajarn was about four years old he recognized her and said, "I am your father." He called her by her name, then started addressing her by her baby nickname. This had annoyed her at first, as she was then a married woman. She said that Phra Rajsuthajarn's character and habits exactly resemble those of her late father. For one thing, he liked to go naked to the waist, as Leng had done, and before becoming a monk he had like Leng showed a great interest in religion, paying regular visits to the temple.

The second daughter, Mrs. Poh, gave much the same account, adding that Phra Rajsuthajarn had mentioned to her many incidents in the life of Leng which she knew were true. Mrs. Pi, the third daughter, confirmed the testimony of the other two. As a child, she added, Phra Rajsuthajarn used to become angry if they did not address him as father. Long before he was able to talk, she said, he made signs of recognition with his hands whenever he saw her and her sisters. When he did this, his gestures were characteristic of those her father used to make to his children.

The three daughters were interviewed in their old house in the village, where they had lived with their father. It is a typical Thai village house of wood, on piles. Phra Rajsuthajarn pointed out the spot on the verandah where in his post-mortem consciousness he had seen his own body lying before cremation. I also visited the house in which he was born. Passing through the village I noticed that he was treated with great respect by the inhabitants, especially by the elders who had witnessed some of the recognitions of his when he was a child. My interpreters on this case were Dr. Thavil Soon Thararaksa, Provincial Health Officer, Surin, and Mr. Sujib

Punyanubhab, a lecturer at a Bangkok college for monks.

The case of Phra Rajsuthajarn is very well known in Thailand, having been the subject of investigation by Prof. Amphai Sutdharitkul of Chulalongkorn University, Bangkok. Prof. Sutdharitkul took films and made tape recordings during her investigation. She had shown them on Thai television. I did not see nor hear them either before or after my own investigation of the case but I understand that the same evidence was given.

The three daughters of Leng all agreed that Phra Rajsuthajarn is completely different from their father physically but resembles him in character. Leng was tall, strong, and good-looking, whereas Phra Rajsuthajarn is below middle height and of meager build. His general appearance is frail but he assured me that he has always enjoyed good health. The fact that he was born before the previous personality, Leng, died, suggests that the psychic current of Leng, through a powerful attraction, must have projected itself into the body of the new-born child, permanently displacing the personality of the individual whose karma had actually formed the body in the womb.

While studying the case I had the opportunity of discussing it with some of the highest authorities on Buddhism in Thailand, including the late Supreme Patriarch of the Thai Sangha. I was interested to find out whether they considered this as a case of rebirth, since it does not fit into the generally accepted pattern of events as defined by Buddhism. According to Buddhist teaching, the karma of a person who has died operates upon the psychophysical organism from the moment of conception, forming the fetus in conjunction with the hereditary biological factors contributed by the parents. But assuming that the case of Phra Rajsuthajarn and of several similar cases on record are genuine, apparently sometimes the disembodied personality projects itself after death into a body already prepared by the karma of another deceased person, displacing the original personality completely and for good. This presumably might happen through a strong force of attraction such as that which existed between Leng and his younger sister, as well as from other causes. It does not therefore necessarily conflict with the Buddhist teaching in this regard, I was told.

If that is what happened in the case of Phra Rajsuthajarn it would account very plausibly for the fact that the robust farmer, Leng, came back in a frail body which was not in the least like his own. It must in fact have been the physical vehicle formed by the karma of another person. Nevertheless, Leng's character traits survived together with his memory, perhaps because of the very short intermission between his death and rebirth. It is also interesting to note that Phra Rajsuthajarn, despite his appearance of debility, has sound health. This could be explained by the possibility that the karma of Leng imbued the frail body with a strength that did not belong to it originally. In this respect the case recalls a parallel one (that of Jasbir) studied in India by Prof. Ian Stevenson and described in his *Twenty Cases Suggestive of Reincarnation.*

These comments, in the present state of our knowledge, cannot be offered as anything more than tentative suppositions. Any phenomenon can be studied only by observing all that has occurred and then by formulating theories, modifying them or even discarding them if and when they are later found to be incompatible with facts. This must be especially so in an area where criteria are not rigidly defined and standards of judgement are not easily established. In studying cases suggestive of rebirth the theory of permanent possession of a given body by another personality is one of the possibilities that must be taken into account in view of the number of cases that seem to fall into this anomalous category.

I have to thank Prof. Ian Stevenson of the University of Virginia, and the Code Foundation, for having made my study of the case of Phra Rajsuthajarn possible. In Thailand I received valuable cooperation from Dr. Chien Siriyanand, psychiatrist of the Medical Section, Bangkok Juvenile Court, Col. Chalor Uthongpatchana, and the Society for Psychical Research, Thailand.

Appendix

A case remarkably similar to the present one has been reported from England. It is almost a rebirth case, but not quite. It is perhaps the most interesting of all, but unfortunately, since it happened many years ago, it has been impossible to obtain confirmatory evidence. The subject (W. Martin) wrote out an account of his experience which was published in the Sunday Express (London) on May 26, 1935. He related that in his youth he was working in a town many miles from his home. One day he was struck on the head by bricks from a collapsing wall. He was taken to hospital in an unconscious state and it was feared that he would die. A telegram was sent to his parents and was received by them at lunch time. They caught the next train and visited him in the hospital, where he was still in a deep coma. After a few hours he revived. As soon as he was able to speak he told them that he knew everything that had happened to them while he was unconscious.

While his body was lying in the hospital his consciousness had been present in his home. He had seen his mother open the telegram, and had been with them throughout the journey. He repeated the conversation his father and mother had had on the train, and described how his father had looked at his watch from time to time, worried because the train was late.

During part of this out-of-the-body experience he had been in the house of a neighbour, where a woman, one Mrs. Wilson, had just given birth to a female child. Seeing the baby he had felt a strong desire to enter its body and so take up life again. He felt that he could have done so, and indeed had to struggle against the temptation. Only the thought of his grieving parents prevented him. Later inquiries proved that the woman he named had in fact given birth to a girl at the time he stated.

The youth afterwards made a complete recovery, but the memory of his experience remained with him throughout his life. His written account of it ended with the words: "I am convinced that if I had willed myself into that baby's body, today I would be a Miss Wilson, instead of still being—W. Martin."

The particular interest of this case is in the fact that it very closely resembles the after-death experiences described by Phra Rajsuthajarn, who entered the body of the child that was born to his sister one day before his death. That such parallel experiences could happen to two persons of widely different cultural background, religion, race, and geographical situation, between whom there could be no connection whatever in thought or belief, is strongly presumptive evidence that such experiences, although not normally remembered, are universal.

XX

What Happens Between Incarnations?

The Cases of Private Keaw; Nang Tong Klub; U Sobhana

There are cases of what I call "spontaneous" recall of past lives. I distinguish these cases from those in which persons claim to remember a previous life during hypnotic regression or have been told of previous lives by psychics such as Edgar Cayce. Nor do I call "spontaneous" those cases in which people attain knowledge of previous lives through meditation—as happens very frequently in the Orient.

In typical cases of spontaneous recall, as soon as the child is able to talk he mentions things relating to his memories of a previous life. Usually the child will talk about a previous family, previous mother and father, sometimes making comparisons not very flattering to the present parents. In many of these cases we have found that the personality described by the child can be identified as someone who actually lived. We have found persons corresponding to the child's description of former relatives and they have confirmed many of the things which the child has said.

It was my privilege to assist Dr. Ian Stevenson, Professor of Psychiatry at the University of Virginia School of Medicine, when he visited Ceylon, and he included several of the cases which concerned us in his book *Twenty Cases Suggestive of Reincarnation*. I have published others in my little book, *The Case for Rebirth*, and in *Fate* Magazine. So in this article I wish to concern myself with cases in which a subject claims to remember not only the previous life but an intermediate state between the two lives.

One such case is that of a private in the Thai army, Private Keaw. (That is his only name; second names seldom were used by ordinary people at that time.) The case was related to me by Keaw's commanding officer, Capt. Luang Varionnakaran, whom I interviewed on September 11, 1966, with Dr. Charoon, a Thai medical man, acting as interpreter.

Keaw was a private in the Fourth Platoon, Eighth Company, Second Regiment of the Royal Guard Division in the year 1912. His home was in Dang village near Wat Anung (a wat is a Buddhist temple), situated in the lower area of Paklad district, Thailand. Private Keaw was 18 in 1912 and had told the story of his previous life to his friends. Captain Luang, then a sub-lieutenant, heard of the case but made no effort to verify it himself.

His commanding officer, Varn Gangasavara, however, went to Paklad and there met Private Keaw's parents, both his present ones and those of his claimed previous life. Private Keaw's previous father had died but the previous mother was still living, as were both his present parents. Varn Gangasavara was able to confirm Keaw's statements about his previous life and learned that his previous mother accepted Keaw as her son reborn. Captain Luang did not remember the names of the previous parents nor the details of the dates but did recall that these had all been confirmed as accurate during Varn's investigation.

Private Keaw had told Luang that in his previous life he had wanted to become a village monk but before he could be ordained had died of cholera at about the age of 20. He remembered that he had not realized that he was dead and tried without success to speak to his relatives and friends. He saw his relatives giving food to monks, the Buddhist equivalent of holding a Mass for the souls of the dead. The monks are given presents and food in the name of the deceased and the merit of the action is thought to be passed on to him so that his state in the next life may be improved.

One day they held a religious ceremony in Keaw's house and *paritta*, a religious chant, was recited. As the monks ceased the chanting and were leaving the house Keaw noticed certain peculiarities about his own body and realized for the first time that he was dead. He then followed the monks. Everything seemed ordinary to him except that he was able to walk through people and as soon as he thought of a place he immediately found himself there. He did not feel hungry. When Luang asked him if he felt afraid of anything during that time Keaw said that he was afraid of a drunken man walking and of a child in case they should fall on him. Keaw seemingly felt himself to be very small. He could not remember being angry but had seen other spirits angry at living persons who threw stones or spat. They feared they might be hit. This is rather a typical example of what you would expect a man in the East to experience after death. The after-death experience seems to be coloured to a large extent by the expectations of the person who has died.

One day Keaw saw a living woman approaching and felt a liking for her. When she came close he got into the basket she was carrying. At the edge of the fence around the woman's house the dog barked at the basket. Keaw became frightened. He ran away and hid by a nearby bridge. There he stayed until dusk when the woman came out to bathe in the *klang* (a canal or waterway in Thailand). He went up to her and embraced her around the neck. He felt comforted and no longer was afraid of the dog. A little while later he lost consciousness. When he again became aware of his surroundings he found he was an infant and had been reborn to that woman.

A similar case, again from Thailand, is that of Nai Chook, who also remembered his previous family. He said that when he recognized his previous mother she said to him, "Why did you not come to my womb to be born of me again?" He told her he had been unable to enter the house because of the sacred thread. The sacred thread is part of the ceremony which follows death in a Buddhist country. In the house of the deceased person the monks chant from the sacred scriptures and hold a thread which is passed around to all those present. Everyone takes hold of it and it is thought to become imbued with magical potency through the chanting. Sections of it are cut off and worn around the right wrist of all those who were present at the chanting, while the remainder of the thread is put around the house to keep out spirits. In the East people have a great fear of spirits, even of their own deceased relatives. Accordingly Nai Chook was afraid to enter the house because this thread hung over the door and windows. He waited outside for his mother but she did not come out. Then he went to the well thinking she would go there.

Instead, his present mother in his present life had come to the village to exchange sugarcane for rice. When she stopped by the well he attached himself to her by getting into the basket she was carrying—just as in the previous case. Nai Chook remembered and could name the place she stopped on her way home, Wat Tao It, 17 kilometers (about 10.5 miles) south of her home. There she took a drink of water from the canal by the wat. He got into the water and as soon as she drank it he lost consciousness.

The informant who told me this story was under the impression that Nai Chook gave all these details before he identified any of these people and he claimed they were memories of his post-mortem state.

Another of my cases from Thailand is that of a young monk named Phra Som Pit Hancharoen, who lived some distance from Bangkok in Ban Sae village, where he was born on November 3, 1939. When he started talking at the age of three he spoke of his memories of a previous life, although they were blurred in places as if he were remembering a movie he had seen. He claimed his previous name had been Nai Soey and that he had lived at Klong Bang Paklad, some distance from his present home. He mentioned these names to his mother and told her that in his previous life he had been stabbed to death at Khoo Sang Wat, Bang Paklad, about two kilometers (one and a quarter miles) from his present home.

He was about 45 when he died and he gave this account of his death. He had gone to a cremation ceremony at the Khoo Sang Wat. There he met a woman, Nang Hom, whom he had known previously. Under the influence of alcohol he had tried to make love to her. When he touched her she drew a knife and stabbed him on the left breast just where he now has a birthmark. I have seen this birthmark, situated below the left nipple. It is a slightly pigmented raised mark and about three-eighths inch in diameter. His present mother told him that when he was born the birthmark was an open sore exuding pus and that it had to be treated like a wound in order to heal it.

All this was verified. There had been such a person and such a crime. Phra Som Pit also recognized some of his relatives from his previous life and gave their names. After his death, he reported, he felt as if he were in a dream. He wandered for a long time. He had been very drunk at the time of his death and that undoubtedly was one cause of his bewilderment. He moved along a path with dense jungle on either side; there were no houses to be seen. He felt clumsy but had no pain nor any sense of the wound. He could not recall having seen his body on the ground. This is an important point in cases where there are birthmarks which correspond to a wound on the body of the previous personality. Usually they have seen the wound and through some psychosomatic reaction it is transferred to the new body in the form of a birthmark. However, in this case Pra Som Pit said he did not look at his body. While he was wandering around he felt just as usual. He wore his usual form of dress; he was barefoot, in black villager's clothes with no headgear, just as when he was killed.

At last he came to a wooden cottage where an old man and woman lived. He asked them for a drink of water. The old woman gave him a bowl of water and a red fruit. She told him to drink the water and eat the fruit and went back into her house. He drank the water but did not eat the fruit. The woman came out again and asked if he had eaten everything and he said that he had, although actually he had thrown the fruit away. Leaving this house, he continued to walk but suddenly lost consciousness. He remembered nothing more until he was three years old in this life, at which time he saw a person whom he recognized as having been one of his children in his former life.

The fact that the old woman offered him the fruit is interesting. This occurred also in the case of Nang Tong Klub, a young woman I interviewed in 1963 in northern Thailand. She had been born to her present mother for the second time. The mother told this story: She had a daughter of whom she was very fond but the girl unaccountably was drowned one day in the canal beside the local temple. Shortly after the girl's body was buried the mother had a dream in which a man dressed in white entered her room. He was a big man, rather stout. White, of course, is not worn by Buddhist monks—they wear yellow—but it is worn by yogis who practise the religious life but have not been ordained into a Buddhist monastic order. This man told her not to worry about her daughter. He said she was safe and with him and he was prepared to give her daughter back to her if she would donate so many gold and so many silver images to the temple in his name.

After having this dream the mother hurried to carry out the instructions of the man in white. She donated the images to the temple and at the same time made the wish that her daughter would be returned to her and that she would have specified marks by which she could be recognized. One mark was to be a slight crinkle in the fold of the left ear and the other was to be a number of small black dots, like blackheads, just below the lip. Finally, she asked that the child be born on a Thursday, which is a more fortunate day according to Thai ideas than the day on which the previous child had been born.

Shortly afterwards the mother became pregnant and in the course of time a girl was born to her on a Thursday. Her mother named her Tong Klub, which means "my treasure restored." The child had the little crinkle in the left ear—it is still quite visible in Tong Klub—but the marks that were supposed to be below the lip somehow were displaced to the chest. As soon as Tong Klub began to talk she called herself by the previous child's name. She spoke of many things her mother knew to be true, of clothes and household things she had used and of how she used to work hard to make money for her mother.

Tong Klub also remembered what happened to her after she drowned. She said she found herself in a place where there was a tall, stout man dressed in white whose description matched her mother's dream man. This man said he would keep her with him and he made her work for him but he also was very kind to her. He offered her some fruit, saying it would make her forget her previous life. But she didn't wish to forget and refused to eat the fruit. Instead she kept asking him to let her go back. Then he told her that if her mother would donate the Buddha images to the temple in his name he would let her be reborn as the daughter of her same mother. Thereafter, the next thing she knew she was back with her mother.

This is the second case in which a mysterious fruit plays a part. There are others. I have been unable to trace it but it seems to me there must be a legend in Thailand and possibly in Burma also, that after death we are offered fruit which causes us to forget our previous lives. It could be compared to the waters of Lethe, the river of forgetfulness, in Greek mythology. If you don't eat the fruit you retain your memory. I have not come across this idea in any reincarnation cases in Ceylon or India, though we do have recurring the idea of a man who appears to the disembodied entity, takes charge of him, and sometimes leads him to a new birth.

One such case is that of the Venerable U Sobhana, a Burmese Buddhist monk who was born on November 5, 1921, and died in Myingyam Hospital in Thailand in 1964. He told me that from his earliest years he remembered his previous life. He had been a land surveyor named Maung Po Thit and had married Ma Shwethin. He had had one son, Maung Po Min, aged three. They had lived in Thanaungdaing village in Upper Burma. At the age of 36 he had contracted a severe fever and was sent to Myingyam Hospital. He remembers going by oxcart to the hospital and arriving there during a heavy monsoon rainstorm. After his arrival at the hospital he remembered nothing more until he found himself alone in the jungle feeling horrible, hungry and thirsty. He was in great distress and did not realize he had died. After about two or three hours he saw a very old man with a white beard and moustache, dressed in white and carrying a staff. On seeing this yogi his distress vanished.

The old man called him by name and told him he must follow him. He did so for about an hour at which time they reached a place he recognized as being near his village. They entered the village and went to his old home. The old man told him to wait outside by the fence while he went into the house. The disembodied entity waited and the old man emerged again after about five minutes. The old man then said, "You must follow me to another house." They went in a westerly direction about seven houses from his former home, to the house of the village headman. Again the yogi told him to wait outside. The old man came back out of the headman's house about five minutes later and beckoned U Sobhana to enter. Once inside he told him, "You must stay here. I will go back." Then the yogi disappeared. The subject saw people in the house but then remembered nothing more.

Meanwhile, his dead body was removed from the hospital and buried. Seven days later the monks were fed according to custom. That night his wife dreamed that she saw an old man dressed in white who said to her, "I am sending your husband to the village headman's house."

In the early morning she got up and went to the headman's house and told his wife about her dream. The headman's wife said she too had had a dream in which an old man appeared to her and told her he was entrusting Maung Po Thit to her family. He led Maung Po Thit into the house and then disappeared. From that day the headman's wife became pregnant and in time U Sobhana was born.

At the age of two he was able to tell her all the above things and they believed that the man he had seen in his prenatal state was the same old man she had seen in her dream and that his former wife had seen in her dream. He recognized all his previous relatives, friends, and property. He even remembered his old debts. U Sobhana told me he had seen the old man once again in this life. At a time of great crisis the old man appeared and cautioned him that, at all cost, he must tell the truth; otherwise things would be very bad for him. Venerable U Sobhana promised and indeed did follow the old man's advice and everything turned out well. It was not a dream but a vision, he told me. It was very late at night but he was not asleep and his vision was vivid and real.

This case echoes the almost universal belief that there is a guardian spirit or angel who comes to people's aid at times. It is reminiscent, too, of the spiritualist teaching that when one dies and enters the spirit world one is met by someone who instructs and even informs one of one's condition. Spiritualists and Buddhists agree that often the deceased does not realize he has died. They also agree that in the afterlife the deceased continues to experience what he experienced in life or what his training and cultural background have conditioned him to expect. Thus we may suppose that at death a Christian will go to a Christian-type heaven or a Christian-type purgatory and a Buddhist will go to a Buddhist-type heaven or purgatory.

I think it is really irrelevant to ask whether these experiences are objective realities or purely subjective creations. When we dream we undergo experiences that at the time of dreaming are as real to us as any we experience when awake. I think it would be arbitrary to make any distinction between the reality in the dream state and the reality in the waking state except to observe that the latter is a state which we share with others whereas the dream state is a private world of experiences.

We now come to the problem of what sort of bodies "disembodied" entities or spirits may possess. Some mediumistic controls claim they possess a body analogous to a human body, having eyes, ears, sex organs, and so forth. Prof. C.D. Broad comments that although we may find such claims hard to swallow we have no right to ignore them. The fact that such statements are made must presumably indicate something genuine and important even if it is only in the psychology of the medium, he says.

But here we have evidence indicating the same sort of body, but evidence which does not come through mediums but from living persons who say they remember being in that state between earthly lives. We also find a curious similarity between these prenatal experiences and those reported by individuals who claim to have had out-of-the-body experiences. Such OOBEs are called variously astral projections or projections of the etheric body. In Buddhism the etheric body is called *manomayakāya*, the mentally-formed body. I think it amounts to the same thing. There is such a body, of a different substance from the physical body and possibly existing on a slightly different vibrational level. When we consider how many living people experience being outside their bodies we must grant that very real experiences are represented here and that they throw an important light on the state in which we may find ourselves when we die. This also is in accord with the teachings in *The Tibetan Book of the Dead*, the treatise of Tibetan lamaism translated by W.Y. Evans-Wentz and designed to instruct newly disembodied consciousnesses.

I have collected many more cases of memories of post-mortem and prenatal states. Many feature the yogi in white and several of them feature the fruit of forgetfulness. The cases I have quoted are representative of the material I have gathered. It must be understood that there is nothing evidential in those stories; they are purely on an anecdotal level. We have no means of checking up on them as we have checked on the memories of previous earthly lives such as I have helped Dr. Ian Stevenson collect. So far as research on reincarnation is concerned the cases that can be neither proved nor disproved must be put aside. But I do think that in the context of psychic research as such they still have considerable value.

It would be useful to compare the experiences related by Asians with those Westerners have put on record—we have many instances of the latter also. In fact, the material we have on hand is enough to furnish substance for a great deal of research.

XXI

Notes on Miscellaneous Cases of Rebirth Memories

Introduction

The following cases investigated during the 1960s are for one reason or another lacking in verifiable details, but they have been investigated so far as circumstances allowed. Such strength as they have comes for the most part from the character and status of the persons who furnished them, from the fact that the subjects have nothing material to gain by their claims to recollect (using the word in its widest sense) previous lives, and from the general impression of probity and sincerity they made in offering their experiences. In some of the cases the circumstances related have been known for many years to friends of the subject, and wherever possible their testimony has also been taken. In some instances there is a possibility of further verification from sources not accessible at the time these notes were made.

Ceylon (Sri Lanka)

I

Ranjith Makalanda, son of Mr. Makalandage Sam de Silva, of Kotte, Ceylon, at about the age of three and a half years, told his mother, brothers, and sisters: "You are not my relatives. My father and the others are in England." He said his father was employed on a big steamship, and used to return home after going on voyages round the world. He used to carry his father's lunch to the place where he worked, and would take his sister to church on Sundays on his motorcycle. He described wintry conditions in England, with snow and frost, such as he had never experienced in his life in Ceylon. He gave other descriptions of his previous life, which fitted in with conditions in England.

Once, on his birthday, his parents told him that his English mother was going to speak to him over the radio. They had previously sent birthday greetings to be broadcast for him from Radio Ceylon on that date. When the time came he pressed close to the loudspeaker, and when the woman announcer's voice was heard reading his message, he said: "That's my Mummie! That's the way she speaks." The English accent of the announcers on Radio Ceylon is closer to standard English than is normally heard there. Ranjith Makalanda, according to his father's statement, was a misfit in his environment. He considered himself to be an English boy, and showed many of the characteristics of one, preferring English food to Sinhalese, and exhibiting an independent spirit and many mannerisms that were more Western than Sinhalese. At the age of fourteen he wanted to leave school and work. Later on, he realized his cherished ambition to go to England, where he at once felt at home, obtained work, and in general adapted himself better toconditions there than to those in Ceylon.

Among the many un-Sinhalese characteristics Ranjith showed were a preference for bread and butter to rice, and the use of knives and forks instead of eating with his fingers. Unlike other Sinhalese children he would never go barefoot, but always insisted on wearing shoesand socks. From his earliest years he showed no affection for his parents, but was constantly talking about his home and mother in England. His family are all Buddhists, but Ranjith insisted that he was a Christian. He is now a Buddhist.

There is no objective verification of this case, since the boy could not recall names or other precise data, but the psychological evidence is very strong. It may be mentioned that at the time when Ranjith started talking about his previous life, some twenty years ago, his father had a strong dislike of the English on political grounds, and there was nothing in the child's environment to encourage him in a belief that he was English. On the contrary, everything was against the development of such a fantasy.[60]

2

In Ambalangoda, Ceylon, a girl of seven, Prasantha Ramani Senawardena, claimed to remember a previous life in Manipur, India, when she was a dancer. This child, without any previous instruction, was able to perform very intricate Indian dances at a very early age. She described the place where she had formerly lived as being very far from Ceylon. It was beside a river, with a suspension bridge close by and a few shops on the further bank. The house was a large one, with six rooms, and could be seen from the bridge. In the household there were her uncle, elder sister, elder brother, two younger sisters, and one younger brother. One of her elder sisters was a better dancer than she was herself. Her uncle's work was unloading red onions for the ships that plied along the river. She said her own name was Rani, her elder brother's name Chandram, and her elder sister who was the better dancer was named Indrani. These are Indian names not common among the Sinhalese.

She often talked about this previous life, usually after periods of silent thought. Once she said: "Some distance from our home there is a place where films are shown. My elder sister and I went there several times. The name of the hall is Dharani."

When she was asked how she came to be born in Ceylon she replied: "One day my elder brother was bathing in the river. There is a huge rock at the bathing place on the river, part of it on the bank and the rest in the water. I sat on the rock and watched my brother, and while doing so I fell down from the big rock onto another pile of rocks. My leg was broken. My elder sister took me to the hospital and I was put on a bed. From there I came here."

Prasantha said that if she was taken to Manipur she would be able to recognize and point out all the places and people she had mentioned. Her parents expressed their willingness for her to be subjected to the fullest investigation, but it has not been possible to take her to Manipur for the purpose. She has undoubted talent as a dancer, having been awarded several prizes at Sinhalese dance festivals. Professional dancers are of the opinion that she ranks with the best of them.

(Case investigated by Francis Story in 1962.)

3

Ranjith Anura Senanayake, a boy of three living at Rattota, Ambagasthanne, Ceylon, began giving information about a previous life, saying that he had lived at a place called Butanne. He said his former father wore a striped sarong and had small "blisters" on his head. He went to his office daily and came home late at night. His mother used to go to the market and buy food, bringing back a lot of *pakkade*, a certain kind of cake, of which he was very fond. He remembered how she used to milk the cow and boil the milk before giving it to him. He said he loved his previous mother more than his present one. The house they had lived in was larger than his present home; it had a tiled roof and fruit trees in the garden. There was a lot of furniture inside, including a big almirah, at the bottom of which there was a money-box in which he used to keep his savings. Ranjith used several words which he had never heard in the present life, among them some English ones. He said that his former schoolteacher was called "Madam," that he used to wear a necktie. His schoolteacher used to pat his head on parting and say "Ta-ta!" This is an English form of saying "goodbye"

179

to children. It was another of the words Ranjith had never heard in his present life.

He gave several other items of identification. It has not, however, been possible to verify these, presumably because the previous life was a long time ago. Even the name of the place Ranjith claims as his former home seems to have been changed. Nevertheless, the child clearly has a very vivid memory of his previous birth, and often cries to be taken to Butanne.

(Case investigated by Francis Story in 1963.)

Burma

I

U Ba Hlaing (alias Peter Knight), born on January 2, 1927, at Maymyo, Upper Burma, was one of twins. When he started talking he said that he had been a captain in the British Army, and his younger twin had been his Indian servant. He had been a European (presumably English) and was married to a European girl. He remembered having many horses, and that there was a war. They invaded a number of countries, fighting with firearms. Finally his army was defeated, and as he did not want to be taken prisoner he killed his wife and servant, then himself.

Many other details were given by the child to his mother, who wrote them down at the time, but unfortunately her record was subsequently lost. The child always treated his younger twin as a servant, and called him by that name instead of addressing him as "brother." Although the children were twins they were completely different in appearance; Ba Hlaing was fair and thin, while his brother was dark and stout. This fact was attested by their sister. Whenever the father beat him, Ba Hlaing would hold his hands above his head in the military attitude of surrender. The younger twin reacted to beatings quite differently, standing rigid and silent. He was a quiet, sad, submissive boy, quite different in temperament from Ba Hlaing. The latter was more intelligent. The twin brother died in 1942.

Ba Hlaing always had a liking for English clothes; he preferred to dress in white, whereas the Burmese are fond of colours. He always insisted that his clothes should be very clean.

(Ba Hlaing and his sister were interviewed by Francis Story in Rangoon, 1961.)

2

Michael Ohn Gaing was born of Burmese parents in Bombay on October 28, 1950. His father's name was U Ohn Gaing and his mother was Daw Khin May Yee, otherwise known as Mary Knight (her father was Indian, her mother Burmese).

At the time the child was conceived, the parents were living in Rambagh, Mankhut, some distance from Bombay. Shortly before the boy was born, Mrs. Ohn Gaing had a dream, in which she went to the Fort, Bombay, and bought an aluminium box at the market. An Indian jumped into the box and accompanied her home in it. Michael was born a few months later.

Mrs. Ohn Gaing has had seven children, including one pair of twins. Before every birth she had a significant dream. About two months before the twins were conceived she dreamed of a double cactus, two shoots on a single stem.

At about the age of two years and six months Michael started talking to his elder brother and the servant girl, saying that he had five children in India—three sons and two daughters. He said he was a "doodh-wallah" (milkman) and was very fond of playing cards. He always showed great interest in cows and was always drawing them. Rambagh, where his parents had been living, was a "doodh-wallah" area; his parents had left India and returned to Burma when Michael was two months old, so he could not have known these things by any normal means.

Michael's father had an old station wagon, the engine of which was always giving trouble. When this occurred, the child would say: "Buy a better car, Father. I have plenty of money." He told them he had his money hidden under a mango tree, in a big trunk. He also talked of his house, described it, and drew pictures of it.

As they had left India, his parents were not able to verify any of these statements about the house and family, but the child's behaviour was thoroughly consistent with his claims. He talked much of his previous family and showed great interest in cows. He was fond of drawing them and liked little toy cows, which his mother used to give him as presents. He was continually talking about cattle.

At the age of five he was living in Rangoon with his parents. One day, during the monsoon, they were all sitting at the front of the house, looking out, when suddenly Michael started crying loudly. When asked why, he pointed to a cow outside, saying that it should be fed. Usually Michael was not given to crying without good reason. This interest in cows and their welfare is a decidedly Indian characteristic, and especially one of cattle owners. It is not found among the Burmese.

On another occasion, Michael saw some cows being driven to a mosque for sacrifice. He was very upset. He said the cows were crying, with tears rolling from their eyes. After that he always refused to eat meat.

When he was about eight, Michael was taken to visit an uncle in Upper Burma. There were several cows there, and the boy took it on himself to feed and look after them. "I must feed my cows," he used to say. Instead of playing with other boys, he was concerned only about the cattle. He found a tree with fruit they liked (the *Koke-ko*) and spent his time collecting the fruit.

As the memories of his previous life appeared to make him sad, the parents tried to discourage him from talking and thinking about it.

The case was investigated by Francis Story in Rangoon in December 1961. He questioned the parents and the little boy. In reply to his questions, Michael said that in his previous life he had been an old man. His children had been present when he died. During the interview he showed emotion when talking about his family and the cows he had owned in the previous existence.

India

I

In 1964, Sunil Dutt, the four-year-old son of Mr. Chadammi Lal Saksena of Bareilly, India, claimed that he could remember his previous life.

It began when the child continuously refused to do any work for several days. Whenever he was given an odd job he asked his parents not to bother him but get to the work done by his servants. The parents did not take his talk abut his "servants" seriously. When his father took him to be admitted to a school, Sunil refused to study there; he said that he would study in his own school in Budaun.

When asked about this school, he said that he was Seth Krishna and that he owned a school in Budaun. There had been in fact a Seth Shrikrishna, who was founder of the Seth Shrikrishna Intermediate College, Budaun; he had died in 1951.

The astonished parents took the child to Budaun on December 29, 1963. Sunil at once recognized the college building and remarked that the big

182

signboard bearing his name was missing from the college wall. He indicated the place where it had formerly been fixed.

The little boy entered the college without any guidance and rushed towards the principal's room, but was disappointed on seeing a "stranger" in the principal's chair. In fact, the principal whom the late Seth had appointed had been removed from service after Seth's death.

Sunil was then taken to the Shri Krishna Oil Mill where he rushed to the "gaddi" and sat on it as Seth had been accustomed to do. Then he called for Shafaat, an old servant, and enquired about his well being.

Sunil then moved about happily in the mill and at one place he pointed out the signboard bearing his name. It was lying on a verandah, covered with dust.

Suddenly the child rushed to the side of the mill where Seth used to live and asked about his "wife." Seth's wife had been Mrs. Shakuntala Devi, but after Seth's death she had started living with Seth's adopted son in Mohalla, Birampur. When Sunil was told this he was extremely sad.

When shown a photograph of Seth's family, Sunil recognized Seth as himself, and also identified other members of the family.

When Sunil saw Seth's elder sister and brother-in-law among the people in the mill he touched their feet. He was very reluctant to leave the mill. While they were moving about the town Sunil pointed out the lofty gate of Gandhi Park, which he said he had erected himself in 1948.

Sunil recognized Mr. S.D. Pathak, the former principal of the S.K. College, among thirty people. He rushed up to him and embraced him. Then he seated himself in Mr. Pathak's lap. Sunil told his father, Mr. Saksena, that he would like to be taught by Mr. Pathak.

Later, Sunil was taken to the residence of Seth's widow. When they met they stood gazing at one another and tears came into their eyes. Sunil then asked her about the image of their family deity which, as Seth, he had presented to her. He recognized the box in which Seth kept his clothes. At parting, Sunil patted his "former wife."

A tonga was brought to carry him and his parents. The child then asked about his tonga, drawn by a black horse, and was distressed to learn that it had been sold.

When asked if he knew Mr. J.D. Shukla, I.C.S., who was District Magistrate of Budaun in 1947–49, the child replied in the affirmative. When shown a group photograph he recognized Mr. Shukla, who later became Commissioner of the Allahabad Division. The bewildered parents of Sunil did not allow the child to be photographed. They rushed him back to Bareilly and no one was allowed to question him any further. At a later date, however, a thorough investigation was made and the facts of the case were amply confirmed.

(This case was investigated by Francis Story and Dr. Ian Stevenson in 1964.)

2

The subject, S.B. Barua, was a Chittagong Buddhist who was born and reared in Upper Burma. He was living in Calcutta in 1963. A few years before 1963 he had practised meditation at the Kammayut Meditation Centre in Rangoon. He was unable to make any progress in developing the trance states because he was always disturbed by a continuous jingle of bells. The sound was like that of harness bells. At the same time he had a sensation of moving along and from time to time prickling and tickling sensations were felt in various parts of his body, as though he were being bitten by flies. He felt a desire to brush them off and was surprised to find that there were no flies in the room.

Considering the nature of his physical and auditory sensations during these attempts at meditation, he decided that the general impression they gave was that he was a horse drawing a carriage of some sort to the sound of harness bells. As he could not overcome this disturbance, he finally gave up meditation.

He stated that from his earliest years he had had a great affection for horses and a feeling of affinity with them. He was always moved by the sight of a suffering horse—a sight so common in India that scarcely anyone notices it. Furthermore, he had a knack of being able to tame horses and gain their confidence. He had often calmed restless horses when other people had failed.

His physical structure, he thought, was rather suggestive of a horse and, in fact, he was unusually tall and large boned for a Chittagonian. His face was long, with a long, slightly curved nose, large teeth and a receding forehead. He was aware of his horselike face but apparently did not know that the resemblance was even more striking in profile. His voice was nasal, sometimes drawling, and had a horselike quality in its timbre, particularly when he spoke meditatively as though to himself, which he often did. As a boy he had been active, fond of games, and a good runner. Psychologically, he had a rather slow mind and was highly suggestible.

I showed him a method of obtaining mental concentration and while doing so put him under hypnosis. This was repeated several times at intervals of a few days until he was able to carry out a post-hypnotic suggestion. (He was made unable to speak or understand Bengali, his mother tongue.) Under regression he again heard the jingling bells and had the same sensations as in meditation. The regression, however, was not complete.

Comments on the Case

Very little by way of comment is possible in this case. There is no obvious reason why a man should wish to identify himself with a horse; at the same time no objective proof of his belief can be obtained. This subject had a strong conviction that his previous life was an equine one but whether this suggested itself to him by reason of his "horsy" appearance and his empathy, and was later reinforced by a meditation-induced fantasy, it is impossible to say. The case is not one that could be offered for scientific appraisal.

Thailand

I

Phra Kemy was a Cambodian Buddhist monk staying, in 1963, at Wat Mahamakut Buddhist University, Bangkok. He spoke French and English. He stated that when he was about ten years of age his parents told him that in his infancy he had said that he was their dead eldest son reborn. He made this claim when he first began to talk, saying that he had followed his parents from the cremation ground and stayed with them until he was able to get reborn. He told them his former name, Teav Seang, correctly.

Both his parents were then dead, but his sisters and brothers were still living at his birthplace in Cambodia. They called him by his former name, Teav Seang, and he regarded his (present) elder sister as his younger sister. He did not remember anything else and was inclined to doubt the rebirth story. His only reason for doubting it appeared to be the fact that he could not remember what he told his parents when he first began to talk; yet he did not think they would have deceived him or have been deceived themselves. He did not know how old Teav Seang was when he died but believed his age was between 16 and 17. He could not say whether he resembled Teav Seang in any way. He believed a period of several years elapsed between Teav Seang's death and his birth.

185

Phra Kemy was highly cooperative and readily submitted to hypnosis by Dr. Chien Siriyananda but regression was not successful. As he was returning to Cambodia soon after this session, there was no opportunity for further attempts at regression.

In relating his story, the young monk showed himself deeply interested in his case but hesitant about believing it and obviously very scrupulous in not going beyond what he could assert from his own knowledge. It is most probable that his doubts are the result of being exposed to modern (materialistic) ideas in the course of his education. He reads widely in French and English.

There is a possibility of further investigation of his case at a later date in Cambodia. He is a good hypnotic subject and regression might be achieved in a second or third session. Further evidence could be obtained from his relatives and others in his native village.

2

Lam Sam Kantapurar's father was a Punjabi Sikh who had become a Buddhist; his mother remained a Sikh. The child (born in 1955) was attending the Sammajiva-silpa Mulnidhi Buddhist School, Bangkok. He started talking soon after reaching the age of two. At that age he saw a picture of a deva (Buddhist minor deity) and pointing to it said: "That is a yakkha." ("Yakkha" is the Buddhist scriptural term for a certain class of deity; it is not in common use today in that sense.) His parents were certain that he had not heard the word in his present life. The child told them that formerly he had been a Chinese, after that a deva, and now he was an Indian. He liked to listen to Chinese music on the radio more than anything else and showed some marked Chinese characteristics. He would never drink milk, but always asked for tea; even in 1963 he would not drink milk unless it was coloured. When sleeping he would always roll up his singlet as the Chinese often do. His parents and teachers said that his voice had a Chinese inflection, and that his pronunciation of Hindi was not clear and good like that of his brother and sisters. But what struck them as most peculiar was the fact that Lam Sam always preferred to play with Chinese children and refused to associate with his Indian school fellows. If his Chinese friends came to watch his television he welcomed them, but he drove Indians and Thais away. The headmistress of the school, Mrs. Sisalab Kokilananda, who was present at my interview, corroborated this; she had often noted that he preferred to play with the Chinese boys and considered it very remarkable.

186

Questioned through an interpreter, the boy said that he clearly remembered certain facts of his life as a Chinese. He had owned a meat shop and used to kill animals—chickens, ducks, and pigs—for sale and for his own table. But towards the end of his life he had given up killing animals and eating meat, which is why he was subsequently reborn as a deva and then as an Indian. He could not remember anything about his family as a Chinese but believed that life was a long time ago and that he was a deva for a long period. Asked what kind of clothes the devas wore, he said they dressed in Chinese style. He said he would prefer to be a Chinese now but would not kill animals. In his present life he had always refused to eat meat.

Comments on the Case

The child's environment and family background presented some interesting features. The father, who·was the proprietor of a bookshop in a quarter of Bangkok where there was a small Sikh community, had been domiciled in Thailand for a number of years and became a Buddhist through environmental influence. He had discarded the characteristic Sikh insignia, but his wife still wore Punjabi dress and had not adopted Buddhism. The boy, Lam Sam, was being given a Buddhist education but through his mother's influence he still wore the long hair of a Sikh. It appeared that there was no tension in the family on account of religious differences and the children were not in any way affected. None of the family spoke English.

In view of the strong communal feeling among Indians, which is, if anything, even more marked among those domiciled abroad, Lam Sam's preference for Chinese playmates was something quite extraordinary. Questioning of the father and mother failed to reveal any possible psychological cause for it in the present life. It was agreed by all who knew the boy that he differed markedly from his siblings in his tastes and behaviour patterns and in several respects still refused to conform to the norms of Indian life. For example, he disliked sitting cross-legged to eat, preferring to take his meals seated on a chair at a table.

Physically, he was slender and fair skinned and, although not abnormally fair for a Punjabi, was lighter in colour than his parents. His siblings were not present for comparison. Mentally, he was alert and appeared to be intelligent. When questioned about his previous life, he seemed to be making a strenuous effort to remember, but could not recall any factual details which might have given an indication of the period to which the Chinese life belonged. Neither could he give any detailed information concerning the intermediate birth. (According to Buddhist doctrine, life in the heavenly realms may extend over a period of many centuries.) Lam Sam's parents said that at a very early age he knew some Chinese words but the possibility that he might have learned these from the Chinese children with whom he liked to associate cannot be excluded.

The mother, Amrit Gaur, was interviewed separately, with an Indian Buddhist monk, Ven. Nāgasena, of Wat Benchamabophitr, interpreting. She confirmed the evidence given by the father as to the boy's preference for Chinese companions. There were no Chinese people living near her at the time the child was conceived or at his birthplace. She remembers that whereas the births of her other children had been difficult, the delivery of Lam Sam was an easy one. While acknowledging all the facts related above, she seemed disinclined to believe that her son was a Chinese in his previous life. Asked directly about her impression, she replied that she could not be certain whether she believed it or not. Her reluctance obviously sprang from an emotional bias.

3

The next case differs from others in that the subject, Bua Pun, was not seen and it was approached from the viewpoint of those associated with the personality of the supposed previous life whose name was Snien (pronounced Sunyin).

Information about the case originally came from Mrs. Sawaeng Kamphol, of Dhonburi. She could not remember the present name of the subject but said that the mother of Snien was a relative of hers. She gave a present address for the subject and letters were sent to officials of the district to trace the man but no reply was received up to the time I left Thailand so that the case could not be fully investigated.

According to Mrs. Sawaeng Kamphol's first account, Bua Pun was (in 1963) between 32 and 33 years of age. When a child, he said that his mother of the present life was not his real mother and went on to describe another person who, he said, was his true mother. He also gave a description of the clothes he wore just before his death and made references to his cow. These statement were later found to agree with the facts of Snien's life. Mrs. Sawaeng spoke no English and the account she was able to give through an interpreter was very sketchy. She had not been an eyewitness of any of the events.

Subsequently, Mrs. Sawaeng Kamphol arranged a meeting for me to interview the parents of Snien, Nai Phoon, and his wife, Sai, both aged sixty.

Nai Phoon and his wife stated that they had five children, the first two being twins named Snien and Snun, both boys. Snien died in 1930 at the age of two years, six months. Some years after his death, his mother, Sai, met the grandmother of Bua Pun at a temple and was told by her that the child, Bua Pun, claimed to remember his previous life and said that his name had been Snien. The grandmother said that the description he had given of his former mother seemed to indicate that he had been Sai's son. She went on to say that at the age of three or four he had said to his present mother: "My own mother is much better than you." He had also said to his brother: "Your mother is no good. Mine is much better." When he was asked where his own mother was living he pointed towards the north. The former parents' house was actually to the north of where he was living and about three kilometers distant.

The child was then brought to Nai Phoon and Sai, and a large crowd gathered to witness the meeting. The boy was told to sit on his former mother's lap. He went straight to Sai without any prompting and climbed onto her lap. He showed her every sign of affection to be expected from a child greeting its mother. After that he spontaneously recognized Nai Phoon who until this happened had not believed the story. Nai Phoon said to the child: "Baby, if you are mine, can I keep you here?" The child replied, "I have always longed to be here." He then began roaming about the house examining things. Sai followed him around and saw that he behaved just like someone returning to his old home. Sai said to him from time to time: "Do you remember this and that?" The boy said he did, but presently he remarked, "The house is different now. It has been altered." This was true; the roof had been altered and a part of the house where their son used to sleep had been pulled down. Then Bua Pun asked: "Where is my cow, Sau?" Snien had had a cow of that name but it had been sold after his death. He also asked to be given his gold necklace (chain). The mother had actually given gold chains to both the twins. She brought them both out and asked Bua Pun to take the one he thought was his own, which he did without hesitation. This chain had a pink stone, the other a white one. Nai Phoon and Sai stated that Bua Pun was almost identical in appearance with their child, Snien.

Comments on the Case

The investigation of this case had only begun when I was obliged to leave Thailand and it is necessarily incomplete. Apart from the fact that the subject, Bua Pun, was not seen, there are many obvious gaps in the testimony of Nai Phoon and Sai. Dates are completely lacking and from the given data it cannot be said that Bua Pun could not have been primed with the necessary information by his parents. The only substantial fact was the strong conviction of Nai Phoon and his wife that Bua Pun was their son reborn. One other point should be mentioned. When asked whether Bua Pun later received any gifts from them, Nai Phoon replied that he often came to them for help, as his present parents were in poor circumstances.

4

The subject of the next case, John Coleman, was a 33-year-old American who agreed to participate in an experiment in hypnotic regression to a possible previous life. The experiment took place in Bangkok on January 12, 1963. The subject had already been hypnotized several times by Dr. Siriyananda.

On this occasion, Dr. Chien hypnotized him again and then "transferred" him to me for regression. He was regressed to fifteen by counting down; then to six; then to two. He answered well, using the present tense. From two, he was regressed ten years back. He made no response to repeated questions, but showed definite physical reactions. At the count down to nine, he gave a start, as though experiencing a shock. This would coincide with the transition to the prenatal stage. After that his head sank down and he became as if comatose. He was regressed another ten years and questioned again.

What is your name?	(It sounded like) Powell.
Where are you?	(No reply)
What can you see?	House.
What kind of house?	Leaves and mud.
Anything else	Cows.
What are you doing?	Leaning on a stick.
What is your age?	Twenty-seven.
What is your father's name?	Michael.
His other name?	(No answer)
What is your mother's name?	Anna.

190

Any brothers or sisters?	Sister.
What is her name?	Olenka.
Where are you now?	(No answer)
Name the place.	(No answer)
What is the nearest big city?	Bucharest. (*At this stage I realized that the name which had sounded like Powell must have been Pavel.*)
Have you ever been there?	No.
What do you do?	Farming.
Do you read newspapers?	No.
What is the Government doing?	Making war.
With whom?	Hungary.

(*He was regressed another ten years*)

Now what is your name?	Pavel.
Father's name?	Mikhail (Here he gave the Slavonic pronunciation.)
Mother?	Anna.
Other name?	(No reply)
Tell me in you own language what you are doing.	(No reply)

When the question was repeated Coleman replied after a long pause, with some unintelligible words. As he was showing signs of uneasiness, he was brought back to the present. To test the depth of the trance he was then given a post-hypnotic suggestion which he carried out on awakening.

After the session, I asked the subject some questions and it transpired that he was a first generation American whose parents came from Yugoslavia.

I hypnotized the subject on three subsequent occasions and he gave the same replies. Each time his trance was tested by a post-hypnotic suggestion which he carried out. During the hypnotic trance his replies were laconic and apparently made with effort; it was found difficult to make him speak any language other than English, but he occasionally muttered some unintelligible phrases which sounded like a foreign language, although his utterances under hypnosis were always indistinct.

5

The subject of this case, Bongkuch, was born in February 1972 in the province of Nakhon Sawan. His parents were Pamorn Promsin and his wife, Sawayi.

Bongkuch started talking at the age of one year and six months. He said he wanted to go home. The first occasion of speaking of the previous life occurred when he had been sleeping and woke up. He said that he had another home. When he said this was not his home, his father became angry. Three or four months later he said his parents were not his real father and mother. He said he lived at Hua Tanon, and he told his former parents' names. He said his father was 'Chan Man (he meant to say "Achang" or teacher). He said he knew the way to his former home, but he was not taken there at first. But once when his father took him to Paknam Po the bus stopped at Hua Tanon and Bongkuch cried to get down. He told a neighbour he had been killed in his previous life. To an old woman of seventy named Kio he told the name of his murderer in the previous life.

When he was three he carried a big stick and beat the house post, saying, "I will kill you," at the same time naming Mr. Ban as one of his murderers. This occurred three or four times in one year. For the Thai word "Nai" (Mr.) he used the Laotian word "Bach," which is a somewhat derogatory form. He also called strangers by the Lao word "Maung" (?) instead of the Thai word. He called guava "bugsida," which is Lao, instead of using the Thai word "farang." His parents did not know the Lao word. He liked to eat glutinous rice with raw fermented fish instead of as a dessert. This he explained by saying that he was not a Thai, but a Lao.

One day the previous mother (and some other persons) came to see him. They called him Chamrat, and asked him about the murder. He said he went to a fair at the Wat, wearing shorts, a white shirt, a wrist watch, a gold ring, and a gold chain. Coming back he was hit in the back by one man and stabbed by the other. They took the watch and the chain, but could not get the ring off. Mr. Ban had been his friend. The harvest that year had been bad, the labourers had not been well paid, and that was the cause of the murder. When Chamrat's father, mother, niece, and nephew went to Bongkuch's home they (Bongkuch and the other children) played together and he talked to them in Laotian. He used a Laotian word his parents did not know. Two days later Bongkuch told his mother that he remembered the name of his former sister. When taken to the place of the murder Bongkuch told his father he felt afraid. He named twelve teachers and one monk at Hua Tanon.

His family had never heard of the previous family before. The second time Chamrat's mother visited Bongkuch she saw his father's bicycle and asked Bongkuch if he had had one in the previous life. He said: "Yes, a maroon coloured one." He also mentioned to Chamrat's mother a knife he used to own. It was hanging on the wall in her house. Bongkuch gave the names of the previous parents long before any contact was made with them; he also gave his own name as Chamrat. He had Laotian eating habits. Once he was sharpening a knife, and on his sister asking why, he replied, "To kill somebody." When she tried to stop him he became very angry, threw the knife, and cut her foot. He was rather bad tempered.

Chamrat was eighteen years old when he died in 1954. His father, Nai Man Poo Keo (aged 63), was interviewed. He confirmed that everything stated by Bongkuch about the murder and robbery was true. The official police record was found; the murder had occurred on April 9, 1954. Chamrat was a good-tempered boy; he was also cowardly, and always went everywhere with friends. He preferred glutinous rice to other kinds, and ate it with raw fermented fish. Chamrat had had a bicycle. His father took it with another to Bongkuch's house, and he identified Chamrat's, which was maroon. Bongkuch resembled Chamrat in features. The murderers had left the district, but were still living at the time of the investigation. Bongkuch recognized Chamrat's girl friend, Thien, and called her by name. He often acted like an adult. He said that he wanted to be a monk. He described two cows, giving their colouring. He said that when the murderers removed his gold chain they wounded his neck; this was confirmed. Sometimes Bongkuch used to say that he was eighteen years old. He described the roof of his former home, which was not like that of his present one. When the previous mother died Bongkuch cried; he asked to be taken to his other home and offered 300 bahts, all his savings, for her funeral ceremony.

Bongkuch's mother, Mrs. Sawai Promsin, said that Bongkuch told her that after the murder in Hua Tanon, he stayed by a bamboo tree close by. Chamrat's mother confirmed that there was one in that area. Bongkuch said he stayed there seven years and was not hungry. He said it was raining and that a bamboo shoot scratched him. He tried to go to his (previous) mother, but got lost in the market. He then saw his (present) father at a bus stop and came with him. Bongkuch's father said that it *was* raining on a day when he visited Hua Tanon about the time his wife became pregnant with

Bongkuch. Pregnancy started that month. Bonkuch saidthat he came with his (present) father by bus in his spirit form.

Sgt. Phoo Thatman (age 57), of Police Headquarters, recalled the murder case, which he had investigated. He described the wounds on the body and confirmed what Bongkuch had said about the clothing—white short-sleeved shirt, dark shorts, and no hat. There was a bamboo tree about twenty meters from the body. Some arrests were made, but the witness could not tell the subsequent history of the accused men. Two other police witnesses, however, said that the body was in long trousers.

(The case was investigated with Dr. Stevenson in 1966.)

6

The subject of this case, Somkroon Meetuam, was thirty-five years old at the time of the investigation in 1963. She was born at Bangmuang Village, Nakhon Sawan, where she was still living when I met her. She was the third child out of four. Her parents were Wan Meetuam and Ub Meetuam.

Somkroon remembered having been a Chinese woman, Nek Oiy, in her previous life. Her father had been Nai Sow, and her mother, Suan; they had lived at Payooha Village, Nakhon Sawan, about twenty miles from Bangmuang.

When Somkroon was about six years old she told her mother she did not want to live with her. She had been playing, and her mother told her to clean the house. Somkroon complained that her (present), mother was always troubling her and she wanted to return to her former mother. She said she lived in Payooha Village. Some time later an old woman came from Payooha selling oranges. When Somkroon learned of this she asked the old woman to take her back there. She told her mother's name correctly. On her return the old woman found the mother Suan and verified the fact that she had lost a child. Her only daughter, Nek Oiy, had died at the age of six. After that, Suan came by boat to Bangmuang to see Somkroon. Somkroon saw her on her way to school and immediately recognized her. She ran to her, calling "Mother!" She took her to the present parents' house, and there the two women had a quarrel because Suan wanted to take Somkroon home with her. Eventually, however, Somkroon was allowed to go with Suan on a visit. During that visit Somkroon asked about her clothes of the previous life and mentioned many things which convinced Suan that she was Nek Oiy reborn. Suan staged an identification with her husband, who was sceptical. Before Somkroon had seen him he placed himself among a number of other Chinese men in an opium hall he owned. Somkroon identified him immediately, though he had his back turned to her when she entered. Somkroon also showed that she knew her way about the house and village. She always preferred Chinese food to Thai. She used some Chinese words in her childhood, but her mother forbade her to use them.

When her mother asked Somkroon how she came to be born where she was, Somkroon replied, "You don't know anything about it. Of course I came with you. You took the bus and a boat, and I hung onto your clothes. That's how I came to you."

III

The Case for Rebirth

First published in 1959, as BPS Wheel No. 12/13.
Reprinted from the second, enlarged edition (1964).

XXII

The Case for Rebirth

Foreword to the
Second Edition

The first edition of this book was published in 1959. Since then, thanks to valuable assistance given by a parapsychology foundation in the United States, which is here gratefully acknowledged, I have been enabled to extend my researches over a wider field of cases of the recollection of previous lives in Ceylon, Thailand, and India. I am particularly indebted to the Society for Psychical Research of Thailand, under the patronage of His Holiness Somdej Phra Mahavirawongsa, and its members, including Dr. Chien Siriyananda, psychiatrist in charge of the Medical Division, Central Juvenile Court, Bangkok, for the help they have freely given to my researches in Thailand.

The cases I have personally studied, together with reports of others received from various parts of the world, are now being evaluated and classified, and the results will be published in due course. Until the work on them is completed it is not possible to publish the cases in detail, but I have added at the end of the book, in the form of notes, some tentative conclusions which at the time of writing seem to be indicated. It must be understood that these represent my own interpretations based upon my reading of the case histories as a Buddhist, and in the light of Buddhist doctrine as I understand it. I may find cause to modify them later on, and if that be the case I shall not hesitate to do so.

The body of evidence for the truth of rebirth has increased substantially since this book was first written. One highly interesting fact which has emerged is that despite the wide range of experiences the cases present, which is to be expected in view of the diverse religious, cultural, and racial backgrounds of the persons claiming to have these memories, they show many striking features in common. The similarities are especially noticeable in the accounts given of experiences in the intermediate state between one human life and another. These seem definitely to point to a universal type of post-mortem experience—one which may be coloured by the individual's preconceived ideas and his customary background of living, but is erected upon a psychological groundwork common to all peoples in all ages. One man may travel by jet airliner, another on horseback, but different though their means of transportation may be, they have one thing in common, the fact of travel. So it is with the state between one life on earth and another; the post-mortem experiences vary according to the individual karma and the details of the preconceived ideational worlds of those who undergo them, but fundamentally they follow the same pattern for all. This being so, it may be possible in time to extract from these cases some fundamental principles which will enable us to formulate a psychology of rebirth, and perhaps even to bring the process under some measure of control. The ethico-psychology of Buddhism already offers the means of doing this, but until the fact of rebirth is more widely accepted and its principles more generally understood, the greater portion of mankind will still continue to blunder along from birth to birth in ignorance of the moral laws that govern human destiny.

As individuals, each with his own particular karma, we cannot know precisely "what dreams may come when we have shuffled off this mortal coil," but by an extension of knowledge man may ultimately learn how to control them for his own well being, and in learning how to die, discover the way to live.

FRANCIS STORY

December 1963

The Case for Rebirth

I

The doctrine of reincarnation, the ceaseless round of rebirths, is not, as many people imagine, confined to Buddhism and Hinduism. It is found in some form or another in many ancient religious and philosophical systems and in many parts of the world.

In the oldest records of man's religious thinking we find traces of a belief in the "transmigration of souls." Some of the forms it took were naturally primitive and crudely animistic; there is, for instance a theory that the ancient Egyptians embalmed their dead to prevent the *ka*, or soul, from taking another body. If the idea existed in Egypt, it almost certainly must have been familiar also to the Babylonians and Assyrians, who shared many of the most important religious beliefs of the Egyptians.

Coming to later times we find reincarnation prominent in the Orphic cult of Greece in the sixth century B.C., when it formed part of the teaching of Pherecydes of Syros. In the Orphic view of life man is a dualism, part evil and part divine. Through a succession of incarnations the individual has to purge himself of the evil in his nature by religious rites and moral purity. When this is accomplished he becomes liberated from the "circle of becoming" and is wholly divine.

This corresponds very closely to the Buddhist, Hindu, and Jain teaching, and there may have been a connection between them; but it is not possible to establish one on historical evidence. Although by the sixth century B.C. the doctrine had already been developed in the Brāhmaṇas and Upanishads, and may have travelled West along the trade routes, there is still a possibility that it arose spontaneously in Greece. The emphasis on ritualism differentiates it from the Buddhist view, but it is significant that it was at about the same time in both Greece and India that the idea of reincarnation first became linked with a scheme of moral values and spiritual evolution.

The connection of Orphism with the mysteries of ceremonial magic must not be allowed to blind us to the fact that it represented a great advance in religious thinking. Hitherto, reincarnation had been regarded in primitive cults as a merely mechanical process, to be controlled, if at all, by spells, incantations, and physical devices. This is the idea still prevalent among undeveloped peoples in certain parts of Africa, Polynesia, and elsewhere, where, far removed from Indian influences, the idea of metempsychosis must have sprung up spontaneously.

Through Orphism reincarnation came to be taught by, among others, Empedocles and Pythagoras. In the hands of the latter the Orphic mysticism was converted into a philosophy. This philosophical aspect of the teaching was inherited by the Platonists, while its mystical character was preserved in the traditions of Gnosticism.

In many respects Greek Gnosticism resembled Hinduism; it was syncretic and eclectic, capable of absorbing into itself ideas from outside sources while at the same time it impregnated with its own thought the beliefs peculiar to other systems. Its influence was felt over many centuries, persisting into the Middle Ages of Europe. In the early centuries of the Christian era we find it in the teachings of men as dissimilar in the general character of their outlook as Plotinus, Cerinthus, and Marcion.

Clement of Alexandria, about the second century C.E., wrote very largely from the Gnostic standpoint. He combined reincarnation with the necessity of striving for an enlightened moral elevation: a result that could be achieved only through a development taking place not merely in the present life but in past and future incarnations as well. This belief was shared by the *Pre-existiani*, a sect that numbered among its adherents some of the most advanced thinkers of the period, including Justin Martyr and the great theologian Origen. They represented a very powerful intellectual movement, one in which the natural freedom of Greek intellectualism was struggling for survival in a world that was sliding towards the Dark Ages. Many of their ideas survived in Neo-Platonism; but for the most part they were driven underground, to find an insecure refuge in the suppressed teachings of the so-called heretical sects that came to be known collectively as the Cathars, or "illuminati."

A not dissimilar doctrine of transmigration is found in the Kabbalah, where it goes under the Hebrew name Gilgul. It forms an integral part of the Kabbalistic system and is one of the features that distinguish Kabbalism from primitive Judaic thought. The Hekhāloth, a Kabbalistic work of the Gaonic era, gives Gnostic and Pythagorean ideas along with the orthodox stream of Talmudic teaching. The result may be regarded as Hellenized Judaism, but modern research on the Kabbalah tends to suggest that its original sources may be much older than has hitherto been granted.[61] It may in fact preserve a very ancient Rabbinical tradition which was not intended for the masses. Much of its philosophical content is of a high order and reveals a creative expansion of Jewish thought in which reincarnation occupies a significant place.

The idea of a transmigrating soul is the central theme of the Bhagavadgītā: "As the soul in this body passes through childhood, youth, and old age, even so does it pass to another body. As a person casts off worn-out garments and puts on others that are new, so does the incarnate soul cast off worn-out bodies and enter into others that are new" (2:13, 22).

Throughout the Upanishads the idea of "soul" (*ātman*) in this sense persists; it is the totality of selfhood and personal identity which transmigrates, occupying successive bodies, becoming now a man, now a god or an animal, yet in some way preserving its uniqueness as the personal ego throughout. Because of certain difficulties attaching to this concept, however, it was somewhat modified in Vedānta, the last phase of Upanishadic thought. In its place arose the theory that the *ātman*, as an unborn, unoriginated principle in no way affected by the activities, good or bad, of the phenomenal being, was not identical with the individual at all, but with the "Supreme Soul," the *paramātman* or (neuter) *brahman*.

Mahāvīra, the founder of Jainism (the Niganṭha Nātaputta of the Buddhist texts), held unequivocally to the "individual soul" theory. Jainism teaches that there are an infinite number of individual souls transmigrating in happy or unhappy states according to their deeds. But whereas in Vedānta release, or *moksha*, comes with the realization that the "I" is really identical with the *paramātman* or *brahman* (the idea summarized in the formula *"tat tvam asi"*— Thou art That), in Jainism it is believed to come only with the complete cessation of rebirth-producing activities. Since automatic and involuntary actions are considered to bear resultants as well as those performed intentionally, the Jain ideal is complete inactivity. As will be seen later, the Buddhist doctrine concerning what it is that undergoes rebirth, and the nature of the moral law that governs *kamma* and *vipāka*, or actions and results, differs from both these theories and eliminates the teleological and ethical difficulties to which they give rise.

The faith in survival after death, which is basic to religious thought, has its natural correlative in reincarnation. If life can extend forward in time beyond the grave it must surely be capable of having extended from the past into the present. "From the womb to the tomb" has its complement in "from the tomb to the womb," and to be born many times is no more miraculous than to have been born once, as Voltaire pointed out.

The opposite view, that a being comes into existence from non-existence, implies that it can also—and most probably will—come to an end with the dissolution of the body. That which has a beginning in time can also cease

203

in time and pass away altogether. The doctrine of a single life on earth therefore holds out no promise of a future life in any other state; rather does it make it improbable. But if we accept that there is a survival of some part, no matter what, of the personality after death, we are accepting also a very strong argument for its existence before birth. Reincarnation is the only form that after-death survival could logically take.

So it is not surprising that wherever religion has developed beyond its simplest beginnings some idea of spiritual evolution through a series of lives is found to be a part of its message. The doctrine of reincarnation together with that of the moral law of cause and effect not only provides an explanation of life's inequalities and the crushing burden of suffering under which countless millions of people labour, thus disposing of the problem raised by the existence of pain and evil in the world; it also gives a rational and practical hope where none existed before. It is, moreover, the supreme justification of moral values in a universe which otherwise appears to be devoid of ethical purpose. It is evident that the Orphic and Gnostic cults recognized this fact when they introduced the concept of moral values into their theology.

II

In all of these systems of thought, rebirth is seen, as it is in Buddhism, to be the only means of spiritual purgation. It is necessary for the moral and spiritual evolution of the individual that he should, through a variety of experiences, by his consciously directed efforts struggle upwards from the lower planes of sensuality and passion to a state of purity in which his latent divinity becomes manifest. That the Cathars, the Kabbalists, and others mixed up this reasoned and enlightened doctrine with the practice of what was later to become known as ritual magic, and with theories of the immortal soul that were frankly animistic, is no argument against the essential truth of their belief. Reason has to emerge slowly and painfully from unreason. It was in like manner that the true principles of science were unfolded at the time when scientific method was growing up alongside the occult practices of the astrologers and alchemists.

We may smile at the alchemist's faith that he could find a means of transmuting base metals into gold, but in this age of nuclear physics the idea does not seem quite so crazy as it once did. The alteration of atomic patterns in the structure of metals is no longer entirely outside the range of possibility. The alchemist's methods may have been hopelessly wrong; his basic assumption was not. Similarly, the transformation of the base metal of human nature into the pure gold of divinity is still a possibility. It is only a question of finding the right key to unlock the doors of the mind.

To understand how the Buddhist doctrine of rebirth differs from all those that have been mentioned, and why the term "rebirth" is preferable to "reincarnation" or "transmigration," it is necessary to glance at the main principles of Buddhist teaching.

These are summed up in the Four Noble Truths:

The truth concerning suffering
The truth concerning the cause of suffering
The truth concerning the cessation of suffering
The truth concerning the way to the cessation of suffering.

The first proposition is nothing more then a self-evident fact: that suffering is inherent in all forms of existence. No one can go through life without experiencing physical pain, sickness, disappointment, and grief; none can escape old age and death. Suffering is even more prevalent in the life of animals than in that of human beings, and Buddhism takes into account all forms of sentient life. But aside from these obvious aspects of the universal world-suffering there is the fact that all conditioned existence is unstable, restless, and lacking in fulfilment. It is a process of *becoming* which never reaches the point of completion in *being*. This in itself is suffering. In brief, life even at its best is unsatisfactory.

In the formula of the "three characteristics of being," all phenomenal existence is defined as being impermanent, fraught with suffering, and devoid of self-essence. These three characteristics derive from one another; because existence is transitory it is painful; because it is transitory and painful it can have no enduring essence of selfhood. There is no "soul" in the sense of a total personality-entity, for what we call the self is merely a current of consciousness linked to a particular physical body. This current of consciousness is made up of thought-moments of infinitesimal duration succeeding one another in a stream of inconceivable rapidity. The psychic life of the individual is just the duration of a single moment of consciousness, no more. We are living all the time what is in reality a series of lives. The life-stream is the rapid succession of these consciousness-moments, or momentary existences, resembling the running of a reel of film through a projector. It is this which gives the illusion of a static entity of being where nothing of the kind exists. The general characteristics of personality are maintained, but only in the same way that a river maintains the same course until something diverts it or it dries up. Thus there is no "immortal soul" that transmigrates, just as there is no river, but only the passage of particles of water flowing in the same direction. *Anattā*, soullessness, is therefore bound up with *anicca*, impermanence, and *dukkha*, suffering. The three characteristics are three aspects of the same central fact.

Yet this state of soullessness is capable of producing rebirth. How can this be so, if there is no transmigrating entity—no "soul" to reincarnate? The answer is to be found in the Buddhist system of ethico-psychology, the Abhidhamma. There it is shown that the act of willing is a creative force, which produces effects in and through the conditions of the physical world. The thought-force of a sentient being, generated by the will-to-live, the desire to enjoy sensory experiences, produces after death another being who is the causal resultant of the preceding one. Schopenhauer expressed the same idea when he said that in rebirth, which he called "palingenesis," it is the *will*, not an ego-entity, which re-manifests in the new life. The being of the present is not the same as the being of the past, nor will the being of the future be the same as the being of the present. Yet neither are they different beings, because they all belong to the same current of cause and effect. Each is part of an individual current of causality in which "identity" means only "belonging to the same cause-effect continuum." Since mind and body are alike continually undergoing change—or, more precisely, they are made up of constituent factors which are arising and passing away from moment to moment—this is the only kind of "self-identity" that connects the various stages of a single life through childhood, youth, maturity, and old age. Buddhism presents a dynamic view of existence in which the life-continuum is merely the current of momentary existences, or successive units of consciousness, linked together by causal relations, both mental and physical. The process may be likened to a current of electricity, which consists of minute particles called electrons. An electron is much lighter in weight than an atom of the lightest chemical element, hydrogen, yet waves of these particles in the form of an electric current can produce many different effects in heat, light, and sound, and can produce them on a tremendous scale. In the same way the units of consciousness constitute an energy-potential which, in the Buddhist view, is the basic energy of the universe, operating through and in conjunction with natural laws.

So we see that mental force is a kind of energy, which Buddhism has linked with moral principles by way of *kamma* (= Sanskrit *karma*), actions, and *vipāka*, moral resultants. Buddhism maintains that the physical universe

206

itself is sustained by this mental energy derived from living beings, which is identical with their karma. The energy itself is generated by craving. It operates upon the atomic constituents of the physical world in such a way as to produce bodies equipped with organs of sense by means of which the desire for sensory gratification, produced by past experiences, may be satisfied again. In this world the mind-force which produces rebirth has to operate through the genetic principles known to biology; it requires human generative cells and all the favourable physical conditions of heat, nutrition, and so forth, to produce a fetus. When it does so, the fetus and the infant that it later becomes bear both biologically inherited characteristics and the characteristics carried by the past karma of the individual whose thought-force has caused the new birth.[62] It is not a question of a "soul" entering the embryo, but of the natural formation of the foetus being moulded by an energy from without, supplied by the causative impulse from some being that lived before. It is only necessary to conceive craving-force as an energy-potential flowing out from the mind of a being at the moment of death, and carrying with it the karmic characteristics of that being, just as the seed of a plant carries with it the botanical characteristics of its type, and a mental picture is formed that corresponds roughly to what actually takes place. Mind force is creative, and its basis is desire. Without desire there can be no will to act; consequently the "will" of Schopenhauer is identical with the Buddhist *taṇhā*, or craving.[63]

The second of the Four Noble Truths, therefore, is that the cause of suffering in the round of rebirths is craving. But one cause is not enough to give rise to a specific result. In this case, craving is conjoined with ignorance. The mind generates craving for sensory experience because of ignorance of the fact that these experiences are impermanent, unsatisfactory, and so themselves a source of suffering. So the circle of becoming, without discernible beginning and without end, is joined. This wheel of existences does not exist in time: time exists in it. Hence it does not require a point of beginning in what we know as time. It is the *perpetuum mobile* of cause and effect, counter-cause and counter-effect, turning round upon itself.

But although, like the revolution of the planets round the sun, it goes on perpetually simply because there is nothing to stop it, it can be brought to an end by the individual for himself, through an act of will. The act of will consists in turning craving into non-craving. When this is accomplished and Nibbāna (= Sankrit *Nirvāṇa*), the state of desirelessness, is reached, there is no more rebirth. The life-asserting impulses are eliminated and there is no further arising of the bases of phenomenal personality. This is the objective set forth in the third of the Four Noble Truths, that concerning the cessation of suffering.

The way to that cessation, which is the Noble Eightfold Path of self-discipline and meditation leading to perfect purity and insight-wisdom, is the subject of the last of the Four Noble Truths, and gives epistemological completeness to the whole.

The Buddhist system of thought is thus presented as a reasoned progression from known facts to a conclusion which is ascertainable by the individual and is also accessible to him as a personally experienced reality. The round of rebirths, or saṃsāra, does not come to an end automatically, neither is there any point at which all beings revolving in it gain their release by reason of its ceasing, for it has no temporal boundaries. But anyone can bring to an end his own individual current of cause and effect, and the whole purpose of the Buddha's Teaching was to demonstrate the theoretical and practical means by which this can be achieved. The painful kind of "immortality" conferred by rebirth in conditioned existences is not to be regarded as a blessing, but rather as a curse which man pronounces upon himself. Nevertheless, by understanding it we are able to gain assurance that there is in truth a moral principle governing the universe; and by learning to use its laws in the right way we become able to control and guide our individual destinies by a higher spiritual purpose and towards a more certain goal.

III

Of late years interest in the doctrine of rebirth has been greatly stimulated by the publicity given to several cases of people who have remembered previous lives. For a long time past it has been known that under deep hypnosis events in very early infancy, outside the normal range of memory, could be recovered, and this technique has been increasingly employed for the treatment of personality disorders. It cannot be used with success on all patients because of the involuntary resistance some subjects show to hypnotic suggestion, which inhibits the co-operation necessary to obtain deep trance. But where it can be applied it has definite advantages over the usual methods of deep psychoanalysis, one of them being the speed with which results are obtained.

The technique is to induce a state of hypnosis and then carry the subject back in time to a particular point in childhood or infancy at which it is suspected that some event of importance in the psychic life may have

208

occurred. In this state, known as hypermnesia, the subject becomes in effect once more the child he was, and relives experiences that have long been buried in the unconscious. Memories of earliest infancy, and in some cases prenatal memories, have been brought to the surface in this way.

Some practitioners have carried experiments in regression even further, and have found that they were uncovering memories that did not belong to the current life of the subject at all, but to some previous existence. In cases where nothing could be proved, the rebirth explanation has been contested, and various theories such as telepathy, fantasies of the unconscious, and even clairvoyance, have been put forward to account for the phenomena. But apart from the fact that many of the alternatives offered call for the acceptance of psychic faculties which, if what is claimed for them is true, themselves bring rebirth nearer to being a comprehensible reality, none of them alone covers all the phenomena which have been brought under observation. If, for example, xenoglossy, the ability shown by some subjects under hypnosis to speak languages unknown to them in their normal state, is to be explained by telepathy, we are brought face to face with a supernormal faculty of the mind which itself contributes to our under-standing of the manner in which mental energy may operate in the processes of rebirth. But although telepathy has now been acknowledged as one of the unexplained phenomena of parapsychology—along with clairvoyance, telekinesis, and psychometry—it cannot legitimately be expanded to include all the phenomena these experiments have disclosed. To account for all of them on these lines it would be necessary to combine every one of the known extrasensory faculties into one concept, that of a freely wandering, disembodied intelligence, independent of spatial and temporal limitations. If we are to apply here the scientific law of parsimony, the more likely alternative is the obvious one that they are simply what they purport to be—memories of previous lives.

As to the theory that the memories are products of the unconscious mind, it cannot survive the proof to the contrary, which comes from the revelation of facts that could not have been known to the subject in his present life. These are objective and circumstantial and they exist in abundance, as any reading of the literature on the subject will confirm.

The best-known example of this kind is the case of Bridey Murphy in America, which raised a hurricane of controversy when it broke into the news a few years ago. It was followed some time later by a similar case in England in which the subject, Mrs. Naomi Henry, remembered under hypnosis two previous existences. The experiments were carried out under test conditions by Mr. Henry Blythe, a professional consultant hypnotist. In the presence of several witnesses tape recordings were made of the sessions, which were held under the supervision of a medical practitioner, Dr. William C. Minifie, who testified that the hypnotic trance was genuine. It has been said of these recordings that they provide "what must surely be the most thought-provoking, absorbing, and controversial angle ever offered" on the subject.

What happened was this. Mrs. Naomi Henry, a 32-year-old Exeter housewife, the mother of four children, was cured of the smoking habit by hypnotic treatment given by Mr. Henry Blithe, of Torquay, Devon. He found her to be "an exceptionally receptive hypnotic subject," so much so that without informing her of the purpose of his experiments he began a series of sessions in which he succeeded in taking her back beyond her present life.

Mrs. Henry remembered two previous existences. In the first she gave her name as Mary Cohan, a girl of 17 living in Cork in the year 1790. Among other circumstances she told how she was married against her wishes to a man named Charles Gaul, by whom she had two children, Pat and Will. Her husband ill-treated her, and finally caused her death by a beating which broke her leg. While describing these events in the trance she was evidently reliving the intense emotional experiences of the past with the vividness of a present reality rather than of a mere memory. Intervening time had been obliterated and she was once more the illiterate Irish girl she had been over a century and a half before. Her marriage, she said, took place in St. John's Church, in a hamlet named "Grenner." Several of the facts she related were afterwards verified on the spot but no village of the name of "Grenner" could be traced. Eventually, however, some records dating back to the seventeenth century were found in the possession of a parish priest, and in them mention was made of a Church of St. John in a village named Greenhalgh. The name is pronounced locally just as Mary Cohan gave it—"Grenner."

Next she remembered a life in which she was Clarice Hellier, a nurse in charge of twenty-four children at Downham in 1902. After relating what she remembered of this life she went on to describe her last illness, her death, and her funeral, which it seems she had been able to witness. She was even able to give the number of the grave, 207, in which she had been buried.

When Mrs. Henry emerged from her trance she had no recollection of what had taken place and it was only when she heard the recording that she learned the purpose of the experiments. The authenticity of this case had been established beyond reasonable doubt.

One of the most remarkable men of recent times, Edgar Cayce, obtained evidence of an even more striking nature. Born in Christian County, Kentucky, in 1877, he suffered as a young man from a psychosomatic constriction of the throat which deprived him of his voice. Orthodox medical treatments having failed, he was treated by hypnotic suggestion, which was not a recognized form of therapy in those days. In deep trance his voice returned to normal and he diagnosed his own condition. Not only did he describe the physiological symptoms in terms of which he knew nothing in his waking state, but he also prescribed treatment.

His self-cure was so remarkable that he was persuaded, rather against his will, to try prescribing cures for others whose illnesses would not respond to medical treatment. This he did with great success, using technical terms and prescribing remedies which, as a man of only moderate education, he was quite unfamiliar with in his normal state. Sometimes the medicines he prescribed were conventional remedies in unusual combinations; sometimes they were substances not found in the standard pharmacopoeia. Cayce himself was puzzled and somewhat dismayed by his abnormal faculty, but since it was proving of benefit to an increasing number of sufferers he continued to use it, only refusing to take any payment for the help he rendered. He soon found that a hypnotist was unnecessary; his trances were really self-induced, and he worked thereafter solely through autohypnosis.

One day while Cayce was giving a consultation a friend who was present asked him whether reincarnation was true. Still in the trance, Cayce immediately replied that it was. In answer to further questions he said that many of the patients who came to him for treatment were suffering from afflictions caused by bad karma in previous lives. It was because of this that they resisted ordinary treatment. Asked whether he was able to see the past incarnations of his patients and describe them, he said that he could.

When he was told what he had said in the trance, Cayce was more disturbed than before. The thing was getting decidedly out of hand. He had never heard the word karma, and his only idea of reincarnation was that it was a belief associated with some "heathen" religions. His first reaction was to give the whole thing up, as being something supernatural and possibly inimical to his Christian faith.

It was with great difficulty that he was persuaded to continue. However, he consented to be questioned further under hypnosis, and after having given

211

some readings and more successful treatments he became convinced that there was nothing irreligious or harmful in the strange ideas that were being revealed. From that time onwards he supplemented all his diagnoses by readings of the past karma of his patients. It was then found that he was able to give valuable moral and spiritual guidance to counteract bad karmic tendencies, and his treatments became even more effective. He was now treating the minds as well as the bodies of the patients who sought his help.

When Cayce discovered that he was also able to treat people living at great distances, whom he had never seen, the scope of his work broadened until it ultimately extended all over the United States and beyond. Before he died in 1945 Cayce, with the help of friends and supporters, had established an institution, the Cayce Foundation, at Virginia Beach, Virginia. It is now operating as a research institute under the direction of his associates. Cayce left a vast number of case histories and other records accumulated over the years, and these are still being examined and correlated by the Foundation. For further information on Edgar Cayce, his work, and the light it throws on rebirth, he reader is referred to *Many Mansions* by Gina Cerminara, *Edgar Cayce, Mystery Man of Miracles*, by Joseph Millard, and numerous publications issued by the Cayce Foundation.

There is a great deal in the evidence to suggest that Cayce in his hypnotized state had access to lost medical knowledge, as well as the power to see the previous lives of others. In the Buddhist texts of a very early date there are references to advanced medical knowledge and techniques of surgery in some ways comparable to our own. Jīvaka, a renowned physician who was a contemporary of the Buddha, is recorded as having performed a brain operation for the removal of a living organism of some kind. But there are still older records than these. The Edwin Smith Papyrus (c. 3,500 B.C.) describes the treatment of cerebral injuries, and the writings attributed to Hippocrates include directions for opening the skull. The great Egyptian physician, Imhotep, who lived about three thousand years before the Christian era and was a many-sided genius comparable to Leonardo da Vinci, had such skill in medicine that he became a legend. He was deified under the Ptolemies and identified with Asklepios, the god of healing, by the Greeks; but there is no doubt whatever that he was an actual historical personage. Without venturing beyond what is naturally suggested by Edgar Cayce's statements concerning rebirth, and their linking up with the often unusual but brilliantly successful treatments he prescribed, it is possible to see that there might be a direct connection between the knowledge possessed by these ancient physicians and the abnormal knowledge released from Cayce's unconscious mind under hypnosis.

But even Cayce was not altogether unique. Egerton C. Baptist, in *Nibbāna or the Kingdom?*, quotes the following from *Life and Destiny* by Leon Denis:

> In 1880 at Vera Cruz, Mexico, a seven-year-old child possessed the power to heal. Several people were healed by vegetable remedies prescribed by the child. When asked how he knew these things, he said that he was formerly a great doctor, and his name was then Jules Alpherese. This surprising faculty developed in him at the age of four years.

In Buddhism, the faculty of remembering previous lives and of discerning the previous lives of others is one that is developed in the course of meditation on selected subjects. But it is acquired only when a certain precisely defined stage of jhāna, or mental absorption, has been reached. The subject is dealt with in the canonical texts of Buddhism, and at considerable length in the *Visuddhi-magga* of Buddhaghosa Thera.[64] Those who have practised meditation to this point in previous lives without having attained complete liberation from rebirth may be reborn with the faculty in a latent form. In the case of others, hypnosis seems to provide a short-cut technique to releasing some at least of the dormant memories of former lives, just as it provides a short cut to results ordinarily reached by deep psychoanalysis. There is much to be done in the way of more extensive and systematic investigation before definite conclusions can be tabulated. The chief difficulty is to obtain suitable subjects for the tests.[65]

IV

A question that is often asked is: If rebirth is a fact, why is it so rare for people to have any recollection of their previous lives?

There are several answers to this. The first and most obvious is that even ordinary memory is very restricted, and varies greatly in extent and vividness with different people. Death itself, the Lethe of psycho-mythology, is an obliterating agent, for it is necessary for each consciousness to begin its renewed course more or less as a *tabula rasa* with the formation of a new physical brain. Another factor is the nature of the lives intermediate to one human birth and another. There are, as Buddhism maintains, rebirths in states that are non-human and in which the consciousness does not register impressions clearly, so that a series of such lives between one human birth and another may erase all traces of memory connecting them. A study of the earliest behaviour patterns of children, however, will furnish much evidence to suggest that they bring with them into the new life certain dim type of types of awareness that do not belong to their present range of experience. The aptitude certain children show for acquiring some particular skills strongly suggests remembering rather than learning.

The head-mistress of a kindergarten school told the author that a few years after the end of the First World War she noticed that some of her boy pupils were showing a maturity of mind and a facility in gaining knowledge which was so unlike anything in her previous experience that it roused her curiosity. After making a study of these children she came to the conclusion that they were not learning but remembering. She became convinced of the truth of rebirth when one small boy, born after the war and exhibiting a highly strung nature which she had formerly attributed to post-war conditions, one day became violently agitated by a sudden explosive noise close behind him. The fear he showed was out of all proportion to the cause; in fact he fell into an almost cataleptic state. When he recovered he told her that he had a vague memory of a tremendous explosion and a brilliant flash of light, and that the loud noise had brought it back to him so vividly that he felt as though he was dying. From that time she was convinced that her extremely intelligent but often nervously unstable pupils were the reincarnations of men whose immediately previous lives had been cut short by the war, and who had been reborn almost at once into the human state to complete the interrupted karmic continuity of that particular life.[66]

Many children lead vivid lives of the imagination, or so it is supposed. They sometimes speak of things that bear no relation to their present experiences. Parents as a rule do not encourage this kind of imaginativeness, particularly if some of its manifestations cause them embarrassment. They then peremptorily forbid the child to tell any more "untruths." But are these always untruths? May they not in fact be residual memories of past experiences? In any case, they are driven under by the parents' unsympathetic attitude and quickly become obliterated by new impressions. In the East, where children are allowed greater latitude to prattle of what they will, this does not happen. The difference may account for the frequently noted fact that instances of people recollecting past lives are more numerous in the East than in Western countries. The son of a distinguished Indian doctor practising in Burma started talking of his "wife" and of events and people

214

belonging to another realm of experience as soon as he was able to speak. The boy was living in a trilingual environment where Hindi, English, and Burmese were spoken, but his father noticed that from the start he used words to denote familiar things, such as doors, tables, and houses, which were not Hindi, English, or Burmese. The doctor noted down a number of these words phonetically, with the intention of later on trying to identify them. Unfortunately, at that time the Japanese occupation of Burma took place and the records were lost, so it was never possible to establish whether the words belonged to any existing language or not.

Cases of children remembering their previous lives in considerable detail are not uncommon in Asian countries. An example which bears all the classic features of this phenomenon is that of Pramod, the son of Babu Bankey Lal Sharma, M.A., Shastri, a professor in an intermediate college at Bissauli in the district of Badan. The boy was born at Bissauli on March 15, 1944. As soon as he was able to utter any words clearly he pronounced the names "Mohan," "Moradabad," and "Saharanpur." Later he said quite distinctly, "Mohan Brothers." When he saw his relatives purchasing biscuits he told them that he had a big biscuit factory in Moradabad, and on being taken to large shops he would frequently say that his shop in Moradabad was bigger than any other shop. As time went on he became insistent that he should be taken to Moradabad, where he had a brother, sons, daughter, and a wife.

When he was able to give a clear account of himself he said that he was Paramanand, the brother of one B. Mohanlal, the proprietor of a catering firm, Messrs. Mohan Bros., having branches in Saharanpur and Moradabad. As Paramanand, he said he had died of a stomach ailment at Saharanpur on May 9, 1943. The date was just nine months and six days before his birth as Pramod.

Early in the year 1949, when the boy was five, a friend of the family, Lala Raghunandanlal of Bissauli, told one of his relatives living in Moradabad about the boy and his assertions. It was then learned that there was actually a firm of caterers called Mohan Brothers, caterers, the proprietor of which was named Mohan Lal. When the story was told to him, Mr. Mohan Lal visited Bissauli with some of his relatives, and there met the boy's father. Young Pramod, as it happened, was paying a visit to some relatives in a distant village at the time (July 1949) and could not be seen. Professor Bankey Lal however consented to take him to Moradabad during the forthcoming Independence Day holidays.

215

They arrived in Moradabad on August 15th. On alighting from the train the boy at once recognized his brother and ran to embrace him. On the way to Mohan Lal's house Pramod recognized the town hall and announced that his shop was close at hand. They were riding in a tonga which, to test the boy, was being driven past the shop. Pramod recognized the building and called out for the vehicle to stop. He then alighted and led the way to the house in front of Mohan Lal Brothers' premises where the late Paramanand had lived. There he entered the room which Paramanand had kept for his religious devotions and did reverence to it. He also recognized his wife and other relatives, and recalled incidents known to them, by which he established his identity to their complete satisfaction. The only person he failed to recognize was his eldest son, who had been thirteen years old when Paramanand died and had altered greatly in the five years' interval.

After a touching reunion with the relatives of his former life, the boy expressed a desire to go to his business premises. On entering the shop he went to the soda-water machine and explained the process of making aerated water, a thing of which he could not have acquired any knowledge in his present life. Finding that the machine would not work, he at once said that the water connection had been stopped, which was a fact; it had been done to test him. After that he said he wanted to go to the Victory Hotel, a business owned by a cousin of Paramanand's, Mr. Karam Chand. The boy led the way to the building, and entering it pointed out some rooms on the upper story which had been added since his time.

During the two days of their stay in Moradabad the boy was taken to the Meston Park by a leading citizen of the town, Sahu Nanda Lal Saran, who asked him to point out where his civil lines branch had been. At once the boy led the company to the Gujerati Building owned by Sahu Lal Saran and indicated the shop which had once been the branch of Mohan Bros. On the way to the Meston Park he had already recognized and correctly named the Allahabad Bank, the waterworks, and the district jail. Some of the English words, such as "town hall," were not in use in the small town of Bissauli, and Pramod had never heard them, yet he used them accurately. He not only identified his former relatives but also people who used to visit his shop on business.

The following is the account given by Mr. J.D. Mehra of Messrs. Mohan Bros., Moradabad, a brother of the late Paramanand:

> My brother, Paramanand, aged 39, died of appendicitis on May 9, 1943 at Saharanpur about 100 miles from Moradabad. Pramod, the

boy concerned, was born on 15, March 1944 at Bissauli. As the boy grew up he began to utter things of his previous life. For instance, he would say to his father when offered biscuits that he would have biscuits of his own shop and that he owned a big shop at Moradabad. He used to refer to his four sons, daughter, and wife. When his mother would prepare meals he would say to her, "Why should you prepare meals? I have an elderly wife, send for her."

As requested by us it was decided to bring this boy to Moradabad on August 15, 1948 ([sic] the day of India's Independence). Shri Karam Chand, the eldest of our brothers, went to the station to receive the boy and his father. When Mr. Bankey Lal, the father, alighted from the station with his boy, Pramod spotted out Shri Karam Chand from the crowd and clung to him, and would not go to his father. When questioned whether he knew the gentleman he at once replied, "Yes, he is my Bara Bhai (elder brother)."

Whilst passing the town hall compound the boy said that it was the town hall, an English word with which he was not familiar in his own small city.... When taken round the place where biscuits were manufactured he said that it was a bakery, another English word not familiar to him in his birthplace. Entering the kitchen he said that he used to sit on a wooden cot there and pray. Before he entered the room he did Namaskar to the place where he used to sit in meditation.

Seeing his wife without the vermilion mark on her forehead he questioned her, "Where is your *bindu* (mark) on the forehead?" This was a very significant remark for a boy of his age....

The boy's own father, Shri Bankey Lal Sharma, wrote the following testimony:

I have read almost all the versions of the statement regarding the rebirth of Paramanand of Moradabad. As I have been the eye-witness of all these things, I can say with emphasis that everything contained in the report is true to its minutest detail.

Paramanand is a wonderful child with a very fine intelligence. He began to utter "Moradabad" and "Mohan Brothers" alone one year back. Since December last he spoke of the firm he owned during his last existence and also of the articles he dealt in. A few days later he made a reference to a shop of his at Saharanpur. Biscuits and tea have been his great attraction. Although nobody attaches any importance to them in my family, he is very fond of them. It was through the association of biscuits that he spoke of his previous soda water and biscuit firm.

When he visited Moradabad he recognized almost everybody with the exception of a few, especially his eldest son who is much changed.... He recognized other sons, his only daughter, wife, brothers, mother and father, and several others whom he contacted during his previous life....

I am a middle-class man, but the boy is not satisfied with the present status. He often stresses on business and opening a big shop in Bombay or Delhi. In the latter place, he says, he had been several times on business. He wants aeroplanes, ships, mansions, radios, and all modern fashions.

He has a great leaning towards his past relatives and does not want to live with me. He requests me to purchase and have a bank of our own....

It was only with great difficulty that the boy was taken away from Moradabad after the visit. He showed such unwillingness to leave his old relatives and the shop that his present father had to carry him away in the early hours of August 17th while he was still asleep.

On the day prior to their departure, August 16, 1949, a large public meeting was held at the Arya Samaj where Prof. Bankey Lal, Pramod's father, gave a full account of the development of the boy's memories since his early childhood. The case was investigated in the full light of local publicity by people known to all the persons concerned.

Among numerous cases from Burma, the following, given on the testimony of U Yan Pa of Rangoon, is one of the most thoroughly substantiated.

In the village of Shwe Taung Pan, situated close to Dabein on the Rangoon-Pegu trunk line, the eldest daughter of a cultivator named U Po Chon and his wife, Daw Ngwe Thin, was married to another cultivator of the same village, named Ko Ba Thin. This girl, whose name was Ma Phwa Kyin, died in childbirth some time later.

Shortly afterwards a woman in Dabein, Daw Thay Thay Hmyin, the wife of one U Po Yin, became pregnant and in due course gave birth to a daughter whom they named Ah Nyo. When she first began to speak, this child expressed a strong wish to go to the neighbouring village, Shwe Taung Pan. She declared that she had lived and died in that village, and that her name was really not Ah Nyo but Ma Phwa Kyin.

Eventually her parents took her to the village. The child at once led them to the house of the late Ma Phwa Kyin, pointing out on the way a rice field and some cattle which she said belonged to her. When the father, mother, and two brothers, Mg Ba Khin and Mg Ba Yin, of Ma Phwa Kyin appeared, she at once identified them. They confirmed that the house, field, and cattle were those that had belonged to Ma Phwa Kyin, and when the child recalled to them incidents of her former life they admitted that her memories were accurate and accepted her as being without doubt the dead girl reborn. Later she convinced her other surviving relatives in the same way.

The girl Ah Nyo, now about twenty-five years of age, is everywhere in the neighbourhood accepted as the former Ma Phwa Kyin reborn.

More numerous are the cases in which specific skills are carried over from one life to another, rather than any distinct recollection of identity. Among musical prodigies we find Mozart composing minuets before he was four years old; Beethoven playing in public at eight and publishing compositions at ten; Handel giving concerts at nine; Schubert composing at eleven; Chopin playing concertos in public before he was nine; and Samuel Wesley playing the organ at three and composing an oratorio at eight. The musical precocity of Brahms, Dvorak, and Richard Strauss was manifest at an equally early stage. In a less specialized field there is the case of Christian Heinrich Heinecken, born at Lubeck in 1721. At the age of ten months he was able to speak, and by the time he was one year old he knew by heart the principal incidents of the Pentateuch. "At two years of age he is said to have mastered sacred history; at three he was intimately acquainted with history and geography, ancient and modern, sacred and profane, besides being able to speak French and Latin; and in his fourth year he began the study of religions and church history."

This amazing child created a tremendous sensation, crowds of people flocking to Lubeck to see and discourse with him. He died at the age of four, soon after he had begun to learn writing. That he was able to master so many abstruse subjects before he could even write is proof that his abnormal achievements were not the result of learning but of remembering.

Sangayana, the journal of the Union of Burma Buddha Sasana Council, reported in its issue of July 1954 the case of a six-year-old girl, Ma Hla Gyi, who showed remarkable intelligence for her age, combined with a phenomenal memory. "She can read," the report stated, "the most difficult Pāli verses a few times, memorize and recite them promptly and correctly." In a test given to her she recited the final stanza of the sub-commentary on the Buddhist "Compendium of Philosophy" in Pāli without an error, after reading it five times. She was also able to recite without a single error a page of the Pāli *Paṭṭhāna* text (an abstruse Abhidhamma passage) after looking at it for one minute. This might be explained by the possession of a photographic memory, but for the fact that the child could understand what she read and was able to give its meaning.

These and many other instances of the appearance from time to time of child prodigies, although not constituting *direct* evidence for rebirth, present a phenomenon for which biology and psychology cannot account. That memory itself is a something extra to the activities of the brain cells is a conclusion accepted on physiological grounds by Max Loewenthal and others. From the cases available for examination it would seem that memories carried over from one life to another are subject to the same broad general principle as are ordinary memories belonging to the current life: we remember what most interests us, and what we most desire to remember. Therefore a strong karmic predisposition to a particular form of study is more likely to persist from the past life than are the actual details of that life, which may be connected with personal psychological reactions and emotional responses that are in the ordinary course of nature suppressed.

V

Despite great advances in the study of genetics, there is still much that is unexplained in the biological processes that produce living organisms. While the transmission of hereditary characteristics through the genes can be traced in the operation of physical laws, there is as yet no known method of accounting for the sudden mutations that occur from time to time and so give rise to variations of species. Yet these mutations, and the fact that they are possible, is a matter of the first importance, since it is by them that biological evolution takes place. For many generations the structural units of a chromosome, the genes, remain the same, and produce uniform hereditary types; but suddenly, without any intermediary stages, a new type is formed from them which may or may not continue to propagate itself. A well-known example of this is the fruit fly, *Drosophila melanogaster*, which, being normally an insect with a grey body and long wings, produces from time to time a spontaneous mutation having a black body slightly different in shape, and very short wings. Many similar cases are known of this kind of departure from a hereditary form, but precisely what different combinations of genes, chromosomes, or atomic patterns cause the variation, or why they occur, is still a mystery to biologists. All that can be said is that the changes are isomeric transformations of the kind found in simple molecular structures, and that they follow the laws of chemical kinetics which also apply to non-living substances under certain conditions.

Between "living" and "non-living" matter there is no sharp line of distinction, for it is known that the processes by which living cells nourish themselves from their surrounding medium, assimilate material for their sustenance, and divide into other cells capable of independent existence is closely paralleled by processes observable in chemical molecules. For example, virus particles, which are the simplest form of life known at present, have to be considered as living units because they perform all the essential functions of living cells: yet at the same time they are regular chemical molecules, subject to all the laws of chemistry and physics. As living molecules comparable to the genes by which organic life is propagated, they are able to multiply, and they are also capable of producing biological mutations which result in the appearance from time to time of new types of a particular virus. Yet a purely chemical study of them shows each type of virus to be a well-defined chemical compound similar to various complex organic compounds that are not strictly "living" matter. They thus represent a "bridge" between "living" and "non-living" substance, and possibly the point at which the "non-living" merges into the "living."

What has to be sought is the directive principle that prompts the transformation and guides the molecules to combine into more complex organic structures. To be able to follow the process, even right from its earliest stage, is not the same as to know its cause, and it is here that scientific method has to enlarge its scope to include the study of principles and laws underlying the phenomena of the physical universe and functioning on a different level from that to which the scientist has hitherto confined himself. Inasmuch as Buddhism locates these ultimate principles in the mental and immaterial, rather than the physical, realm, the inquiry must necessarily be turned towards the interaction between mind-energy and the material substance through which it manifests itself. If the transformations of non-living into living matter, and the developments which these transformations afterwards undergo, are regarded as the physical manifestation of *kamma* and *vipāka* (karma-result), it is only necessary to add these to the present stock of scientific knowledge as the unknown factors that at present elude identification, for many things still obscure to become clarified, without resorting to the supernatural for an explanation.

The embryo of a human being derives its hereditary characteristics from the genes of the parents, sharing in equal measure the chromosomes of father and mother, the sex being determined by the proportion of what are distinguished as X and Y chromosomes. Female cells always contain two X-chromosomes, while the male has one X and one Y, and it is in the substitution of one Y for an X-chromosome that the basic difference in sex consists. At the time of conception the male sperm cell unites with the female and by the process of syngamy forms one complete cell, which afterwards divides into two, thus starting the process of mitosis by which the complete organism eventually comes into being. Here, what is *not* known is exactly why in certain cases the X and Y chromosomes combine to form a female, while in others they produce a male cell. This may be purely fortuitous; but it is more in accordance with the scientific view of cause and effect to suspect the presence of another factor which in some way determines the combination. The Buddhist view that this unknown factor is karma or energy-potential, the mental impulse projected by another being which existed in the past, is one that science by itself can neither prove nor disprove, but it provides the most likely explanation—in fact, the only one which can be offered as an alternative to the improbable theory of chance.

Kamma as cause, and *vipāka* as result, also provide an explanation of the intermediate conditions in which sex characteristics are more or less equal in one individual, or where it is possible for a complete change of sex to take place. The karma which in the first place produced a male may be weak, or may become exhausted before the life-supporting karma comes to an end, in which case the characteristic of the opposite sex may become so marked that they amount virtually to a sex-transformation, the result of a different kind of karma coming into operation.[67] Similarly, masculine thoughts and habits gradually becoming dominant in a female may bring about more and more marked male characteristics with the passage of time, and these influences may be so strong that they actually reveal themselves in physical changes. On the other hand, they may only affect the psychic life. What is certain, as this analysis will attempt to show, is that the thought-accretions do have the power to affect not only the general outlook and habits but the physical body itself. For "thought-accretions" we may substitute here the Buddhist term *saṅkhārā*, since this is one of the various associated meanings of this highly comprehensive word.

Individual character is usually attributed to two factors, the first being heredity. But simple physical characteristics alone are not always traceable to this cause. Colour-blindness, although it can be followed back through successive generations and shows clearly marked biological transmission, is not invariably hereditary; and in those individual features that partake of both the physical and psychological, such as the sexual deviations referred to above, the hereditary influence does not provide any satisfactory explanation. That they are not hereditary is the conclusion of most authorities. This also applies to the many examples of infant prodigies and to the less striking, but nevertheless significant, instances of children who bear no resemblance whatever to their parents or grandparents. Where hereditary traits transmitted through the genes of the parents cannot account for differences in character, the second factor, environmental influence, is brought in to explain the variation. But this also fails to cover all the ground because the same antecedents and the same environment together frequently produce quite dissimilar personalities, and there are numerous examples of pronounced characteristics appearing at birth, before any environmental pressure is brought to bear on the developing personality.

In Buddhist philosophy it is axiomatic that more than one cause is necessary to produce a given result, so that while character may be partly drawn from heredity, and partly modified by environment, these two factors do not in any way rule out the third factor, that of the individual *saṅkhārā*, or karma-formation tendencies developed in previous lives, which may prove stronger than either of them. Hereditary transmissions themselves are a part of the operation of the causal law, for it happens that owing to strong attachments the same persons may be born again and again in the same family. This accounts for the fact that a child may be totally unlike either of its parents in temperament, tastes, and abilities, yet may resemble a dead grandfather or some more distant ancestor. Physical appearance may be derived in the first place from the genes of the parents, but it undergoes modifications as the individual develops along his own lines, and it is then that distinctive characteristics, the result of habitual mental tendencies stamping themselves upon the features, become more pronounced.

That the mind, or rather the mental impressions and volitional activities, produce changes in the living structure, is a fact which science is beginning to recognize. Hypnotism affords an opportunity of studying this phenomenon under test conditions. It is only recently that hypnotic suggestion as a mode of therapeutic treatment has been officially recognized by medical associations in many parts of the world, but it is already being used with success as a form of harmless anaesthesia during operations and childbirth, and as a treatment for psychological disorders. Clinical experiments with hypnosis are helping to reveal the secrets of the mysterious action of mind on body, for it has been found possible by suggestion to produce physical reactions which under ordinary conditions could only be obtained by physical means. Doubtless many of the "faith cures" of Lourdes and other religious centres are the result of a strong mental force, comparable with that produced under hypnotism, acting upon the physical body; the force in this instance being the patient's absolute conviction that a miraculous cure will take place. The task of the hypnotic practitioner is to induce this acquiescent and receptive state of unquestioning faith by artificial means. This, of course, requires the consent and cooperation of the subject, and it is here that the difficulty usually arises. The patient must have complete faith in the operator to enable him to surrender his own will entirely, for the time being, to another person. When full control of the subject's mind is gained, the required suggestions can be made with every confidence that the mind of the subject will carry them out, and the astonishing thing is that not only does the mind obey, but the body also responds. If, for instance, the idea of a burn is conveyed through the mind, the mark of a burn duly appears on the flesh on the spot indicated, without the use of any physical means to produce it. Many similar experiments attest to this close interrelationship of the mental and physical, and prove beyond question the truth of the Buddhist teaching that mental conditions precede and determine certain classes of phenomena which we have been wont to consider purely physical and material.

Hysteria also produces marked physiological changes in certain circumstances, among them being the well-attested phenomenon of "phantom pregnancy." The abnormal mental excitation which produces phantom pregnancy is also to be found in states of religious frenzy, when an unnatural degree of strength, insensibility to pain, and even invulnerability to injury are exhibited. These unexplained phenomena point to the existence of a mental force which can not only inhibit normal reactions to sense stimuli, but more than that, can affect the physical structure in a particular way.

All this has a distinct bearing on the manner in which the mental impulses generated in past lives, particularly the last mental impressions at the time of the preceding death, influence the physical makeup, and often predetermine the very structure of the body, in the new birth. Before going more deeply into this a specific example may be offered for consideration.

The subject was a Karen houseboy S.T., aged 20, employed by a friend of the writer.[68] While he was in all other respects physically sound, well built and well proportioned, he suffered from an unusual malformation of his hands and feet. Across his right hand a fairly deep, straight indentation, roughly following the "heart line" of palmistry, but much deeper and sharper than any of the normal lines of the hand, and extending right across the palm, divided the hand into two sections. Above this line the hand was not as well developed as at the base of the palm, and the fingers had something of the childish, unformed appearance that is one of the physical accompaniments of cretinism, although not to the same degree. Lower down on the hand and across the forearm there were similar marks, but not so pronounced as that at the base of the fingers. The left hand was indented in the same unusual fashion, but to a lesser degree; and linear indentations of the same kind appeared less distinctly across both feet and on the calves, the lines being roughly parallel to one another. In addition to this, two toes of the left foot were joined together.

The boy's previous employment had been with a leading Rangoon surgeon who, after examining these marks, had declared that although they had been present from birth they could not have been caused by any prenatal injury or abnormal condition in the womb. Questioned about them, the boy confirmed that they were congenital, and stated that all the indentations had been much more pronounced in childhood. Furthermore, at birth three of his toes had been joined, but his father, with the rough surgery of village folk, had separated two of the toes himself. During his infancy and boyhood these malformations had been a cause of acute suffering to him, for at times, particularly when the attention of others was drawn to them, his right arm would swell, and severe pain would be felt in all the affected parts. At such times he experienced mental as well as physical distress, being conscious of fear and depression in connection with the malformations.

According to the boy's own narrative, as a child he had been very reluctant to talk about his physical defects, but one night, lying under the mosquito net with his mother, he felt a sense of security which enabled him to speak freely. He then told her that he remembered incidents of his previous life which were the cause of his terror and distress whenever he was reminded of the marks. He had been, he said, the son of a rich man, possibly a village headman, who had died leaving him three adjoining houses and a large quantity of silver stored in large vessels of the type known as Pegu jars, besides other treasure secreted in various parts of the buildings. After his father's death he

225

had lived alone, unmarried and without servants, in one of the three houses. One night a band of dacoits, armed with bamboo spears, broke into the house and demanded to be told where the treasure was hidden. When he refused to tell them, the robbers bound him with wire in a crouching position, with his hands firmly secured between his legs. In this position, tightly bound and unable to move, they left him huddled in a corner while they ransacked the other two houses, finally making off with the entire store of silver and jewellery. For three days he remained in that position in acute agony, and one of the things he remembered vividly was that blood, dripping from the deep cuts made in his hands by the wire, fell onto his feet and congealed between three of his toes.

Some time during the third night he suddenly became aware, in his alternating periods of consciousness and insensibility, that he was looking down at a still form crouched in a corner, and wondering who it was. It was only later that he realized the body was his own, and that his consciousness was now located in a different and less substantial form. The rest of his recollection was confused and obscure. It seemed to him that for a long time he wandered about the scene of his former life, conscious only of a sense of loss and profound unhappiness. In this condition he appeared to have no judgment of the passage of time, and was unable to say whether it lasted for days or centuries. His sense of personal identity, too, was very feeble, his thoughts revolving entirely around the events just prior to his death, and the memory of his lost treasure which he felt a longing to regain. He seemed, he said, to have his whole existence in a single idea which was like an obsession: the loss of his wealth and the desire to recover it.[69]

After a long time he again became aware of living beings, and felt an attraction towards a certain young woman. He attached himself to her, following her movements, and eventually another transition was effected, in a manner he was unable to describe clearly, as the result of which he was reborn as the woman's child.

These were the memories that lingered with him in connection with the strange malformations of his hands and feet, and which he told his mother in halting, childish words when he was able to speak. The case history bears several features in common with other instances of the recollection of previous lives that are fairly frequent in the East, and so may be profitably discussed as a typical example. One fact, however, should be noted at the outset: the child who made the claim to these recollections had nothing material to gain by doing so. Neither had the parents. Another noteworthy fact is that the boy was a Karen, of a family that had been nominally Christian for two generations, and would be expected to have no belief in the doctrine of rebirth.

Certain interesting and very significant features emerge from an analysis of this particular case. In the first place, the *craving* motif is strongly marked throughout. The young man's choice of a solitary life in a house filled with valuables suggests a fear of employing servants and a tendency towards miserliness in his character. After death, in the *peta* state (i.e., as an unhappy ghost), his attachment to the lost treasure and to the locale of his previous life persisted as the strongest element in his consciousness up to the time when he again became attracted to another human being. So far, this important part played by the impulse of craving and attachment links the story with other instances of *petas* haunting the spots where their former property was located; but here there is another element, that of fear, combined with the attachment. This fear was generated during the days and nights when the subject crouched, bound with wire, in the empty building, with no possibility of escape. In remote spots on the outskirts of villages and townships it is even now possible for such a solitude to remain unbroken for weeks at a time. An intensely strong mental impression of the wire cutting into the flesh must have been formed during this period, and it was probably the last image present in the consciousness at death. In accordance with the principles of Abhidhamma psychology, this last thought-moment would determine the character of the *paṭisandhi-viññāṇa*, the connecting-consciousness or rebirth-consciousness, and would thus become the chief factor in determining the conditions of the new birth. To understand how this comes about we must turn to a brief consideration of the Buddhist analysis of consciousness.

The process by which thought-impressions register themselves is called *citta-vīthi*, or the course of cognition, and there is a *citta-vīthi* connected with each of the organs and fields of sense cognition; that is, eye, ear, nose, tongue, touch (body), and mind. The passive flow of the subconscious mind-continuum (*bhavaṅga*) is disturbed whenever an external impression through one or other of these six channels impinges upon it. This disturbance is called *bhavaṅga-calana* (vibration of the subconscious mind-continuum), and it lasts for exactly one thought-moment. It is followed immediately by *bhavaṅgupaccheda*, or the cutting off of *bhavaṅga*, which is a definite interruption in the smooth flow of the subconscious current.

At this point the thought-moments begin to follow a set progression of cognitive response beginning with *pañca-dvārāvajjana*, which is the turning towards the sense door (in this case one of the five physical organs). This is followed by the arising of the consciousness-moment appertaining to whichever of the sense-doors—eye, ear, nose, tongue, or body—is involved, which is the actual seeing, hearing, smelling, tasting, or feeling, as the case may be. This is followed at once by *sampaṭicchana,* the mental "receiving" of the sense object. When this has been effected, the function of *santīraṇa*, or investigation, comes into play; at this stage associative ideas arise by which the mind is able to identify the impression that has been received, so that the next stage, that of *votthapana*, or identification, can be produced. *Votthapana* is the stage of conscious recognition, at which the object assumes a definite identity in the mental awareness. This stage is then succeeded in a full course of cognition by no less than seven *javanas*, thought-moments during which consciousness relating to the object arises and passes away; it is at this phase that karma, good or evil, is produced. It is followed by *tadālambana*, which is the holding of the impression and the registering of it upon the mental stream; this stage, which lasts for two thought-moments, completes the *cittavīthi* of that particular impression, making sixteen thought-moments of the course of cognition from the first awakening of attention to the object to its fixing upon the consciousness. Each of these thought-moments is complete in itself, consisting of three phases, arising (*uppāda*), enduring (*ṭhiti*), and passing away (*bhaṅga*).

The relative intensity or feebleness of impressions varies considerably. One single impression may be the subject of thousands of complete *vīthi*, each of them very distinct (*atimahanta*). If the impression is less marked it is called *mahanta* (distinct), and does not give rise to the *tadālambana* stage. Still weaker is an impression that does not even reach the *javana* stage (*paritta*; i.e., feeble); while if it is very feeble indeed (*atiparitta*) it passes away after the *bhavaṅga-calana* (vibration of *bhavaṅga*) without any of the subsequent thought-moments arising. An extremely vivid and clear impression reaching the mind door, accompanied by a full course of cognition, is called *vibhūta* (vivid). It is such impressions as these, repeated over and over again, which influence the mind and may be capable ultimately of influencing the body, with or without the accompaniment of a volitional impulse directed towards that end. Normally the mind is selective, turning again and again to those impressions which are most agreeable, while ignoring the others; but under certain exceptional conditions disagreeable impressions force themselves

228

upon the attention so strongly that they cannot be thrust aside. Very often such impressions may be rejected by the conscious mind, yet linger in the *bhavaṅga* ineradicably.

We are here dealing with states of consciousness arising in the *kāma-loka* (the world of fivefold sense perception) and such as come into being through contact with external sense objects. The course of ideational objects, those entering through the *manodvāra*, mind-door, is slightly different. In the cognitive series (*cittavīthi*) dealt with above, the *javana* thought-moment occurs up to seven times, but in loss of consciousness or at the moment of death it subsides after the fifth repetition. At that moment, representing the end of the final phase of the current life, cognitive thought (*vīthicitta*) is experienced, and this takes the form of an idea-image which may be that of predominant karma, of something associated with that karma and its performance, or else a representation of the destiny to which the past karma has been directed. At the expiry of the cognitive thought (*vīthicitta*) or that of the *bhavaṅga*, there arises the *cuticitta* (death-consciousness), which performs the function of cutting off, and immediately after that the *paṭisandhi-viññāṇa*, or connecting-consciousness, arises in the next life as rebirth-consciousness. In the formula of "dependent origination" (*paṭicca-samuppāda*) this is expressed as: *viññāṇapaccayā nāmarūpa*—"From (rebirth) consciousness arise name-and-form," i.e., the mental and physical aggregates. This consciousness, conditioned by ignorance and actions (*kamma*) motivated by craving, carrying with it the predominant impressions of the last thought-moments, functions as the *bhavaṅga* of the next existence and so determines the key, as it were, in which that life is pitched. Thus the life-continuum flows on from one existence to another in the endless succession of *paṭisandhi*, *bhavaṅga*, *vīthi*, and *cuti*.

There is no actual mental entity that passes across from one life to another, but only an impulse. Each moment of consciousness passes away completely, but as it passes it gives rise to a successor which tends to belong to the same pattern; and this process is the same, whether it be considered from the viewpoint of the moment-to-moment life-continuum that makes up a total life span, or from that of the connecting link between one life and the next. The rebirth is instantaneous and is directly conditioned by the preceding thought-impulse. Since both mind and body are conditioned by it, even the distinctive pattern of the brain convolutions that accompanies a particular talent, say for music or mathematics, is the result of this powerful mental force operating from the past life and stamping its peculiar features on the physical substance, the living cell-tissues of the brain. It is this which accounts for the phenomenon of genius in circumstances where heredity offers no tenable explanation.

In the case of the Karen boy under discussion the most potent rebirth force, craving, was conjoined with a strong impression of physical suffering and physical marks, and this impression had been the central pivot of consciousness for three days and nights—long enough to set up a thought-construction (or a pattern impressed on the *bhavaṅga*) sufficiently emphatic to influence the succeeding phases of consciousness and the new body that was formed under its direction. In some way not yet known to science, the thought-energy released at the time of death is able to control the combinations of male and female gametes and by means of *utu* (temperature) and the other purely physical elements of generation to produce a living organism that embodies the nature and potentialities of the past karma in a new life (*anāgata-vipākabhava*).

Here it should be noted that strongly marked tendencies, both mental and physical, as well as actual memories belonging to past lives, are most in evidence when the rebirth is direct from one human life to another. The memories themselves are transferred by impressions on the brain cells, so that the ordinary rules of memory obtain here, and it is the most recent and vivid impressions that survive. Intermediate lives in one or other of the remaining thirty planes of existence can efface altogether the memory of previous human lives, and if these intermediate existences have been spent in any of the lower states, where consciousness is dim, or spent in the inconceivably long life span of the deva realm, it can hardly be expected that there should be any recollection at all. This is only one of the many reasons why most people altogether fail to remember having existed in a previous state, and yet may have a vague feeling that they have done so.

In the case under review the subject spent an undefined period in the state of a *peta*, or what is popularly known as an "unhappy ghost." His own belief was that this state lasted for a long time; but in such conditions time is a purely subjective element. His existence as a *peta* may in fact not have lasted for more than a few thought-moments. Questions put to the boy by the writer, however, seemed to indicate that the interval of *peta* existence had actually been of considerable duration, for after his rebirth he had not been able to identify any places or people from the former life. Everything had changed from his memory of it. Other attempts to draw some clue as to the period of the previous life were equally profitless. The primitive weapons of the dacoits did not necessarily indicate that it took place before the invention of firearms; for the statement that they used wire points to a more recent date. It is possible, however, that the boy's use of the word "wire" was a linguistic error; he may have meant thin strands of creeper, which would produce the same effect. The joining of his toes, corresponding to the manner in which they had stuck together with the congealed blood, is a striking instance of the enduring power of a mental impression. Crouched with his head bent down to his knees, his hands and feet would be the central objects of his *cittavīthi*, and what was happening to them must have stamped itself visually on his consciousness, to reproduce itself later in his new body by means of the *paṭisandhi-viññāṇa*.

This case is the most remarkable one known to the writer for the demonstration it gives of the mind's influence upon the physical body in a direct causal sequence from one life to another.[70] That the process of mutation from one existence to the next is carried out without any "soul" or transmigrating entity is another fact that becomes apparent on examination of the case history. The only factor of identity between the headman's son, the *peta* (unhappy ghost), and S.T. the Karen houseboy, was the craving-impulse that carried with it the potentiality of remanifestation: that is, *bhava* (existence) resulting from *upādāna* (attachment). The terrors and physical affliction were the direct outcome of the *upādāna*, or attachment. In terms of dependent origination, *saṅkhārā* (karmic tendencies) conditioned by *avijjā* (ignorance) had produced *viññāṇa* (consciousness), and from that consciousness had sprung a fresh *nāma-rūpa* (mind-body) bearing all the marks that had impressed themselves on the last moments of consciousness during repeated *cittavīthis* on the same object. It is thus that all living beings carry with them, throughout countless existences, the inheritance of their own thoughts and actions, sprung from past tendencies and nourished on the ever-renewed craving that comes from contact between the senses and the objects of the external world. Heredity itself is merely one factor in the multiple operations of the law of *kamma* and *vipāka* (result), and it too is greatly influenced by the direction taken by past interests, activities, and attachments.

In the Buddha's Teaching it is naturally the moral aspect of *kamma* and *vipāka* that is stressed; and indeed there is a moral aspect to every major volitional impulse. The relationship of good *kamma* and good *vipāka*, bad *kamma* and bad *vipāka*, however, is not always obvious at first glance. A child born with a physical deformity, as in the present case, has not necessarily inflicted injury of a similar kind on someone else in a previous life. The physical defect may be the result of a strong mental impression produced by some other means. But as in the case of the Karen boy, the ultimate cause can invariably be traced back to some moral defect of the individual concerned—to some trait of character unduly dominated by the *āsavas*, the taints or fluxes associated with the grasping tendency which in *paṭicca-samuppāda* is shown as the immediate cause of the process of "becoming" (*upādāna*, or grasping, gives rise to *bhava*, or becoming, which in its turn causes *jāti*, arising or rebirth). Thus the whole individual life process, including its physical medium, the (body) *rūpa*, must be viewed as a causal continuum of action and result, all the actions being to some degree tainted by craving for existence, passion, self-interest, and ignorance, until the attainment of arahatship extinguishes these energy-supplying fires.

It only remains to be noted that in the operation of mental impulses upon living cells at the time of their uniting, and during the processes of syngamy and mitosis, Buddhism offers a fully scientific explanation of the biological mutations described at the beginning of this chapter.

VI

Buddhism teaches that there are altogether thirty-one planes of existence on which rebirth is possible; the human plane is only one of them. The thirty-one "abodes" comprise the states of extreme suffering, or "hells," to which people consign themselves by reason of their bad karma; the realm of the unhappy spirits, or *petas*, who on account of attachment to mundane concerns of a low order are more or less earthbound; the animal world into which people may be reborn through the manifestation of bestial characteristics; the realm of superior spirits intermediate between earth and the heavenly planes themselves, which are the abodes of *devas* enjoying sense pleasures as the result of their past good actions; and lastly, the Brahma-worlds, wherein beings who on earth have attained specific spiritual goals live for aeons in pure and immaterial forms. All of these states of existence, however, are impermanent; sooner or later they come to an end, when the karma that has produced them is exhausted. Rebirth then takes place once more, as the result of craving and residual karma of the process of another type from past lives, which then comes into operation. So the process of saṃsāra continues until all craving is extinguished and Nibbāna is reached.

It is important to realize that Buddhism does not teach rebirth only on the human level. If it did so it would leave unexplained all the phenomena of spiritualism and a great deal more besides which has to be accounted for in human experience. Many Western spiritualists have now come to accept rebirth as a fact because it is the only valid explanation of certain data which cannot otherwise be fitted into the spiritualist concept. To give only one example, it is well known that spiritualist mediums find it impossible to "contact" certain people after death, while with others they are able to do so. This has always been a great difficulty to spiritualists, but the Buddhist answer is a simple one: it is not all who are reborn into the so-called spirit worlds; and furthermore some of these planes of existence are too remote from the human world to be accessible to any ordinary "medium."

The idea of other realms of existence is more difficult for those to accept who have become conditioned to thinking in terms of "naive realism," and it sometimes happens that through a misunderstanding of the Buddhist doctrine of *anattā* (no-self) they believe that rebirth can take place only in a physical and human body. This is an error which the Buddhist texts do not support. To deny the possibility of rebirth in the animal world, for example, is a negation of the universal applicability of the moral law of cause and effect which the Buddha consistently proclaimed. Both Theravāda and Mahāyāna Buddhism teach unequivocally that if the karma of the last thought-moment before death is on a low moral level governed by any of the unwholesome factors associated with lust, hatred, and delusion, the next manifestation of the causal continuum will be on precisely that level. In other words, rebirth as an animal, a *peta*, or a being in one of the hell states will result. It must be understood that this does not correspond at all to the Pythagorean idea that the "soul" of one type of being can enter the body of another. For the sake of a clear understanding of the processes of saṃsāra in regard to other realms of existence, the following extracts from letters from the present writer to a friend are given.

Like yourself, when I first studied Buddhism I thought of rebirth as being only in human form. In the beginning that was satisfactory; as you say, "a nice, clear-cut philosophy, rational"—and of course ethical as well. But further consideration revealed certain mechanical difficulties in the way of direct rebirth invariably from one human state to another. It meant, for instance, that at the moment of death some conception must be taking place somewhere which was in all respects ideally suited to be the vehicle of expression for the karmic potential released by the death. Of course, conception is actually taking place in millions of cases all over the world at any moment one cares to name; yet still it seems that too many coincidental factors must somehow be present to bring the thing within the realms of probability. Again, if animals are to be taken into the scheme, which is philosophically necessary in order to make the world view comprehensive and to get away from the anthropocentric idea that ethics and spiritual meanings apply only to mankind—an idea which always seemed to me quite indefensible—it must be that the rebirth concept is somehow extensible to other modes of existence besides the human.

After all, why should we assume that we are the only form of sentient and intelligent existence in the cosmos? Does the scientific outlook forbid us to envisage the possibility of other modes of life, simply because we cannot see, hear, or handle them? Does not science itself tell us that most of the significant things in the universe, the things that really shape the visible world, are themselves invisible and intangible forces? We have to take many things on the authority of science which we cannot see and test for ourselves. True, somebody else has presumably tested these theories and so, science being a body of shared knowledge as distinct from the esotericism of personal revelations, we accept the findings—that the universe is of such and such a construction, that man has evolved from lower forms of life, and so forth. Even when we are led by gradual degrees to Einstein's general theory of relativity, the space-time complex, curved space, the expanding universe, and other ideas which nobody, not even the scientists themselves, can demonstrate in tangible form, we go on believing something that we cannot realize, or ever hope to realize except as perhaps a mathematical concept, simply because we have faith in the former discoveries of science and have seen that the method bears results. In other words, we believe in the method, even when we cannot check its latest results for ourselves. At that stage very few of us are philosophers enough to ask ourselves why we believe in a substantial physical universe when every new concept of science brings us into a more abstract world and proves that the universe is in reality something quite different from the mental picture we have formed of it from the data furnished by our senses. In a universe of energy, what has become of the solid, impenetrable substance of our world? If it is not exactly illusion, it is so different from the reality that its appearance at least may be termed illusion. Because it is a *shared* illusion and one that is necessary to our continued functioning within the framework of a world that we must regard as substantial, we are compelled to go on treating it as though it were actually the thing it appears to be as interpreted by our sensory awarenesses.

But when we try to apply the laws of Newtonian physics to nuclear physics, and Euclidean geometry to the multiple space-time dimension, we find that these laws, while they are still valid in the limited sphere of the material world, are quite inadequate to cope with the abstract and much more complicated world of mathematical (and therefore philosophical) reality. From then on we have to suspect that the relatively simple material universe, in which certain things just cannot be, because they cannot be always seen, heard, or felt, is only a very partial aspect of the whole. What was simple and obvious to Charles Bradlaugh becomes not quite so certain. But still, through habit we go on asserting the validity of materialistic principles in spheres where it is far from certain that they obtain. So people say that there cannot be a heaven because they were always told that heaven existed somewhere up above the clouds, and stellar exploration (even before it becomes a fact) has disproved this.

But on what principle do we insist that heaven or hell must have an objective, external existence? If "heaven" is happiness and "hell" misery, they are personal and subjective states; they exist independently of physical location. To take a concrete example, two men may be sitting side by side in a bus. One is desperately unhappy, perhaps through remorse, unsatisfied longing, anger, or any one of the myriad causes of human misery; he may even be contemplating suicide. The other is blissfully happy: he has perhaps got a promotion in his job, just had his first book published and the reviewers have been enthusiastic, or he has married the girl he loves. Each of these two men is inhabiting his own personal world, which has nothing to do with the world of the other; yet physically they are sitting side by side in this familiar world shared by us all. They may both get off at Sloane Square: but for one of them Sloane Square is a bus stop in heaven, while for the other it is located nowhere but in hell. So these states of being—really the only true states, since the external world has no part in making them what they are, but itself takes on whatever aspect they give to it—are internal, subjective, and purely mental states. As such they have no connection with location in time or space, or the events of the world going on about them. Each of us lives and has his own peculiar experience in a separate world, to which the external world presents only points of contact and general reference.

So, if this can be the case in regard to two living men in a bus, whose physical bodies are touching one another but whose minds— and therefore real being—are living in different realms, why do we insist that if heaven exists as a reality it must be accessible by space travel or anything of that kind? In doing so we are naively applying laws that are relevant to physical space and time to other modes of conscious being where they are not relevant at all.

What I am trying to express is a different vision of the world of reality. To me it seems that the real world is an intangible world of mental events and concepts, to which the external is only incidental. This may of course take the appearance of Berkeleyan idealism or, worse still, mysticism. But in reality it differs fundamentally from both; it is not Berkeleyan idealism because it does not attempt to brush aside the physical world as being non-existent. It accepts that world as a reality; but not the whole or the final reality. It differs from mysticism in that it does not lose touch with the conditions in which we function as living, material organisms, and does not postulate any invasion of the laws governing extra-physical phenomena into the realm of the physical to the disorganization of the latter. The worlds exist side by side, interpenetrating one another and affecting one another in various ways, but only within the limits imposed by the laws peculiar to each, and in conformity with those laws. Each world stands in relation to the others as a teleological necessity.

It may be objected that of the two men in the bus, the happiness of the one and the wretchedness of the other have certainly been caused by external events; something has happened to them to put them into their respective heaven and hell. That is true; but it is retrospective to the cause, while we are dealing with the effect as it now is. Their present conditions, whatever may have induced them, have no reference to one another nor to the objective world they share; they are living in discrete worlds that have been created for them by their reaction to some previous events. Now had they been indifferent to those events they could not have been plunged into hell or exalted to heaven by them. So finally their condition can be traced back to their own minds and the degree of their susceptibility to external occasions for joy or sorrow. A certain thing happening to one man may cause him a mild and fleeting unhappiness; the same thing happening to another may reduce him to suicidal despair. The same kind of event objectively, but vastly different in its results—that is, in the kind of world it creates internally. If that is the case, which is the more significant—the event in itself or the respective mental conditions of the two men, which have invested it with such different degrees of importance? If we say, as it seems to me we are bound to say, that the mental condition is the more significant, it must follow that it is the mental state, not the event, that represents the true reality in any situation. The illustration of the two men in the bus may be a trite and obvious one, but from it we are entitled to draw certain inferences concerning the nature of states of being in terms of isolated experiences. One of them is that the mind has its own habitat and a limitless capacity for creating its own worlds out of the raw materials of any situation. That these worlds of subjectivity have their counterparts in planes of existence other than our own is borne out by the testimony of Swedenborg, William Blake, and a host of others whose independent experience has given them glimpses of their reality.

The part science plays in life is only on the fringe of mankind's collective experience. In any case, when we bring science into the problem of being, we ought to begin by defining just what we mean by the word. The most we can say is that science is a body of knowledge concerning accepted facts, gained by the pursuit of a certain method which has been found to give results in the past and so is presumed to be valid for all investigations. Scientific theories are constantly subject to alteration as knowledge increases, but scientific *method* remains the same. Therefore at any given point it is the method that is more important than any particular stage it has brought us to in the never-ending pursuit. But there can be no assurance that the method will eventually succeed in revealing everything; in fact its progress suggests that the more it reveals, the more there remains to be explored. It continually opens up new vistas, each of which demands that it be explored with new compasses. The "expanding universe" may be just a natural allegory of man's expanding knowledge of the universe; something to which there can be no final limit. It becomes increasingly difficult to apply any sort of scientific knowledge to ontological questions, even when it seems to have some bearing on what we desire to know. Science may destroy religious myth but it has not made any important change in the terms of philosophical thought. It has given us a wider range of symbols and a more exact terminology, but that is all.

We are no longer obliged to talk of the elements of earth, air, fire, and water, but the philosophical concepts they stood for remain fairly constant.

Everything we know is merely a subjective experience based upon data presented by our senses, and these data come to us in the form of impressions which are in most cases far removed from the nature of the object as it really is. All that physics tells us is that the objects of the external world would appear to us quite differently if we possessed a different kind of cognitive apparatus. But even this was known long ago. Things that we see, hear, smell, taste, and touch have no intrinsic properties, only the characteristics we invest them with in the course of cognizing and appraising. Thus the world of aesthetic values lies only in ourselves, and is in some respects different for each of us. In this mental world, made up of highly individualized impressions combined with the concepts that have gathered about them from prior association and, in the field of abstract concepts, the biases, predilections, and prejudices that are personal to the individual concerned, the range of variations becomes limitless. No two people think exactly alike, which means that no two people inhabit precisely the same world. Two persons may agree on all factual points, yet the interpretation they give to the totality may produce two quite different pictures.

So the world we live in is largely, if not wholly, a mental construct. Science gives us information about the external world which we know to be true so far as it goes. It is true because it is seen to work; if we apply the knowledge practically we get the expected results. Constructing a machine in accordance with certain proved laws of physics we get something that flies, defying another law of physics, gravitation. Something which one law seems to make impossible thus becomes practicable by the understanding and use of other laws. It is this form of progression from the impossible to the possible that has made our world what it is. The laws governing the propagation of sound make it impossible for the voice of someone talking in London to be heard in New York, and three hundred years ago the "natural philosopher" would have been content to leave it at that and would have had a hearty laugh at the notion of radio. But Newton would probably not have dismissed it as impossible because the genius of a really great scientist is like all other forms of genius—it includes a large amount of imagination. Had it not been for the old alchemists, with their absurd theory that somehow the elements of one metal could be rearranged to form another, we should never have had modern chemistry. Even those who went further than the elixir of life and the transmutation of metals, and tried to produce the "homunculus," an artificial man, were only in a crude way trying to anticipate something which biochemistry may one day make possible.

And here it may be noted in passing that even if science should ultimately succeed in generating life from non-living matter, the achievement will make no difference to the Buddhist doctrine of rebirth according to karma. The karmic causal current may remanifest through vital elements brought together artificially in the same way as it does through the natural biological processes. The artificial production of living organisms may deal the final blow to the theory of divine creation but it will not in any way affect the Buddhist explanation of life.

The laws that work in science are continually having to give way before the discovery of fresh laws which either cancel them out or modify them, or make them subservient to ends which previously they appeared to obstruct. And as this process develops we find ourselves becoming more and more doubtful as to whether it will reach any conclusive end. The horizon is eternally receding from us, the spiral nebulae forever thrusting outwards into limitless space. The familiar and comfortable world of "things" is meanwhile dissolving into abstract forces, a whirling dance of electrons, of atoms which are never the "same" atoms from one moment to another of their restless existence. Does what we see bear any relation whatever to the external reality? Can we ever be certain that physics itself is "true"?

Speculative thought has been dried up at its source by the realization that science alone can never help to reveal ultimate truth but can show us only expanding areas of what is relatively true. It was because of this that Wittgenstein was constrained to renounce all attempts to erect systems of philosophy, even negative systems, and was particularly averse to theories which take mathematics or natural science as the ideal. But while the scientist remains content to work within the areas of relative truth and to leave teleological questions alone, his self-denial does not forbid others from making use of his knowledge in the attempt to trace a coherent pattern in the diversity of human experience. We have evidence from other sources that it is possible to improve man's perceptual apparatus and extend it, and by that means we may break through the impasse. It is only necessary that the ideas we bring into play should not be of a kind that science has shown to be false on grounds within its own province.

The limits of scientific competence should be clearly understood. It is a common error to suppose that science has accounted for a phenomenon when it has given it a name, and that it has explained a cause when it has merely described a process. To take an example, "natural selection" is accepted as one of the primary factors in evolution. But if we ask what *causes* natural selection—precisely why does a living organism choose one course of action rather than another, or whence comes the instinctive urge to mate in a certain way that "happens" to be conformable to biological needs—science is silent. It does not know the answer. It has named a process, and shown how it works, but it has not discovered the reason for it. To say that there is no reason is to evade the issue. The purpose may be assumed to lie in the final result; but that is legislating after the event. A certain phenomenon may be produced by accident, but for a long and involved series of such accidents to bring forth in the end a highly organized and equipped animal of the type of the higher vertebrates is stretching pure chance too far.

All the evidence points towards some kind of drive behind the process; but this theory is vitiated by the fact that the drive does not go directly towards the fulfilment of its purpose. It blunders along by a painful process of trial and error—stopping, retracing its steps, coming to dead ends and scattering the debris of its failures along the path of geological time, yet always ensuring that in some way its surviving stages are contributory to the ultimate result, whatever that may be. This drive, or demiurge, cannot be a creator-god, for if it were it would achieve its purpose with greater economy and, presumably, with more regard for ethical principles. That these are completely lacking in nature is one of the strongest arguments against the emergent theory. All the indications in fact are opposed to the idea of a supreme deity, whether God be conceived as a complete being or as an evolving and progressively revealed spiritual principle. Yet when all this is granted we are still left with the vacuum created by the lack of a purposive directing force. The question still remains: Can biological processes be explained in purely physical terms, or do the problems of structure, function, and organization necessitate some kind of teleology? The scientist may reject the "vitalism" which Hans Driesch postulated as a necessity, but something of the kind is needed to account for organic evolution.

Buddhism meets the challenge with the concept of the force of craving, an impersonal urge to fulfilment continually renewing itself in successive manifestations. The "demiurge" and the "élan vital" are both functionally represented in this concept. Here we have not a "something" which has visualized the final result from the beginning and has been capable of creating from nothing and moving directly towards its consummation, but a blindly groping urge which shows itself in the instinctive behaviour of animals and on the deeper psychological levels of human beings. It is the one great creative impulse to which all the laws of the universe are subservient.

Far from precluding the possibility of other states of being besides our own, science makes them, by inference, a logical necessity. The facts suggest that, in the words of Sir Oliver Lodge, "an enlarged psychology, and possibly an enlarged physiology—possibly even an enlarged physics—will have to take into account and rationalize a number of phenomena which so far have been mainly disbelieved or ignored."

It is as well to bear in mind that the existence of extraterrestrial modes of being had always been recognized until science, by confining the method and grounds of knowledge to the material level, caused an unprecedented antagonism to metaphysical ideas. The revolution in outlook justified itself in many ways, but a new rationalism is emerging which has its roots in the enigmatic territory that modern physics has revealed beyond the tangible world.

Understanding of how rebirth in the human state takes place is sometimes obscured by misconceptions regarding certain biological principles, especially those relating to the transmission of hereditary characteristics. Here it is necessary to realize that "the various parts of an organism are not received intact from the parents but developed out of comparatively simple structures present in the egg. There is no real analogy between heredity and the legal notion of inheritance of property. One speaks loosely of a given hereditary character being 'transmitted' from parent to offspring, but obviously this is impossible since the only materials which can be thus transmitted are those contained in the uniting sex cells, the eggs and spermatozoa in higher animals. An individual receives from his parents not a set of fully formed characters but a set of determinants or genes, as a consequence of whose activities the hereditary characters are developed. This concept of hereditary determinants is fundamental for an understanding of heredity" (Prof. G. H. Beale, Lecturer in Genetics, Edinburgh University, 1957). The determinants are therefore only a contribution to the sum total of characters, or personality. The extent to which they are decisive must depend very largely on other factors, not all of which are to be accounted for by environment. Heredity and the predispositions from past karma may be complementary to one another, as when attachment leads to repeated rebirth in the same racial group or even in the same family; or the kammic tendencies may modify or counteract the hereditary characteristics. It is only if rebirth is taken to mean the transmigration of a "soul" that there is any conflict between it and the known facts of genetics.

The emphasis laid upon *anattā* is fundamental to the Buddhist point of view. There is no "soul" in the sense of an enduring entity; in its place there is mental energy flowing out from living creatures which, after their death, continues its current of causality by assembling out of physical substances a new being. But this "new being," which is the continuation of the karmic cause-effect current of the previous one, does not necessarily have to be a human being. It may be an animal or it may be a being existing in other realms, where it produces a body in accordance with the particular laws of generation obtaining in those realms. If it has brought about a birth in the *deva-* or *petaloka* (which are justifiably called "spirit" realms, since "spirit" has nothing to do with "soul" but denotes a particular type of body, different from the bodies of the terrestrial plane), it continues with a more or less recognizable personality. It is similar enough in general characteristics to the person who died to be recognizable as belonging to the same current of causal identity, and so we call it the "same" person, just as we say that John Smith at ninety is the "same" person as John Smith the infant which he once was. Actually they are not the same, except in this conventional sense; they merely belong to the same continuum of cause and effect. The new being, *deva* or *peta*, also retains memories of the previous life, and if emotional links or other attachments are strong it continues to share the interests of people living on this, our own plane. Furthermore, when personality is very strongly marked, it is all the more likely to reproduce characteristics which make it identifiable as the "same" person in a new manifestation.

In this way Buddhism accounts for the phenomena of the seance room. Rebirth in these other realms, or *lokas*, does not necessitate a soul any more than does rebirth as a human being or animal. When the result of the karma that has caused the rebirth in the *deva* or *peta* realms is exhausted, the mental energy once more flows out to operate through the conditions of the physical world and human rebirth takes place again. Or it may be that another *deva* or *peta* rebirth will come about, or a rebirth in any other of the thirty-one planes of existence, according to the nature of the residual karma.

There are several lines of inquiry on which investigation into rebirth may be carried out. It has been possible to indicate only a few of them here. The serial continuity of life, which so many people in all ages have felt instinctively to be a truth, however, carries with it the force of an intellectual conviction to all who seek for a purpose and a moral pattern in human experience. It is not too much to say that the whole of man's future development depends upon an acceptance of rebirth and a fuller understanding of the ethical principles it brings to light. Mankind is now ripe for a complete reassessment of values and a restatement of the universal principles on which our moral and spiritual convictions rest. Unless this is undertaken we stand in danger of a catastrophic destruction of all those virtues by which man has risen to his present position in the hierarchy of living beings. It is only by the acceptance of rebirth as a fact that the sense of moral responsibility in an ordered universe can be restored.

Notes

1. Ian Stevenson, M.D., Carlson Professor of Psychiatry, University of Virginia Medical School. See his *Twenty Cases Suggestive of Reincarnation*, 2nd enlarged ed., 1974 (University Press of Virginia).

2. See Part III of this volume.

3. See "Buddhism and the Spirit-World" in *The Buddhist Outlook* by Francis Story (Kandy: Buddhist Publication Society, 1973,) pp. 307ff.

4. See *Reincarnation in World Thought*, ed. J. Head and S.L. Cranston (New York: The Julian Press, 1967).

5. In Buddhism, *ucchedavāda* and *sassatavāda* respectively.

6. The first verse of the Dhammapada says: "Mind precedes all *dhammas* (states): they are mind-made and governed by mind." This relates to the nature of the states; it does not place mind as a first cause but as the chief conditioning factor in all states of existence.

7. *Paṭicca-samuppāda*. See *Dependent Origination* by Piyadassi Thera (BPS Wheel No. 15).

8. The author probably refers here to the Pāli term *"uppāda,"* which, however, is generally not used to signify rebirth. But its verbal form, *uppajjati*, frequently indicates in the Buddhist texts the process of rebirth, e.g., *so devaloke uppajjati*, "he arises in a celestial world." (Editor.)

9. There is also a Pāli word *punabbhava*, which means "re-becoming" or "renewed existence" and is roughly equivalent to "rebirth." (This term is almost identical with the one that Arthur Schopenhauer preferred to use, i.e., "palingenesis." See also Chapter XII of this book ("A Question of Terminology"). (Editor.)

10. See also the author's article on "identity-in-change," in *The Buddhist Outlook*, p.29.

11. *Avijjānusayaparikkhittena taṇhānusayamūlakena saṅkhārena janīyanaṃ*. "It is brought forth by a mental activity which is rooted in such craving as is dormant, and is wrapt in such ignorance as is latent" (*Abhidhammattha-saṅgaha*).

12. It is worth noting that Mrs. Rhys Davids did not go so far towards the Pythagorean misunderstanding of the situation as to write of rebirth in an animal.

13. *Amitāyur-dhyāna Sūtra*, trans. by J. Takakusu. Sacred Books of the East, Vol. XLIX, p.182.

14. This was written over forty years ago, when a more optimistic view was taken of evolution than is held today. We now know that evolutionary processes are reversible.

15. The Nembutsu school in Japan arose from the belief that the Buddha-sāsana came to an end 2,000 years after the Buddha's Parinibbāna. In the succeeding

period, the age of *mappo*, it would be impossible for anyone to attain Nirvāna by his own efforts. Honen (1133–1212) and Shinran Shonen (1173–1262) then popularized the credo that rebirth in the Western Paradise of Amida Buddha could be obtained by repeating his name, as taught in the *Sukhāvati Vyūha Sūtra*. Hence Shinran's famous dictum: "If even a good man can be reborn in *sukhāvati*, how much more so a sinner!" In China the teaching was propagated by Shan-tao (613–81).

"Nembutsu is the most basic thought of the Pure Land school....The utterance of the name of Amida Buddha ... is believed to be the practice of the highest value. Nembutsu had gradually been popularized ... with the significance that the utterance of Amida's name was the most excellent and the easiest way to be born in the Pure Land and attain Enlightenment for those who were not qualified to practise the Buddhist doctrine perfectly." *The Practice of the Development of Nembutsu*, by Ryosetsu Fujiwara (Jodo Shinshu Series No. 1, Bureau of Buddhist Education, San Francisco, Calif., U.S.A. 1962).

Here we have a clear declaration of an exoteric teaching, similar to that found in the Lamaism of Tibet. To these schools it is the doctrine of *Śūnyatā* and *anātman* that are considered "esoteric" teachings for the elite. The sexo-magical practices of Vajrayāna (Tāntra) are also esoteric, but as they form no part of original Buddhism they may be excluded from this discussion.

16. "Le Bouddhisme en Chine," *Presence du Bouddhisme*, p.698.

17. Mahāparinibbāna Sutta, Dīgha Nikāya 16. (See *Last Days of the Buddha*, rev. ed., Kandy: BPS, 1988, p.32.)

18. In Jaina philosophy, *jīva* means "soul" in the sense of a homunculus which leaves the body at death and transmigrates. The Buddha repudiated this doctrine, but the word occurs in the Pāyāsi Sutta (Dīgha Nikāya 23), where Prince Pāyāsi, a sceptic, objects that when a thief is thrown alive into a jar, sealed down with leather and clay, and then roasted on a furnace, the *jīva* of the dead man cannot be seen coming out when the jar is opened. To this the Ven. Kumāra Kassapa replies with a simile of the prince dreaming himself in another place, and asks whether those around can see his "soul" entering or leaving him. "If the living do not see the soul of you who are living, entering or leaving you, how will you see the soul of a dead man entering or leaving him?" Kumāra Kassapa does not assert that there is a *jīva* in the sense of "soul," but that rebirth in other spheres can take place without it as the fruit of karma.

19. "The Place of Animals in Buddhism" (BPS Bodhi Leaves No. 23).

20. The capitals in the quotations are those of Dr. Roos, wherever they occur.

21. "The North Sea," quoted in *Reincarnation: An East-West Anthology*.

22. Properly speaking, karmic effects are *vipāka*. The word "*vāsanā*" means only an impression made upon the mind, a recollection from the past (*pubba-vāsanā*).

23. This assumption is made solely for the purpose of covering Dr. Roos' argument. As I have suggested, there is reason to suppose that some animals do in fact have a marginal choice between good and bad actions. If this is indeed the case, the situation is modified in favour of the animals, but not fundamentally altered.

24. From the French translation by Etienne Lamotte, *La somme du Grand Vehicule d'Asanga* (Louvain, 1938), Vol. 2, p.14.

25. Ibid.

26. Ibid., p.26.

27. Nyanatiloka, *Buddhist Dictionary*, s.v. *bhavanga*.

28. These are the four stages of awakening in Buddhism, the stream-enterer, once-returner, non-returner, and arahat or liberated one.

29. *Xenoglossy* is the ability to speak a foreign language not normally learned by the speaker. *Glossolalia*, "speaking in tongues," is a term used to describe speech in a "language" different from the speaker's native speech. It occurs usually in a religious context and is attributed then to an "inflowing of the spirit." Involved listeners may derive a "message" from the strange speech, but examinations by linguists show that (with perhaps rare exceptions) glossolalia consists only of gibberish, that is, of no known language living or dead.

    For more information on these subjects, see Ian Stevenson, *Xenoglossy: A Review and Report of a Case* (Charlottesville: University Press of Virginia, 1973).

30. Hypnogogic visions: Images occurring to a person as he is falling asleep and thus in a state intermediate between wakefulness and sleep. Corresponding visions or images occurring as the subject is emerging from sleep are called "hypnopompic."

31. Professor Stevenson plans to publish a detailed report of this case.

32. Thanks are due to the Venerable U. Dhammajoti, Mangala College, Colombo, Ceylon, who translated from English into Sinhalese the list of statements and behaviour shown by Warnasiri Adikari according to the informants, which list the two principal witnesses signed as accurate.

    Mr. Godwin Samararatne, Mr. Amarasiri Weeraratne, Mr. L.F. Panangala, Mr. T.B. Disanayake, Mr. Rajah Weeraratne, Mr. P. Premaratne, and the late Mr. E.C. Raddalgoda all gave valuable assistance as interpreters at different stages of this investigation.

33. This refers to Dr. Ian Stevenson with whom F.S. had investigated this case as well as the following one (Disna Samarasinghe).

34. The detail of some food taken or some other seemingly unimportant event occurring just before death occurs quite often in the cases suggestive of reincarnation, for example, in the cases of Ravi Shankar and Pramod Sharma (3). Perhaps food taken or something done just before death becomes specially fixed in the

memory because of the intensity of the experience of dying. Dostoevsky commented on the trivial details noted by men about to be shot of which he himself had personal experience. In the present case, a surviving Ananda, finding his body dead, might have cast around for a plausible explanation of such a sudden death and attributed this superstitiously to something he had recently eaten. Such misplaced assignments of blame in illness and death occur commonly in the East, but also in the West. I.S. has drawn attention to incorrect, or at least unsubstantiated, assignments of causes of death by the present personalities in the cases of Swarnlata and Jasbir (3).

35. The hypothesis of reincarnation by itself implies nothing as to when a personality assumes occupancy of a new physical body. In most of the Asian cases now under study, the interval between the death of the previous personality and the birth of the body of the new personality is more than a year, although it is rarely more than ten years. But in a small number, the interval seems shorter so that conception and some embryonic development of the body of the second personality must have begun before the death of the first. In one (unpublished) case in India studied by I.S., the death of the first personality occurred three days after the birth of the second personality, and in the case of Jasbir (3) the death of the previous personality occurred about three years after the birth of the present personality.

36. Buddhism teaches that release from the cycle of death and rebirth can be attained only by the development of non-attachment to the elements of sensory experience. The release from desire for the unrealities of incarnated existence may be sought and achieved in meditation, which Buddhist monks practise and teach. (See, for example, Christmas Humphreys, *Buddhism*, Harmondsworth, Penguin Books, Ltd., 1951; Francis Story, *The Four Noble Truths* (BPS Wheel No. 34/35).)

37. Thanks are due to Mr. Godwin Samararatne and Mr. Amarasiri Weeraratne who acted as interpreters in the study of this case. They also kindly translated a written record of information related to the case made by the subject's mother. Mr. Samararatne additionally gathered some further information from informants in 1968. Mr. P.K. Perera and Mr. H.S.S. Nissanka furnished some information about details of the case.

38. Stevenson, I., *Cases Suggestive of Reincarnation*, Series II. (In preparation.)

39. Stevenson, I., *Twenty Cases Suggestive of Reincarnation*. Proceedings of the American Society for Research Psychical Vol. 26 (September 1966), pp.1–362.

   Story, F. and Stevenson, I., "A Case of the Reincarnation Type in Ceylon." *Journal of the American Society for Psychical Research*, Vol. 61 (1967), 130–45. (Reprinted as Chap. XV of this volume.)

40. Stevenson, I., "Characteristics of Cases of the Reincarnation Type in Ceylon." *Contributions to Asian Studies*, Vol. 3 (1973), 26–39.

41. Stevenson, I., "Characteristics of Cases of the Reincarnation Type in Turkey." *International Journal of Comparative Sociology* , Vol. 11 (1970), 1–17.

42. Stevenson, I., "Cultural Patterns in Cases Suggestive of Reincarnation among the Tlingit Indians of Southeastern Alaska" *Journal of the American Society for Psychical Research*, Vol. 60 (1966), 229–43.

43. See n.39.

44. See, for example, the cases of Prakash and Pramod in Stevenson, n.39, and the case of Warnasiri, in Chap. XV of this volume.

45. To Western readers we should point out that many Sinhalese place family names first and personal names afterwards. Thus R.M. Gardias and R.M. Romanis are brothers with the same family name indicated by the initials "R.M." Female names are also somewhat inconsistent by Western standards. A wife does not always take her husband's name after marriage.

46. Buddhism does not recognize caste distinctions, this being one of the departures of the Buddha's teachings from doctrine prevailing in his time and later in India. In fact, however, Sinhalese Buddhists have been considerably influenced by a number of Hindu practices, including caste. Caste, therefore, has existed in Ceylon for centuries and it still has considerable strength among certain Sinhalese Buddhists.

47. See n.38.

48. Bana preaching consists of the exegesis of passages in the sayings attributed to the Buddha.

49. The district of Galagedera is in the highland part of Ceylon whose inhabitants (Kandyans) often exhibit a superior attitude towards persons from the coastal plains. Babanona's husband had come from Devundera in the extreme south (near the coast) of the island.

50. See, for example, the case of Marta, in Stevenson, n.39.

51. For a summary of the facts related to the fading of apparent memories in sixteen cases, see Stevenson, n.39, p.326.

52. See Stevenson, n.39.

53. "Identification parades," used by lawyers and police to select out a wanted criminal, are not usually handled in a more controlled manner. Williams has reviewed and castigated the weaknesses in nearly all current legal procedures of this type. See Williams, G., *The Proof of Guilt* (London: Stevens and Sons, 1963).

54. Westerners, uninformed fully about the doctrines of rebirth in Hinduism and Buddhism, may suppose that if a child remembers a previous life in a higher caste, he has the motivation of escaping from present unhappiness by imagining a previous life as a person in a higher station in life. But for a Hindu or a Buddhist such a remembrance is not a creditable memory since it supposes that

the person has fallen from his previous superior position because of his own misconduct which earned him a rebirth in a lower caste.

55. See, for example, the cases of Gnanatilleka and Marta in Stevenson, n.39.

56. Buddhism, which prefers the term "rebirth" to "reincarnation," does not suppose that all aspects of one personality necessarily become manifested in the related personality born after the death of the first personality. Information about the Buddhist doctrine of rebirth will be found in our earlier publications and references cited therein, n.39.

57. See Stevenson, n.39.

58. Venerable Teacher: the usual honorific of Burmese monks.

59. Mi Mi Khaing (Indiana University Press).

60. For a detailed report on this case, see Stevenson, *Twenty Cases Suggestive of Reincarnation.*

61. Since this was written, confirmation of the view that reincarnation beliefs in Kabbalistic Judaism are of considerable antiquity has been found in an article, "Seelenwanderung und Sympathie der Seelen in der Judischen Mystik (Transmigration and the Sympathy of Souls in Jewish Mysticism)," by Prof. Gershom Scholem, in the *Eranos Jahrbuch*, Vol. 25, 1955 (Rhein Verlag, Basel, 1956).

Prof. Scholem finds the first mention of reincarnation in the book, *Bahir*, edited c.1180 in southern France, but notes that it is there spoken of as a matter of course, without apology or explanatory comments. Official Jewish theology emphatically opposed the doctrine, yet Kirkisani. a tenth century writer, in his *Book of the Lights*, affirms that the Karaic teacher 'Anan accepted the doctrine in the eighth century. 'Anan wrote a book on it, and his followers preserved the doctrine.

Prof. Scholem considers it open to question whether the Kabbalists developed the theory of transmigration of souls independently as a psychological assumption, or whether they adopted it from older traditions. But he draws attention to the fact that the *Bahir* contains fragments of an older, undoubtedly Oriental Jewish gnostic source, and concludes: "All things considered, I incline to the view that we are here dealing with an older gnostic Jewish tradition which the book *Bahir* derives through channels unknown to us."

(The author is indebted to the Ven. Nyanaponika Mahāthera for the translation of Prof. Scholem's article from the German.)

62. The formation of personality has to be considered under three heads. There is first the karmic potentiality of the individual, which is the inheritance from his own previous lives. Secondly, there is the set of hereditary characteristics which he derives from his parents. This appears to be connected with the karma by way of attraction, as when the rebirth takes place in the same family or in the same sociological or ethnic group, and accounts for racial characteristics the origins of

which cannot be specifically determined. Thirdly, there is environmental influence, which produces modifying effects upon the developing personality. Since causality in the Buddhist sense implies multiple causality, the karmic character-motif, which represents at once the residuum of the old personality and the matrix of the new, does not exclude the other two formative factors, nor is it excluded by them.

On the other hand, the attempt to erect a theory of the origin of personality solely upon biological heredity and environmental influences is at the outset nullified by the fact that siblings with the same hereditary background and reared in the same environment show marked differences in character and abilities. Such differences are frequently to be met with even in the case of twins.

63. The will to act undergoes a complete reversal when desire is totally extinguished, as in the case of the arahat. It is not, however, converted into what would appear to be its opposite, volitional inertia. The arahat continues to will and to act as long as he lives, but his willing is not prompted by desire; its source is the uniform, practically automatic, functioning of the impulse of disinterestedness. For this reason it is *kiriya*, or karmically neutral and non-regenerative. The personality pattern in which desire is totally absent bears no resemblance to the psychology of the ordinary person who is subject to rebirth. A close parallel to the Buddhist conception of will as a generative force is to be found in Bergson's theory of "creative evolution." If the Bergsonian idea were to be enlarged, as quite logically it could be, to include a succession of lives subject to karma and its results, the parallel would be exact.

64. Translated by Bhikkhu Ñāṇamoli *The Path of Purification,* 3rd ed. (Kandy: BPS, 1975).

65. Hypnotic regression, the technique of carrying a subject under hypnosis back to a previous life, may give negative results from a variety of causes. Due to an unconscious resistance the regression may not be complete; or the existence to which the regression has led may have been on a subhuman level and therefore inarticulate. Several cases are known to the author in which the subject has had fragmentary memories of a previous life while practising meditation. In some instances the descriptions afterwards given of these experiences strongly suggest that they relate to states of consciousness of a subhuman order. If a hypnotic subject is regressed to a previous condition of this kind the response will naturally be negative.

The question of hetero-biological transition in rebirth is a controversial one; but so far as Buddhism is concerned it is disputed only by those who have not succeeded in overcoming the anthropocentric bias that has its root in personality-belief (*sakkāya-diṭṭhi*). It cannot be too often stressed that Buddhism does not subscribe to the belief in the sharp distinction between human and animal life that has dominated Western thought for many centuries, and that continues to colour it on the emotional level despite the discoveries of biological science.

The chief objections to the cases of apparent memories of previous lives under hypnosis may be briefly stated here. The first is that such cases can rarely be confirmed by objective evidence, and that even when such proof is given, as in the cases mentioned in Section III of this essay and in Part II of this book, it is difficult to eliminate the possibility that the subject may have acquired the information either unconsciously by normal means, from books and other sources, or telepathically from other minds. The picture is further complicated by the possibility that the source of information is the "collective unconscious," or race memory. Nevertheless, methods are being devised whereby these possibilities may be either ruled out or confirmed. The "collective unconscious" itself, if it exists, may turn out to be a misinterpretation of what are actually memories of previous lives. Rebirth would seem in fact to imply the existence of a common stock of experiences preserved on the unconscious level in each individual.

Another possibility, in cases where no objective proof can be obtained, is that the suppressed memory of a previous life may be a fantasy. Experience has shown, however, that mental fantasies under hypnosis do not arise spontaneously. They come about in response to suggestions from the hypnotizer, and can readily be distinguished from genuine memories.

In the cases of spontaneous recollection, those in which a child claims to remember a previous existence without assistance from hypnotism, it is easier to eliminate alternative explanations of the phenomenon. These cases present a much broader basis for investigation, particularly in view of the fact that, as recent examples seem to indicate, they occur when the intermediate existence between the former human life and the present one has been relatively short. A number of such cases have recently come under investigation and the findings on them will be published in the near future. They are supported by much evidential material in the form of identifications by the subjects of persons and places known to them in their previous lives. In quite a few instances the subjects have been found to be in possession of information on matters hitherto unknown to the other persons involved, which on inquiry has been found correct.

66. Recent investigations carried out by the author in Ceylon and Thailand appear to indicate that such memories occur when the previous life was cut short abruptly by sickness, accident, or violence. From a survey of these and a number of cases gathered from other parts of the world, it would seem that rebirth in the human world tends to take place more quickly after a premature death, and that it is in such cases that vestigial memories of the previous life are retained in sufficient strength to permit their spontaneous revival. The implication is that a premature death leaves the pattern set by the regenerative karma uncompleted, with the result that it is renewed more quickly, and more of the previous personality structure survives. This, of course, is a tentative supposition which further research may establish or disprove. The accumulation of evidence has to be exam-

ined in the light of the fact that personality is a composite formation, subject to alteration, disintegration, and reconstruction, and that in rebirth it is not the total personality that is transferred from one life-manifestation to another, but only the karmically directed impulse of the previous existence, which may reproduce more or less of the recognizable features of the former personality.

67. The commentary to verse 43 of the Dhammapada relates a sudden change of sex, due to exceptionally weighty karma, in the case of a youth, Soreyya, who became a woman as the result of a thought of lust directed towards an arahat, the Thera Mahā Kaccāna.

68. This case is taken from the records of the Burma Buddhist World Mission. The subject was examined in 1949 in Rangoon.

69. Several cases have been found in which the subject remembers an intermediate life. These memories show an underlying unity of pattern, and in some respects confirm the accounts given in spiritualist communications. At first the disembodied entity is not aware that death has taken place. The sensations described resemble those of persons who have had experiences of the disembodied consciousness under anesthesia or in what is known as astral projection. The term "disembodied" is not strictly correct; the consciousness is always located in, or associated with, a body of some kind, but the physical vehicle (*rūpa*) is of the fine-material type known to Buddhist metaphysics; that is to say, while it is unsubstantial on the plane of human consciousness, it is solid on the plane of a different vibrational frequency on which it manifests.

A feature which frequently occurs in these memories is the appearance of a guide who assists and directs the discarnate entity. In the case of a Burmese Buddhist monk whose rebirth history was investigated by the author, such a guide appeared to him shortly after his death and directed him to his new birth. Subsequently, the same personage appeared to the monk in a dream during a critical period of his present life and gave him valuable advice (see Chap. XX). A close parallel has been found in a case in America. A connection may be traced here with the almost universal belief in the "guardian angel" or spirit guide. It is significant, too that such helpers do not appear to be attached to every individual. The Buddhist explanation is that the guide and protector is someone who has been closely connected by ties of friendship or relationship with the individual in a past life, and who still continues to take an interest in his welfare. The case from America, referred to above, gives support to this explanation. Here again, the post-mortem experience was followed by further appearance of the guiding entity in the present life, in one of which a strong hint was given of a karmic link between the two persons concerned.

70. Cases in which the subjects have birthmarks corresponding to injuries or physical characteristics they bore in the previous life form an important class of the rebirth case histories. They include the following examples:

Thailand. Large capillary naevus on left of cranium, corresponding to a fatal knife wound received in the previous life. Also malformation of big toe, corresponding to a wound present at the time of death. (This is the case of Sgt. Thiang San Kla of which a report is included in Chap. XVIII.)

Thailand. Slight malformation of left ear, reproducing similar irregularity in the previous life. (This is the case of Nang Tong Klub, included in Chap. XX.)

Burma. Birthmark on ankle resembling the mark of adhesive tape, corresponding to a mark on the dead body of the previous life where adhesive tape had been fixed for blood transfusion. (This is the case of Win Win Nyunt, which is reported in Chap. XIX.)

Ceylon. Extensive malformation of right arm and right upper chest. The subject remembers having killed his wife by stabbing, and relates his deformities to the use of his right hand in the slaying. Case confirmed by a number of living witnesses. (This is the case of Wijeratne, reported in *Twenty Cases Suggestive of Reincarnation* by Ian Stevenson, M.D.)

England. Round, reddish area the size of a bullet wound, corresponding in position to fatal bullet wound in the previous life.

Brazil. Pigmented mark on back, below right scapula, with area of increased hair over left ribs in front of chest. The subject as a child said that he had been killed by a bullet in World War II.

America. Scars closely resembling bullet wounds of entry and exit, front and back of left chest. Other particulars of the case suggest death by murder in the previous life.

The case in Ceylon differs from the others in that it indicates a retributive karmic effect. The others in this selection would appear to be psycho-kinetic effects which could be explained on the assumption that the subjects in a post-mortem disincarnate state saw the marks on their own bodies. These were then reproduced on the new body, as in the case of S.T., the Karen house boy, quoted here in Section V (p.252).

Well-authenticated cases of a change of sex in rebirth at present number fifteen. These are being made the subject of special study in view of the light they may throw on sexual deviations where the cause is not traceable in the present life. In a few of the cases so far investigated there is a decided predominance of the characteristics of the opposite sex in the present personality. In others the sexual adjustment is normal. The latter cases are valuable in that they eliminate the possibility that the rebirth memories are a fantasy designed to explain away the sexual aberration. In one case, that of a girl, the previous personality was a boy who had a strong desire to be of the opposite sex. The child not only identified places and persons still living, connected with the previous life, but also showed strong liking for certain persons and dislike of others, exactly as the previous personality had done. She remembers having wished to be a girl, and is happy now that her wish has been fulfilled. One striking feature of this case is that the girl recognized a school teacher who had been kind to her in the previous life and she now shows a strong attachment to him. The teacher testified that the dead boy whom she claims to be had asked him whether it was true that people were reborn after death. This particular case is supported by an abundance of detailed proof and contains many features of psychological interest. (This is the case of Gnanatilleka, reported in *Twenty Cases Suggestive of Reincarnation*.)

Facets of Buddhist Thought

K.N. Jayatilleke

K.N. Jayatilleke was one of the best-known Buddhist scholars in Asia. This book presents a brilliant account of of Theravāda Buddhism and embraces a wide variety of themes ranging from the birth of Buddhism to the Buddha's prophetic teachings regarding the future of mankind.

Topics covered include, among many others, the background of early Buddhism; the significance of the Buddha's birthday; the Buddhist doctrines of karma and reincarnation; the Buddhist conception of truth, good and evil, Nirvana, the individual, the universe and the material world; the Buddhist view of nature and destiny; Buddhism and the caste system; Buddhism and international law; and the contemporary relevance of the Buddha's teachings to the modern world.

Professor Jayatilleke always writes with both the scholar and the lay reader in mind. As a result, this is a highly readable and extremely penetrating book—and one that explores the roots and nature of the Buddha's teachings and examines them in the light of contemporary knowledge.

The present collection contains the essays earlier published by the BPS in *The Message of the Buddha* as well as essays that were published the *Wheel Publication* series. A long essay on the principles of international law in Buddhism is also included.

BP 428H   506 pages

THE BUDDHIST PUBLICATION SOCIETY

The BPS is an approved charity dedicated to making known the Teaching of the Buddha, which has a vital message for all people.

Founded in 1958, the BPS has published a wide variety of books and booklets covering a great range of topics. Its publications include accurate annotated translations of the Buddha's discourses, standard reference works, as well as original contemporary expositions of Buddhist thought and practice. These works present Buddhism as it truly is—a dynamic force which has influenced receptive minds for the past 2500 years and is still as relevant today as it was when it first arose.

For more information about the BPS and our publications, please visit our website, or write an e-mail, or a letter to the:

Administrative Secretary
Buddhist Publication Society
P.O. Box 61
54 Sangharaja Mawatha
Kandy • Sri Lanka

E-mail: bps@bps.lk
web site: http://www.bps.lk
Tel: 0094 81 223 7283 • Fax: 0094 81 222 3679